D1326983

John Jacob Astor

OTHER BOOKS BY AXEL MADSEN

Nonfiction

The Deal Maker: How William C. Durant Made General Motors

The Sewing Circle: Female Stars Who Loved Other Women

Stanwyck: A Biography

Chanel: A Woman of Her Own

Sonia Delaunay: Artist of the Lost Generation

Silk Roads: The Asian Adventures of Clara and André Malraux

Gloria and Joe: The Star-Crossed Love Affair of Gloria Swanson and Joe Kennedy

Cousteau: An Unauthorized Biography

60 Minutes: *The Power and the Politics of America's Most Popular TV News Show*

Private Power

Living for Design: The Yves Saint Laurent Story

John Huston: A Biography

Hearts and Minds: The Uncommon Journey of Simone de Beauvoir and Jean-Paul Sartre

Malraux: A Biography

William Wyler: The Authorized Biography

Billy Wilder

Fiction

Unisave

Borderlines

John Jacob Astor

America's First Multimillionaire

AXEL MADSEN

John Wiley & Sons, Inc.

New York • Chichester • Weinheim • Brisbane
• Singapore • Toronto

Copyright © 2001 by Axel Madsen. All rights reserved

Published by John Wiley & Sons, Inc.
Published simultaneously in Canada

This publication is designed to provide accurate and authoritative
information in regard to the subject matter covered.
It is sold with the understanding that the publisher is not
engaged in rendering professional services. If professional
advice or other expert assistance is required, the services
of a competent professional person should be sought.

Library of Congress Cataloging-in-Publication Data:

Madsen, Axel
    John Jacob Astor : America's first multimillionaire / Axel Madsen.
        p. cm.
    Includes bibliographical references and index.
    ISBN 0-471-38503-4 (cloth : alk. paper)
        1. Astor, John Jacob, 1763–1848. 2. Businesspeople—United
    States—Biography. 3. United States—Economic conditions—to
    1865. I. Title.
    HC102.5.A76 M33 2001
    380.1'092—dc21
    [B]   00-042273

Printed in the United States of America
10 9 8 7 6 5 4 3 2 1

Contents

Acknowledgments

—ɯ—

I could not thank all the people who took time to help me prepare this biography. First and foremost I am indebted to my son Gil, who took time out to research details of the Astoria saga and helped with the final version of the manuscript.

In New York, I want to thank my editor, Hana Umlauf Lane, and the staff at the New York Public Library archives. Diane Hamilton, in Washington, and Michael Hargraves and Carole Cole, in Los Angeles, were more than helpful.

Los Angeles, May 2000

John Jacob Astor

Introduction

—ɯ—

Before Bill Gates and Donald Trump, before the Rockefellers, before Andrew Carnegie, E. H. Harriman, and Henry Ford, there was John Jacob Astor. He might have been born in a village in southern Germany, but his story is American in his desire to reinvent himself and, to an astonishing extent, invent the newly formed United States. The wish to make something of oneself is a perennial in most cultures. Doing so is the American obsession. Doing so supremely is the stuff of legends. Astor was America's first multimillionaire. As his friend Philip Hone, the last of the aristocratic mayors of New York, said of him: "All he touched turned to gold, and it seemed as if fortune delighted in erecting him a monument of her unerring potency." When he died a few months short of his eighty-fifth birthday, he left behind a fortune that represented one-fifteenth of all the personal wealth in America.

The new American democracy's laissez-faire economy gave astute and audacious entrepreneurs unlimited opportunities. Astor was one of the first merchants to imagine the world as a global economy. He traded on three continents and had little patience for prickly nationalism. He didn't think England's quarrel with its former North American colonies was any of his business. Throughout his long life he ignored jingoistic passions while remaining attentive to the money to be made on wars. A beaver skin, he believed, belonged to the trapper who caught the animal and to the person who bought the pelt regardless of maps that statesmen in London, Paris, Madrid, St. Petersburg, and the new

1

capital of the new United States drew up of territories no white man had ever seen. When he entered the fur trade, two of every three Americans lived within fifty miles of the Atlantic Ocean, and only four roads crossed the Allegheny Mountains. California belonged to Spain; Russian traders had footholds on the coast of Alaska. In between, Canadians dominated whatever business was carried out with Indians.

The French Revolution upset Europe's dynastic checkerboard and Napoleon's rise spilled over into sea warfare with Great Britain that tested its relationship with the United States. The new American states suspected England of waiting for an opportunity to reclaim the colonies. Successive governments in London were too focused on conflicts with Napoleon to try to placate the apprehensions of the testy citizens of its former colonies. Thomas Jefferson clung to the illusion that depriving Britain and France of American commerce would make the two enemy nations come to their senses. When he imposed an embargo on all foreign trade, Astor tricked the president into making an exception for him. Wars make for inflation—countries don't tax their citizens in advance; they issue debt to pay for wars—and Astor profited handsomely when James Madison blundered into the War of 1812. With Philadelphia banker Stephen Girard, he lent the Treasury money to finance the conflict, and thumbed his nose at both sides by floating part of the war loan in London. His wartime activities might have verged on the treasonable, but his loan to the Treasury saved him from popular wrath and judicial pursuit. Besides, with the election of James Monroe in 1817, a man in Astor's debt occupied the White House.

—◊—

His time was the eight decades that stretched from the end of the American Revolution to the mid-nineteenth century. When he arrived in Baltimore, the jealous states didn't trust the federal government with printing money. A silver dollar was worth $200 of today's money. A clerk earned $150 a year (again × 200, the $30,000 paid an office worker in today's dollars). A person could live comfortably and even with a degree of style on $750 a year. A night at Astor House, the city's first luxury hotel, cost $2, but room and board in New York could be had for $2.50 a week. Horace Greeley, the newspaper editor and reform politician, taunted Astor in 1844 by writing that the average earnings of two-thirds of New York City's population scarcely, if at all, exceeded a dollar a week. The same year Astor gave his granddaughter Laura a wedding gift of $250,000, conservatively worth $50 million today.

It was a time before a centralized, national economy. People worked for a "livelihood" rather than for money. They grew their own food, wove their own cloth, turned their own furniture. Handicrafts were widespread, shops and factories were interspersed among farms, and traffic in goods and money was limited to narrow regions. Fortunes, especially in New York and Virginia, were based on ownership of land. Along the Atlantic coast, wealth was created in the shipping trade, although the pace was slow and temperate. It was a time before railways and telegraphs, when commerce was carried on rivers and the construction of the Erie Canal was a wonder of progress. To reach the Pacific took the better part of a year. The easiest way was to start in the fur capital of Montreal, float down the St. Lawrence through the Great Lakes, cut down to the bottom of Green Bay, haul canoes overland to Lake Winnebago, continue to the upper Mississippi, and run down to the confluence of the Missouri above the frontier town of St. Louis. From here it was three thousand miles up the Missouri, past the friendly Mandan villages and, hopefully, past the fierce Blackfeet, trek overland across the Rockies to the Snake or one of its tributaries, travel by river until reaching the Columbia, and then head down to the coast. The sea route was barely any faster. A Chinaman or East Indiaman sailed south from New York, caught the tradewinds, navigated the treacherous Roaring Forties off Argentina, stopped at the Falklands for freshwater, rounded Cape Horn, ran up the west coast of South America or, more often, cut across to Hawaii for freshwater again before heading for Canton on the Pearl River.

To find passage in Hawaii for what was called the Northwest Coast was difficult. Below the Russian trading post at Sitka, Alaska, Neweetee, on the southern tip of Vancouver

Island, was the sole Indian settlement of consequence. Only fur traders navigated the foggy waters lapping the jagged shores of the Strait of Georgia and Puget Sound and the inlets inhabited by fierce Indians, always alert for pillage and massacre. It was a time before political correctness decreed that the continent's aborigines had lived in peace and harmony until violated by white intruders. Cruelty can be practiced by anyone. President Zachary Taylor, whose soldiering during the Black Hawk War brought him into contact with the American Fur Company's representatives, considered Astor's agents "the greatest scoundrels the world ever knew."

It was the best of times and the worst of times, said Charles Dickens, who visited the new Astor House hotel in New York shortly after it was built. Astor was by then the courtly widower fastidiously fond of music, never happier than when he was surrounded by his grandchildren. Yet the silver-haired patriarch was also a slumlord, a war profiteer, and a ruthless jobber who shipped opium to China, and sold liquor to Indians knowing the devastating consequences. He prospered not only by maximizing profits, but also by riding out storms that sank less well-capitalized rivals. He was perhaps the first entrepreneur to diversify, and, as he said, to see "how one form of commerce could be linked with another to the advantage of both." Best of all, he knew when to get out of a business. He liquidated his China clippers and New York warehouses as tea from Japan and India cut into the China tea trade. He dropped the fur trade as fashions changed and North American beaver pelts and other animal coats became scarce after a century of devastating trapping. Converting the profits from China and the fur trade into Manhattan real estate made him and his descendants for generations the wealthiest Americans.

Astor was in Paris in 1826 when Joseph-Nicéphore Niepce took the world's first photograph. He was still alive when a collection of daguerreotypes went on display in New York in 1839 (his friend Philip Hone thought Louis Daguerre's Parisian landscapes constituted "one of the wonders of modern times"). No photo exists of John Jacob or his immediate family. The lack of photographs is perhaps the reason the American Revolution and the Napoleonic era feels remote compared, say, to the Civil War with its images of soldiers and commanders in the field. Astor had himself painted by the leading portraitists of his day: Gilbert Stuart, who painted George Washington twice, and John W. Jarvis, famous for his portrait of the War of 1812 hero Oliver H. Perry and the Illinois Indian leader Black Hawk. Astor was not handsome and the portraits we have of him are, in the manner of his time, celebratory, posed images.

He was not eloquent and had little talent for flattery, but from an early age his character commanded trust and confidence. He was not a man who lost his temper easily, nor was he given to bragging. He was formal and guarded, but knew how to lead people almost without their knowing they were being led. He and his wife, Sarah, didn't let money go to their heads. When he took over the indebted Aaron Burr's Manhattan manor, the Astors didn't move into Richmond Hill. Instead, they leased it to Governor George Clinton, who, like Burr, found politics expensive and soon had to sell land to Astor.

With the exception of New York's first luxury hotel, he never built anything. He preferred to lease his land and let others do the developing. That put taxes and assessments on the lessee, who usually built a two-story dwelling, often financed by an Astor mortgage. When the typical twenty-one-year lease was up, the builder had ten days to remove the structure, have a neutral committee appraise the property, or see the building revert cost-free to Astor. The extraordinary growth of New York City during his lifetime assured an ever-growing number of tenants and a healthy—reformers would say "obscene"—return on the family investment. His grandson liked to quip that "a man who has a million dollars is as well off as if he were rich."

"Decadence," wrote Thomas Mann in *Buddenbrooks,* the story of the decline of a North German merchant family, "is detectable in the third generation and fatal in the fourth." John Jacob's son William had none of his father's entrepreneurial energy. By the time grandson John J. Astor III inherited the empire, the financial flair was lost, and the rest of the descendants never *made* any money. Many of them, however, had the good sense or luck to marry women smarter than them.

Inherited wealth was new to the United States—and to the Astors. The country believed, and openly declared itself, to be a classless society. One great-grandson bought a British peerage because elitism and wealth inequality were tolerated in England. Some of the Astors were not very talented; some were arrogant dilettantes. Not all were slumlords. They were not famous for their humor, even though journalistic legend has it that great-grandson John Jacob IV came on deck after the *Titanic* hit the iceberg saying, "I asked for ice, but this is ridiculous." They were mostly a dour lot, eccentric and shy in public. One granddaughter-in-law gave balls at her Fifth Avenue mansion that cost $200,000, and refused to invite the Vanderbilts because she thought it ungentlemanly to manipulate railway stocks. Another granddaughter-in-law financed a regiment of black Union soldiers. Some of them tried politics, others gave away a lot of money. All married extravagantly. Great-great-grandson Vincent, who married three times, said that if the Astors were successful it was because the men in the family married clever women, which allowed one great-great-granddaughter-in-law to quip, "I married beneath me—all women do," and to become the first woman elected to the British Parliament. There were no children from any of Vincent's three marriages, and his death in 1959 marked the end of the house of Astor on American soil.

Whatever they all did, old John Jacob's wealth kept them from ruining themselves.

"His story makes for marvelous reading—particularly as he never learned to write English properly," Brooke Astor, the last wife of great-great-grandson Vincent, said over two hundred years after his birth.

1

—⁓—

The Hard Years

At a time when most people lived and died within a hundred miles of where they were born, John Jacob Astor's birth in the German territory of the margrave of Baden-Baden was almost accidental. The Astors—the name was variously spelled Astore and Aoster—were Italian Protestants from the Alpine village of Chiavenna high above the northern end of Lake Como. A medieval ancestor was supposed to have been Pedro de Astorga, a knight from León, in northwestern Spain, whose coat of arms featured a goshawk—*azor* in Spanish—and who was killed in Jerusalem on the Fourth Crusade in 1203. Tracing the lineage back to the Castilian grandee was the genealogical handiwork of John Jacob's great-grandson, William Waldorf Astor, when the latter pressed his case for British peerage. The first documented ancestor is Jean-Jacques d'Astorg, who embraced the Reformation. He and his family are assumed to have been followers of the persecuted Waldensian Puritan faith originating in southern France and existing chiefly in Savoy, a small duchy in northwestern Italy. The religious wars, which broke out in 1618, resulted in brutal persecutions.

Like most subjects of the duke of Savoy, d'Astorg spoke French and Italian, and answered both to Jean-Jacques and Giovan Pietro Astore. The duke of Savoy was a boy of ten and a vassal of Louis XIV in 1685 when the Sun King revoked the Edict of Nantes, which for nearly a century had protected French Calvinists and Lutherans. The massacre of Protestants in Valtellina high up in the Adda Valley sent d'Astorg-Astore, his wife, and their two children fleeing north across Switzerland to Heidelberg, the old university town and Calvinist stronghold where freedom of worship was respected. The family was uprooted again in 1693 when the troops of Louis XIV razed the town. They settled in Zurich, the birthplace a century earlier of Ulrich Zwingli's Reformation. Astore found work as a silk maker and changed his name to Hans Peter Astor. He died in 1711 at the age of forty-seven. His grandson Johann Jakob moved north to Nussloch in Baden, one of the three hundred German principalities, duchies, free cities, and estates forever changing shapes and allegiances as a result of wars and dynastic marriages.

Records show that Johann Jakob and his wife, Anna Margaretha Eberhard, had only one child, Felix Astor. He, too, moved. After Felix married Eva Freund and came into property settled on his wife, the couple established themselves in Walldorf—from the German words *Wald* and *Dorf,* meaning literally "wood village"—a community of a thousand souls on the edge of the Black Forest twenty miles south of Heidelberg.

Baden was a long strip of territory stretching from Mannheim to the Swiss border on the south and on the west facing French Alsace across the Rhine. Baden was divided into two states, Catholic Baden-Baden and Protestant Baden-Durlach, a rift that provided little incentive for commerce and industry. Because the Catholic and Protestant halves had pursued diverging policies, Baden had been left helpless during French expansion across the Rhine. Towns and citadels had been destroyed. Felix Astor bought a vineyard in Walldorf in 1713, but he and Eva were never part of the landowning class, although he achieved the honorable position of churchwarden. They were enterprising in commerce. Johann Jacob chose to stay while his half brother Georg Peter—one of the six sons born to Felix Astor's second wife, Susannah—sought his fortune in England. Johann Jacob became the town butcher and, in 1750, married Maria Magdalena Volfelder, when she was seventeen. Five sons and one daughter were born of the union. The first boy died in infancy. Georg Peter, Johann Heinrich, Catherine, and Melchior followed.

The future empire builder and founder of the Anglo-American dynasty was the fifth and youngest son, born on July 17, 1763. Johann Jakob, as he was christened, was three when his mother died. The widowed butcher remarried, but his new wife, Christina Barbara, proved to be of little benefit to her stepchildren as she bore her husband six children of her own. The first set of children resented their stepmother and the second brood. The loathing was mutual. Perhaps because he was only three when his birth mother died, young Johann Jakob seemed not to have suffered the problems so often associated with boys and stepmothers. No letters indicating his affection for Christina exist, but as a mature man he hired an artist to paint portraits of his father and stepmother. Like modern-day police sketches, the portraits were painstakingly drawn from the adult John Jacob's memory. The portraits showed the elder Johann Jakob, toothless and scrawny, selling fish and game. Christina is thin and wrinkled. She holds up one egg from a basket of eggs in the Walldorf market square.

Maria Magdalena's offspring left the overcrowded home as soon as they were old enough to fend for themselves— Catherine to marry, the boys to seek their fortunes elsewhere. There was little motivation for their father to keep them at home or for them to stay. Johann Jakob Sr. was a stubborn, careless, and optimistic man. After a few steins of beer, he could turn nasty and cruel. None of his children apparently liked him. But he ran Walldorf's leading butcher shop for forty years and after that enjoyed good health for another three decades. He was ninety-two when he died in 1816.

—⚉—

The margrave Karl Friedrich was a benevolent ruler of Baden-Durlach and, after the other line of margraves became extinct in 1771, of Baden-Baden. In his youth, he had visited France, the Netherlands, England, and Italy and for a time studied at the University of Lausanne. With his wife, Caroline Louise of Hesse-Darmstadt, he was devoted to art and science beyond mere patronage, and became a friend of Mirabeau and the benefactor of Goethe, Voltaire, and Linnaeus. His concern for improving farming made him an acquaintance of Pierre S. du Pont de Nemours, who would flee the French Revolution for the United States and make a fortune in gunpowder.

Karl Friedrich introduced reforms that were much admired in other German states. Among them was early schooling, from which the Astor children benefited. Johann Jakob came under the influences of schoolmaster Valentin Jeune, a French Protestant who had settled in Walldorf, and the village pastor, John Philip Steiner. Both men seemed to have recognized an able mind in young Johann Jakob because both made special efforts to broaden the boy's horizons beyond reading, writing, and ciphering. The boy was no dreamer. His talents were practical and analytical, and he was an avid reader of the few books and newspapers available in Walldorf. Since his brothers Georg and Heinrich had emigrated, he was especially interested in foreign countries.

Georg, the eldest son of Johann and Maria Magdalena, had been the first to leave. In London, Uncle Georg Peter secured him a job in a company making musical instruments. Young Georg was a gifted musician and craftsman who did well in his uncle's workshop. In 1777, he borrowed enough money to set out to make his own way in the London music scene. He wooed a young girl named Elizabeth Wright. Because she was under the age of consent, her father had to agree to their union. The fact that he did so suggests Georg was not regarded as a penniless foreigner.

The second son, Heinrich, seized his opportunity when German princes began raising regiments to help the Hanoverian King George III of England fight dissidence in his American colonies. Wars were remarkably passionless in eighteenth-century Europe, restricted by conventions and fought for dynastic reasons, with limited objectives. Nationality made little difference to allegiance. Armies were immobile and expensive, and mostly recruited from nobles, vagabonds, and sons pushed out of large, hardscrabble families. The officer corps was permeated by corruption and ineptness, and was separated from the enlisted men by arrogance and incompetence. Heinrich enlisted in Frankfurt, one of the 29,166 men rented out to George III by German rulers for the gross sum of £850,000 a year. Germany was the British army's traditional recruiting ground. German mercenaries were cheaper to recruit than working-class Englishmen who, although poor, enjoyed a high standard of living and were rarely driven by hunger to enlist. Besides, procuring mercenaries for Britain was all in the family. The ruler of Frankfurt was Prince William of Hesse-Kassel, King George's nephew.

Heinrich sailed in a Royal Navy man-of-war in 1775 and arrived in British-held New York, not as a soldier but as a butcher. His job was to procure and prepare meat to feed the Regiment of Hesse. He Anglicized his name to Henry, but the way he pronounced his last name made people spell it Ashdour. He discovered that a third of the colonists were for accommodation with the Crown, a third were for independence, and a third had no opinion.

When his regiment moved out, he deserted and soon opened a butcher's stall in Fly Market. To overcome the shortage of meat, he slipped out of New York City on horseback and somewhere in Westchester County bought stolen livestock from a raiding party. Under cover of night he drove the animals into town, slaughtered them, and sold the meat. Since his prices were generally lower than those of other butchers, competitors protested.

—⚅—

On Palm Sunday of 1777, fourteen-year-old Johann Jakob was confirmed in the Lutheran Church. For peasant and village boys the ceremony marked the end of schooling. Thanks to Karl Friedrich's education reforms and to schoolmaster Jeune's teaching and interest in him, Johann Jakob was better educated than the majority of poor youths of his time. However much his head was filled with ideas of striking out on his own like George and Henry, he followed his father's edict and learned the butcher's trade.

The next two years were the unhappiest in his life. He hated the slaughterhouse and the butcher shop where he worked skinning animals, jointing carcasses, serving customers, and delivering orders. At fifteen he was an expert meat cutter and, with his knack for calculations, a competent would-be tradesman. He was serious, and eager to improve himself. From his mother he was said to have inherited an alert mind. Physically, he was a lanky blond youth, strong and sturdy.

The letters from his brothers made him realize that Walldorf was, economically, the sticks. Henry wrote from New York that even a butcher boy could earn three times as much as he could in Walldorf. Letters from George in London also stirred John Jacob's imagination, and he showed the letters to Reverend Steiner and Schoolmaster Jeune. The trio gravely discussed the contents. It was hard to believe that the rebels in America could possibly win against the powers of the English king. But George reported that London merchants were uneasy over the way the fighting was going in the colonies.

George suggested Melchior join him in his expanding flute-making business. But Melchior could not or would not leave home. He either had no interest or his father could not do without him. Late in life John Jacob would remember how he tramped miles to collect the letters his brothers sent, how his imagination was stirred by descriptions of life in London and the New World. Melchior eventually left their father's shop and joined a community of the evangelistic Moravian church near Koblenz. There he managed a community school and became a tenant farmer on the estate of the prince of Neuwied.

Johann Jakob wrote back to his brothers, asking if he could take Melchior's place. The answer came from London after many weeks, from New York after many months. Yes, they said, he should leave. We do not know why he chose flute making in London over slaughtering in New York: perhaps one step at the time was sensible, or perhaps money for passage to America was out of the question; after all, the king of England had paid for Henry's Atlantic crossing. Johann Jakob discussed the opportunities with Steiner and Jeune. The choice no doubt came down to what was common sense. Other Germans worked in George's instrument factory. Pastor and schoolmaster put in a word with Butcher Astor. It apparently took months before Johann Jakob Sr. agreed to give the youngest son of his first wife the chance he had afforded his other sons.

Two months short of his seventeenth birthday, Johann Jakob stood at the edge of Walldorf and gravely said goodbye to Steiner, Jeune, and one of his half sisters. Only the teacher was cheerful, saying Johann Jakob had a good head and that the world would hear of him. Out of their sight, Johann Jakob knelt under a tree and, according to a story he probably originated himself, promised *der lieber Gott* he would be honest, industrious, and never gamble. With that he walked to the Rhine and, in the town of Speyer, became a deckhand on a raft transporting Black Forest lumber downriver. Two weeks later he was in Holland with enough money for passage to England. In London he found his way to the Astor & Broadwood musical instrument factory.

Johann Jakob stayed four years in London and Anglicized his name to John Jacob. In 1778, the musical instrument firm of George and John Astor opened its doors at 26 Wych Street, off Drury Lane, in the heart of fashionable London. The brothers made wooden flutes, clarinets, and other wind instruments, slowly broadening their range. As John matured, he learned the business from his brother, and became fluent in English, though he never lost his heavy, guttural accent and never learned the spelling. George was an astute merchant who expanded and diversified into keyboard instruments. John proved to be a born salesman.

News from the American colonies told a confusing story. Letters from Henry spoke of opportunities for ambitious young men and suggested John Jacob come and try his luck. France entered the war on the side of the American rebels the year George and John Jacob opened their shop, and bolstered George Washington's resistance to Britain's veteran troops. The surrender of Cornwallis at Yorktown in 1781 did not settle the conflict, but peace negotiations were started. Thomas Jefferson, President Washington's ambassador to France, was particularly anti-British. "Mr. Jefferson likes us because he detests England," wrote the French minister Pierre Adet, "but he might change his opinion of us tomorrow, if tomorrow Great Britain should cease to inspire his fears." Even after the peace treaty was signed in Paris in 1783, Jefferson brought Anglo-American relations close to war again after a 1790 flare-up between Britain and Spain over English navigator George Vancouver's claims for Britain of a stretch of the Pacific coast of North America.

Twenty-year-old John Jacob possessed both imagination and caution. Peace meant the ex-colonists would turn to cultivating the arts, meaning they would want musical instruments. On the other hand, if the music business failed, there was always the butcher's trade. Flutes were a luxury, but people always needed meat, leather, and furs. The brothers dissolved their London partnership and, with his own modest resources, John Jacob embarked aboard a vessel named the *North Carolina* or the *Carolina* in November 1783. His luggage included a consignment of flutes.

The average transatlantic crossing took sixty-six days. Because of an unusually severe winter, the ship taking John Jacob to America was four months at sea. Captain Jacob Stout veered south toward Baltimore to avoid pack ice, which clogged the more northerly ports. The ship was nevertheless immobilized in the frozen waters of Chesapeake Bay. The ice encasing the vessel was thick enough to walk on, and by February and March 1784 a number of John Jacob's fellow passengers clambered overboard and made their way on foot to the Maryland headland. There are two versions of how John Jacob reached America's shore. In 1929, Arthur Howden Smith would write in *John Jacob Astor: Landlord of New York* that John Jacob waited until the ice broke and the captain was able to move the ship to her berth. In his 1993 biography, *The Astors 1763–1992: Landscape with Millionaires,* Derek Wilson would claim John Jacob stayed on the ship because the shipping company was obliged to provide bed and board until the end of the voyage. However, by March 24 or 25, he, too, had enough and, with no sign of an imminent thaw, made his way across the frozen Chesapeake Bay to Baltimore.

Half a century later, when he commissioned the best-selling author, historian, diplomat, and gossip Washington Irving to write his life story, he dictated this sketch of his first day in the New World:

> I took a walk to see the town, getting up Market Street. While standing and looking about, a little man came out of his shop. This was Nicholas Tuschdy. He addressed me saying— young man I believe you are a stranger, to which I replied yes. Where did you come from—from London—but you are not an Englishman, no a German. Then he says we are near countrymen. I am a Swiss—we are glad to see people coming to this country from Europe. On this he asked me into his house and offered me a glass of wine and introduced me to his wife as a countryman. He offered his services and advice while in Baltimore and requested me to call again to see him.

John Jacob stayed three weeks in Baltimore. Tuschdy displayed some of John Jacob's instruments in his shop window. Several sold. When it was time for J. J. to move on, he had money enough to take a coach for New York.

2

—ɯ—

Flutes and Miss Todd

O n his twenty-first birthday, or shortly before or after July 17, 1784, John Jacob stepped ashore in
Manhattan from the New Jersey ferry. No imposing figure, he was strikingly blond, but short, with a slim
face, brown eyes, a prominent nose, pale complexion, and
long, straight hair. He had rough manners, and spoke un-
couth English.

Henry was doing well, but like so many newcomers writing home had embellished his success to his kid brother. He
was no longer hawking meat from a wheelbarrow. He was delivering his victuals by horse cart and vying for a stall of his
own in Maiden Lane. A month before John Jacob's arrival,
he had acquired a wife, a girl still in her teens. Dorothea
Pessenger was the stepdaughter of John Pessenger, a meat
seller who occupied Stall #1, the most advantageous location, in the Fly Market. Henry and Dorothea had set up
housekeeping in a small house at First and Fisher Streets.
John Jacob was given a warm welcome, but was not invited
to stay with his brother and sister-in-law. Whether Henry
thought it imprudent to leave his young wife with John
Jacob or didn't have space for his young brother, he arranged

for John Jacob to become the lodger of a baker named George Dietrich at nearby 150 Queen Street. Dietrich had known the Astors in Germany. Henry suggested that John Jacob work for him, but J. J. turned down the job offer. No more butchering.

Dietrich needed a peddler boy to hawk his cakes, cookies, doughnuts, and rolls, and John Jacob's first job was to sell the Dietrich confections in the streets. With a basket of wares, he walked up and down cobble-laid Broad Street, with its rattling handcarts, spangled phaetons, and lines of shops. John Jacob no more wanted to become a baker's hawker than be a butcher's assistant, but peddling for Dietrich taught him the layout of the city. His next job was with an elderly Quaker. Robert Browne was a fur dealer, and during the summer of 1784, J. J.'s main chore was beating the furs to keep the moths away. The pay was $2 a week and board. Astor carried out Browne's orders with competence and within a few weeks, Browne increased his new employee's wages. J. J. was quick to learn. The best beaver skins were from Canada. The most highly prized skins for hatters were *castors gras d'hiver* ("beavers taken in winter"). Indians scraped the raw side, a process that weakened the roots of the long hairs and made them fall out. Next, the Indians sewed a number of pelts into a dress, which they wore next to their bodies for several months. This made the pelts soft and greasy, the fur downy—the most desirable for the finest hats. Pelts worn only a short time were called *demi gras*. Beavers killed in the summer were *castors gras d'été*. *Castors secs* were skins that had not been worn at all, and their value depended on the season in which they had been killed.

Working for Quaker Browne, as he was called, didn't prevent John Jacob from disposing of the rest of the instruments he had brought with him from London. As was the custom for people who had articles to sell but did not own a shop, he made arrangements with Samuel Loudon, a job printer and publisher of the *New York Packet*. The September 20, 1784, ad read:

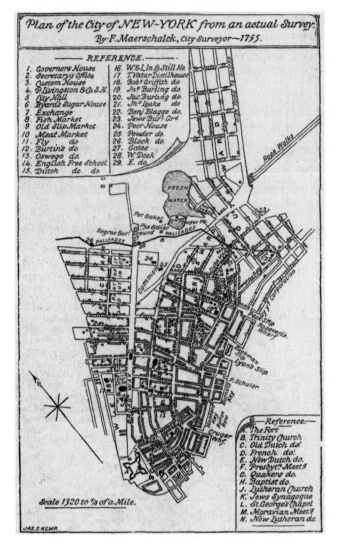

New York City map

GERMAN FLUTES of a Superior Quality to be Sold at this Printing-Office.

We do not know whether advertising the flutes as German was homage to his and his brother's homeland or whether, ten months after the end of the war with England, it was a diplomatic way of distancing the merchandise from the former colonial power. In any case, George sent John Jacob a new shipment of flutes. Quaker Browne, meanwhile, was happy with his energetic assistant, and showed his appreciation by giving him a pocket watch. The silver time-piece of the so-called English bulldog type was engraved: "Presented to John Jacob Astor by R. Browne, 1785."

John Jacob invested his money in flutes and skins. On Sundays and evenings he could be found on Beekman Slip, Hunter's Key, Schermerhorn's Wharf, and other docks and quaysides on the East River, going aboard sloops and barges to ask river men if they might have a pelt or two for sale. Back in his room at Quaker Browne's, he beat the skins, then cleaned and packed them. He didn't sell them but put them in storage. In the fall of 1785, he had enough pelts to make it worth his while to sail across the Atlantic to dispose of his consignment in London at a good profit. Once there, he picked up flutes from George and convinced two reputable British piano makers to name him their American agent.

Profit margins were sizable, as fashionable New Yorkers demanded the luxurious trappings of sophisticated European society. Within a few years, John Astor built a business not quite rivaling that of New York's two established music dealers, Messrs. Dodd and Wilks of 66 and 235 Queen Street, respectively. Still, he also located his musical emporium in Queen Street, albeit in a walk-up room at number 81.

He informed the readers of the May 22, 1786, edition of the *New York Packet* that he had imported a new supply of instruments:

JACOB ASTOR, 81 Queen Street, Two doors from the Friends Meeting House, has just imported from London an elegant assortment of Musical Instruments, such as pianofortes, spinets, pianoforte guitars, the best of violins, German flutes, clarinets, hautboys, fifes, the best Roman violin strings, and all other kinds of strings, music books and paper, and every other article in the musical line, which he will dispose of on very low terms for cash.

His landlady was Sarah Cox Todd. Mrs. Todd was related to the Brevoorts, a notable old New York Dutch family. Her two sons and a son-in-law were sea captains, but she lived in reduced circumstances herself. Her husband's death had left her almost penniless and obliged her to take in lodgers. She liked her young German tenant and so did her daughter, also named Sarah. On Sundays after church, the two young people went walking under the tulip trees and chestnuts that made the Bowery deserving of its name. On September 19, 1785, John married Sarah.

No details of the nuptials have come down to us. Brother Henry and sister-in-law Dorothea might have been generous, and the Brevoorts may have sent a gift on the occasion of their poor relations' wedding. Perhaps Widow Todd gave a dinner and the other lodgers chipped in with drinks. We don't know. We don't even know what the bride looked like. Several biographers have said she was no beauty, that she was not even conventionally pretty. The only portrait extant of Sarah Todd Astor is an engraving executed when she was a middle-aged woman. It shows her as a woman of regular features with a frank gaze and full, sensuous lips.

Calculation no doubt played a bigger role than passion. A year older than her husband, young Sarah brought with her a dowry of $300. No doubt she, in turn, appreciated John Jacob's initiative, knowledge of music, dexterity with a carving knife, and serious attitude toward life. Many of the young men boarding with her mother were veterans of the War of Independence, given to booze and restlessness. Both mother and daughter appreciated that John Jacob was a hard worker. They also liked his taste for fine music and the fact that he regularly, if not assiduously, attended church. Perhaps more important for John Jacob, his new in-laws had strong maritime and commercial connections. He much admired the Brevoort farm out in the country at Broadway and Fourth Street, where Broadway detoured because the elder Brevoort refused to let the city run a road across his property.

Mrs. Todd gave the newlyweds two rooms. The front first-floor space was the showroom for the music business. The rear room on the same floor served as the newlyweds' living quarters, bedroom, and kitchen. Sarah threw herself into

Sarah Todd Astor

her husband's affairs and encouraged his entrepreneurial bent. Besides her $300, John Jacob had hoarded a couple of hundred from the music business and the transaction in pelts he had learned from Quaker Browne and his trip to London. Within a few weeks of their marriage, Sarah waved good-bye to her husband as he took a boat up the Hudson River to Albany to try his hand at fur trading.

3

—ɯ—

Into the Woods

The Old World conquered the Americas largely for commercial gain. The desire for the wealth to be made from the acquisition of animal skins led to the opening up of North America. The French were the pioneers. Operating out of Montreal and traveling by the continent's waterways, hunters, trappers, *coureurs de bois* ("woodsmen," or ambulant traders), and *voyageurs*, or boatmen, built up a highly profitable trade with Indians who arrived at the trading posts every spring, their canoes laden with pelts. At the end of the Seven Years' War, in 1763, when the French lost Canada, this fabulous trade fell into British hands.

As John Jacob tramped through the wilderness of upstate New York, buying beaver skins from trappers—mostly European adventurers, Indians, and mixed-race men cheating, fighting, and outwitting one another—the Union Jack still flew over Niagara and Detroit. To regulate the trade north and east of the Great Lakes, leading merchants in Montreal formed the Northwest Company. To monopolize the vast, unexplored hinterland of the new, confederated States, assorted Scots and French Canadians set up the

Mackinac (or Mackinaw) Company on the strait between Lake Huron and Lake Michigan.

During the next years, John Jacob was a harbinger of spring in Albany, arriving with the first sloop to get through from New York City after the ice melted. He struck out on foot along the Indian trail snaking westward through the Onondaga settlement to the Finger Lakes country, the Allegheny Valley, and the mountains of Pennsylvania. He ranged west to Buffalo and north into the Adirondacks. He drove himself unsparingly. One contemporary wrote that before the Canandaigua settlement was founded in 1789, John Jacob Astor, with a backpack of Indian goods, one night strayed from the Indian trail, got lost in the low grounds at the foot of Seneca Lake, and wandered amid the rustling of wild animals until almost morning, when he was attracted by the light of an Indian cabin. James Wadsworth, whose father remembered meeting J. J. in the woods of western New York, told one of the few anecdotes extant of Astor's humbler years. "His wagon had broken down in the midst of a swamp," the elder Wadsworth reported. "In the melee all his gold had rolled off the tail-piece and vanished into the ooze, and was irrevocably lost; and Astor was seen emerging from the swamp covered with mud and carrying on his shoulder an ax—the sole relic of his property." To which Astor's business biographer Kenneth W. Porter would sensibly add: "It was doubtful he would carry any considerable quality of gold while engaged in Indian trade."

John Jacob discovered that Mohawks and Senecas liked music, and when the occasion was right he took out a flute and tootled a few Baden-Baden folk tunes. He was seen in the taprooms of the frontier taverns and was remembered for his insatiable thirst for knowledge of geography, tribes, and, of course, furs. Muskrat, raccoon, deer, wolf, and bear had always been used for clothing, but smart men and women in London and New York wanted to adorn themselves in finer furs—beaver, marten, ermine, mink, and otter.

Peter Smith was a salesman of books, beeswax, lace, walking sticks, and snuffboxes who became a friend. In

1788, Smith and Astor made a number of trading trips together to Fort Schuyler, where Smith opened a general store
and became a founder of the future city of Utica. Of Astor's
utilitarian business correspondence only his letters to Smith
show a capacity for affection and kindness. John Jacob had
advanced money in a land deal in which Smith and he were
associated with the New York fur trader William Laight.
In November 1794, when Astor needed money to finance
another trip to Europe, he wrote a "Dear Peter" letter: "You
Know that I would as soon injure myself as to do it you . . .
you Know that I have put every Confidence in you that One
man can in another & which I have found you have always
kept Sacred altho' its probably that I may want money very
much next Summer yet I would no ask you for any more
than what you can pay without injuring yourself . . . I have
and wish to Show you as much real Friendship as can be
expected from any person who art the same time wishes you
do his duty to his family I wish you well god Bless you &
keep you in health."

John Jacob was a canny trader. Few trappers or Indians
got the better of him. He did it all himself, hauling the
furs back to Albany, baling and loading them on barges
down to New York for reshipment to London. The profits
were as much as 1,000 percent. Still, he realized, it was all
exceedingly small beer. To make it big in the fur trade he
had to be in Montreal.

Lack of capital held him back. Henry refused to lend him
money, but gave his brother $200 on the condition that he
never asked again. To raise more capital, John Jacob made
deals with established furriers. Two years after he entered
the business, he journeyed up the Hudson past Albany to the
Hudson Falls, where the river turned west. On horseback,
he reached Lake George. From there a sloop carried him onto
Lake Champlain to Plattsburgh, New York, where he stayed
with Peter Sailly, the newly appointed collector of customs.
After spending a night in front of Sailley's big open kitchen
fire, J. J. boarded a lake boat that took him to Rouses Point,
on the border. In a smaller craft he sailed down the Richelieu
River to Saint-Jean, Quebec. From here he traveled in a

wagon to the St. Lawrence River, and in August 1787, he reached Montreal.

Canada's largest settlement was a growing city. Twelve years earlier, the American Revolution had led to an unsuccessful attack on Montreal, and since the end of the war, Americans loyal to the Crown had swelled the ranks of the town's British element and opened up the adjacent eastern townships. Astor met one of Montreal's prominent Britons, Alexander Henry, who had been a British soldier fighting the French during the Seven Years' War. This legendary trapper and frontiersman was a man of some education who recorded his observations and experiences in *Travels and Adventures in Canada and the Indian Territories*. He had entered the fur trade and traveled widely from the St. Lawrence to the Great Lakes and beyond to the Saskatchewan. Trying to hang on to the remnants of their great empire, Montreal's French merchants at first refused to work with him. However, he had established his own house in Montreal and had worked his way to becoming a shareholder of the Northwest Fur Company.

Unlike the formidable Hudson's Bay Company, which operated with a royal charter, the Northwest Company was a partnership formed in 1783. The twenty-three shareholders, or partners, employed two thousand clerks, guides, interpreters, and voyageurs. William McGillivray was the president and Simon McTavish the organizer of the company. The roster included some formidable names, including Alexander Mackenzie, who was planning a journey across Canada to the Pacific via the Peace and Fraser Rivers, and Benjamin and Joseph Frobisher, descendants of Martin Frobisher, the navigator who had searched for the Northwest Passage and given his name to a bay in Arctic Canada. Some of the partners administered the company from Montreal; others lived year-round at the trading posts on the lakes and rivers as "wintering partners." The "Northwesters" were successful. During the year 1793, for example, the company shipped 106,000 beaver, 2,100 bear, 1,500 fox, 400 kit fox, 16,000 muskrat, 32,000 marten, 1,800 mink, 6,000 lynx, 6,000 wolverine, 1,600 fisher, 100 raccoon, 1,200 dressed deer, 700 elk, and 550 buffalo skins.

Tracing the Northwest Company's organization, Washington Irving wrote:

> The goods destined for this wide and wandering traffic were put at the warehouses of the company in Montreal, and conveyed in bateaux, or boats, and canoes, up the river Attawa, or Ottawa, which falls into the St. Lawrence, near Montreal, and by other rivers and portages, to lake Nipising, lake Huron, lake Superior, and thence, by several chains of great and small lakes, to lake Winnipeg, lake Athabasca, and the great Slave lake. This singular and beautiful system of internal seas, which renders an immense region of wilderness so accessible to the frail bark of the Indian or the trader, was studded by the remote posts of the company, where they carried on their traffic with the surrounding tribes.
>
> The company, as we have shown, was at first a spontaneous association of merchants, but, after it had been regularly organized, admission into it became extremely difficult. A candidate had to enter, as it were, "before the mast," to undergo a long probation, and to rise slowly by his merits and services. He began, at an early age, as a clerk, and served an apprenticeship of seven years, for which he received £100, was maintained at the expense of the company, and furnished with suitable clothing and equipments. His probation was generally passed at the interior trading posts; removed for years from civilized society, leading a life almost as wild and precarious as the savages around him; exposed to the severities of a northern winter, often suffering from a scarcity of food, and sometimes destitute for a long time of both bread and salt. When his apprenticeship had expired, he received a salary according to his deserts, varying from £80 to £160, and was now eligible to the great object of his ambition, a partnership in the company; though years might yet elapse before he attained to that enviable station. Most of the clerks were young men of good families, from the Highlands of Scotland, characterized by the perseverance, thrift, and fidelity of their country, and fitted by their native hardiness to encounter the rigorous climate of the north, and to endure the trials and privations of their lot.

Irving had visited Montreal "in the days of the McTavishes, the McGillivrays, the McKenzies, the Frobishers and the other magnates" and would remember one or two partners showing up in New York. "On these occasions there was always a degree of magnificence of the purse about them, and a peculiar propensity to expenditures at the gold-smiths and jewelers for rings, chains, brooches, necklaces, jeweled watches, and other rich trinkets, partly for their own ware, partly for presents to their female acquaintances; a gorgeous prodigality, such as was often to be noticed in former times in southern planters and West Indian creoles, when flush with the profits of their plantations."

Once a year the Northwest partners traveled to their Fort William outpost in today's northeastern Wisconsin. "They ascended the rivers in great state, like sovereigns making a progress or rather like Highland chieftains navigating their subject lakes," Irving would write. "They were wrapped in rich furs, their huge canoes freighted with every convenience and luxury, and manned by Canadian voyageurs, as obedient as Highland clansmen. They carried up with them cooks and bakers, together with delicacies of every kind, and abundance of choice wines for the banquet which attended this great convocation." When Irving wrote this passage in 1835, the Northwest Company was a thing of the past.

At the height of its opulence, Philip Turnor, a Hudson's Bay officer, expressed his disgust at the extravagance of Northwest officers in a letter to the Hudson's Bay headquarters in London. A Hudson's Bay employee was expected to do his own paddling, and at the end of a day eat whatever game or fish there was to eat before rolling himself up in a blanket under a tree for the night. The Northwest partners, Turnor wrote, "give men who never saw an Indian one hundred pounds PR. ANNUM, his feather bed carried in the canoe, his tent, which is exceeding good, pitched for him, his bed made, and he and his girl carried in and out of the canoe, and when in the canoe he never touches a paddle unless for his own pleasure. All of these indulgences I have been an eyewitness to."

—ɯ—

Alexander Henry was impressed by Astor's grasp of the business, and helped the young German conclude deals for expertly dressed and bundled furs. An agreement in the archives of Palais de Justice in Paris shows that on September 30, 1788, Astor and one Roseter Hoyle, a Canadian merchant, signed a contract for shipping furs from Montreal to New York and Rotterdam. This first document of Astor's fur trade stipulated that he was to ship "two thousand dollars in Furrs and Peltries more or less" to the order of Hoyle in London. Hoyle was to reship half the pelts to Astor in New York, and half to Rotterdam. The furs shipped to Astor were invoiced at £704 14s 3d. It is a tribute to the savvy of the twenty-five-year-old newcomer's first trip to Montreal that he could muster credit to contract for furs valued at $3,000.

Undoubtedly with Henry's help, Astor got to travel to Fort William, near Grand Portage on today's Minnesota-Ontario border. Space was at a premium in canoes and Henry must have used his considerable influence to secure a seat for John Jacob. The big canoe to which he was assigned was forty feet long, made of birch bark and caulked with pine resin. The cargo, weighing two tons, was wrapped and tied in hundred-pound packs, which could be carried over portages. Fully loaded, the canoes had only six inches clearance in the water, which forced the voyageurs to hug the shores instead of crossing the often-choppy waters of the Great Lakes. In good weather they could make six miles an hour. Overland, the canoe was carried on the shoulders of ten or twelve men.

Once on Lake Huron some of the big canoes reached the end of their outward voyage at Michilimackinac on the peninsula, where Lake Huron meets Lake Michigan. Michilimackinac was an Algonquin word meaning "Great Turtle" and referred to a turtle god that was supposed to inhabit the peninsula. Trappers and traders set out from here for Lake Superior and its tributary waters as far as the shores of Lake Winnipeg and the Saskatchewan River or for the Mississippi, the Arkansas, and the Missouri. Most of the year Michilimackinac was a village. However, when crews returned, often after a year or more, the place swarmed with people. The broad beach was a kind of public promenade. Again Washington Irving:

Voyageurs frolicked away their wages, fiddling and dancing in the booths and cabins, buying all kinds of knick-knacks, dressing themselves out finely, and parading up and down, like arrant braggarts and coxcombs. Sometimes they met with rival coxcombs in the young Indians from the opposite shore, who would appear on the beach painted and decorated in fantastic style, and would saunter up and down to be gazed at and admired, perfectly satisfied that they eclipsed their pale-faced competitors.

John Jacob stayed with the canoes that pushed up St. Mary's River to Lake Superior, then hugged the northern shore of the huge body of water until at last they came to Grand Portage and Fort William. Here on the northern shore of Lake Superior, 1,500 miles west of Montreal, he grasped the sheer scale of the Northwest Company's operations. Here packs of furs from the previous winter and spring were waiting to be loaded for the return trip. The pelts came from as far as the shores of Lake Winnipeg and the Saskatchewan River. Here he learned of the rough diplomacy that prevailed on the frontier, the knowledge of when to say no and when to make a joke or turn an ugly confrontation into a reasonable counteroffer. Indians required deft handling. They should not be hurried in driving a bargain, and should always be sent away with the impression they had bested the white man. Brawls were frequent and could be deadly as knives and tomahawks flashed and victims fell screaming to the ground. Canadian traders were forbidden to supply Indians with alcohol. Yet a large part of the canoe cargoes was cheap New England rum made from West Indies molasses. The Quebecois voyageurs were touchy, as ready as Indians to drink themselves into a stupor. Their religion was a mixture of errant Catholicism, Indian folklore, and superstition. Around campfires they told John Jacob of rivers, prairies, and mountain ranges that could be found on no maps.

Loaded to the gunwales with packs of furs, they set off on the return trip, joined at Michilimackinac by boats carrying furs from as far south and west as the Illinois, the Wisconsin, and other streams of the Mississippi basin. At Michilimackinac, John Johnson, the Irish husband of Whitefisher, a chief's daughter, told John Jacob of western rivers, prairies,

and mountains. There he also met George and Charles Er-
martinger, sons of a Swiss merchant, who switched to German when they recognized his accent. Why didn't he stay
with them? They had plenty of pelts for trade and he might
trade for himself with nearby tribes. He was tempted, but
wanted to get back to Sarah. Talks with them and others
at Michilimackinac made him realize how difficult it was
to keep a monopoly together. In a settlement on the Mississippi called St. Louis, Spanish and Louisiana French traders
clashed with hunters from the Michilimackinac who claimed
exclusive rights to the Illinois country and along the Wabash
and the lower Ohio. To the north, the formidable Hudson's
Bay Company squeezed the Northwest men.

Chartered by Charles II in 1670 to promote trade in
the Hudson Bay region and to seek the fabled Northwest
Passage to Asia, the company not only controlled the fur
trade but governed immense expanses of territory. Although
it ruled by right of charter, whereas the Northwest partners controlled by right of possession, there were also sim-
ilarities. Both were essentially feudal in the traditions of
eighteenth-century Europe, with class divisions and func-
tioning on top-to-bottom loyalties. The Britons provided
leadership and kept the books, the French Canadians han-
dled the boats and sometimes trapped, and hired Indians
both trapped and did the menial tasks. Freelancing Iroquois who traded with Yankee upstarts were accused not
of breaching a legal obligation but of disloyalty, and never
mind that the Americans paid more for pelts.

There was talk of merging Hudson's Bay and the Northwest Company. Alexander Mackenzie, who in 1793 became
the first white man to cross the Rockies north of New Spain,
suggested that if the two companies combined, the fur trade
from the Great Lakes west through today's northern Minnesota, North Dakota, Montana, and Washington and north
to the pole would be theirs. Jealousy and mistrust killed the
plan.*

---

*The two companies' "fur trade war" ended in 1821 when the British
government imposed a merger under the name and charter of Hudson's Bay Company.

It dawned on John Jacob that to reach the front ranks of fur dealers, he would have to set up trading posts of his own and, like the Northwest Company, have Indians and traders bring their pelts to him. He also realized the real money was not in selling pelts in New York but in exporting the furs to Europe.

—ɯ—

He was back home in New York in October or early November 1788, and immediately inserted additional information into an advertisement for musical instruments in the *Packet*:

> He gives cash for all kinds of Furs; and has for sale a quantity of Canada Furs, such as beaver, beaver coating, raccoon skins, raccoon blankets, and spring musk rat skins which he sells by large or small quantities—a considerable allowance will be made to every person who buys in quantity.

Sarah gave birth to a daughter that year. They named her Magdalen, after John Jacob's mother. The new parents lived frugally and worked long hours. John Jacob spoke of his wife as a business partner and acknowledged that when it came to gauging the quality of pelts, she was the better judge. To get extra cash and experience, he sometimes worked for other furriers and plowed every penny back into the business. Still, he, Sarah, and little Magdalen moved from Mrs. Todd's boardinghouse into larger premises they bought at 40 Little Dock Street (later Water Street). They needed extra space for the increased quantities of furs and lived in the three-room apartment above the ground-floor warehouse. Sarah was pregnant again. The child, a girl, died in infancy. A year later, Sarah gave birth to a boy they named John Jacob II.

They prospered. Contemporary records show a dealer could sell a beaver pelt in London for 25 shillings, or $3. For that amount he could buy a musket for which, in trading with Indians, he could get ten first-quality beaver skins.

—ɯ—

John Jacob duplicated the Northwest Company on a modest scale. Instead of tramping the wilderness trails of upstate

New York, he established his own depot at Schenectady on the Mohawk River. He also spent half the year journeying to and from Montreal to personally buy supplies. When in New York, he could be found on the docks of South Street helping to load or unload a ship. In association with the London fur dealer Thomas Backhouse and Company, he imported an ever-widening range of general goods. After an initial transaction in 1790, J. J. regularly shipped casks of peltries to Thomas Backhouse and Company. Backhouse's brother William lived in New York and was a partner of William Laight. At the recommendation of Laight, with whom Astor and Peter Smith had been in business, the elderly Backhouse invited the young trader to his home, offered help and advice, and, apparently, loans when John Jacob's business outgrew his capital.

Sarah urged her husband to use his gift of persuasion by making contacts with people frequenting the Tontine Coffee House, the favorite meeting place of the mercantile class. The owner was Nesbitt Deane, an Irishman famous for his extravagant hats who, besides breakfast and coffee at all hours, offered lodgings "suitable for gentlemen either of divinity, law, or physic, and fit for a notary public or insurance office."

John Jacob became a Freemason. He knew the power of Masonic lodges in Germany and England and decided to seek to join the prestigious Holland 8 lodge. There are indications that his in-laws, perhaps at the urging of Sarah, sponsored his application. In 1790, the Holland lodge, whose members included Governor George Clinton and Robert R. Livingston, an influential merchant who had helped draft the Declaration of Independence, accepted Astor and Governor Clinton's nephew, DeWitt Clinton, whose political career would make him a U.S. senator and mayor of New York. Besides DeWitt, with whom he passed through the various grades of membership, John Jacob rubbed shoulders with the likes of Stephen Van Rensselaer, a New York legislator of his own age, and, he noted, made several "useful" acquaintances. To meet younger men destined for fame and fortune, Sarah took John Jacob to a Mrs. Keese's boardinghouse

Tontine Coffee House

on the corner of Broadway and Wall Street, across from the Trinity Yard. Mrs. Keese's was both the residence and meeting place of politicians and lawyers. Here, John Jacob and Sarah made friends with John Armstrong, a future secretary of war, and William Van Ness, a young lawyer who was to become a prominent Democrat and judge of the Southern District of the State of New York. Astor was to become involved in several land deals of historical significance with another lawyer he met at Mrs. Keese's: Aaron Burr, the mercurial leader of the radical wing of the Jeffersonian Democratic-Republican Party.

Politics and the soundness of John Jacob's business saw him through the Duer Panic in 1792. William Duer was Treasury Secretary Alexander Hamilton's assistant and, like his boss, a proponent of a national currency and of the creation of a national bank. To strengthen the national government, Hamilton asked the Federalist-controlled Congress to assume the states' war debt and pay off the liability with excise taxes and import tariffs. In March, Duer's arrest on corruption charges led to the country's first financial panic. Insolvency and ruin were widespread as property values plummeted. The fur trade, however, held steady. In a letter to Peter Smith, John Jacob commented on the number of bankruptcies affecting him. That Duer went to prison one day after a branch office of the Bank of the United States opened in the city intensified anti-federalist sentiments and gave a strategic edge to the Republicans.

John Jacob's benefactor William Backhouse died that same year. A month later, when Sarah gave birth to a second son they named him William Backhouse. John Jacob and Sarah moved again, this time to 149 Broadway, where leading citizens lived among maples and tulip trees.

If Astor had a philosophy it was to let the chips fall where they may, to make the best of opportunities and not cry over spilt milk. He was forceful and compelling in meetings, but he had little interest in parties, balls, lavish dinners, and theater outings (which didn't prevent him from becoming the half owner of the Park Theater on Broadway). Devout Sarah had even less taste for leisure and distractions. Still, they attended functions where convention and business required their presence. As their fortunes grew, Sarah liked to entertain her husband's friends at home, especially when they brought their families. She was a giving, thoughtful hostess. When he was not traveling, she insisted he go to church with her on Sundays to be seen by respectable lawyers and bankers.

On a rare occasion she took a boat trip up to Albany, but she never went to Montreal or London with him. Road travel was often painful and sea voyages hazardous. Besides, it was not customary for eighteenth-century wives to accompany their husbands on business trips. What kept wives close to the hearth, besides household duties, were frequent pregnancies. Sarah bore John Jacob eight children, five of whom survived infancy. Only two would outlive their parents.

4

—⁀⁀—

Politics

During Astor's lifetime the fur trade was a contentious activity. Long before the creation of the new United States, the fur trade's fabulous riches—and its reliance on unruly frontiersmen and unpredictable Native Americans—exasperated Britain and France and led to proxy wars between the two old enemy powers. Roving English, Portuguese, and French captains had found little of interest along the coasts of North America until Jacques Cartier ascended the St. Lawrence River in 1535 and, in the name of King Francis I of France, took possession of the land. He found no equivalent of Aztec or Inca treasures, however, and interest in the interior waned. Breton and Basque fishermen were drawn to the sea riches of the Gulf of St. Lawrence and incidentally began a trade in furs with local Indians. By 1600, American furs, particularly beaver, were sufficiently prized in Europe for French monarchs to establish a fur trade monopoly. Over the next century, French fur merchants ventured farther and farther inland. Because of hostility by the Iroquois, they initially avoided the lower Great Lakes and followed the Ottawas into the interior. After a British-French rapprochement during the later years of Louis XIV's long reign, the traditional rivalries flared again. In 1740, the War of the Austrian Secession, which once more pitted England against France, featured a New World chapter. In 1745, New Englanders attacked and captured Louisbourg, on Cape Breton Island in Nova Scotia. The war ended three years later with New France recapturing Louisbourg, but both sides regarded the peace as little more than a truce.

For the Europeans of North America who did not yet think of themselves as Americans or Canadians, the theater of conflict shifted west to the Ohio Valley and the lands which later became Michigan, Wisconsin, and Minnesota. Both English and French traders needed the friendship of Native Americans. In 1749, the French laid claim to the Ohio Valley and five years later built Fort Duquesne at the forks where the Monongahela and Allegheny Rivers join to form the Ohio (today's Pittsburgh). The leader of a British expedition sent out to dislodge the French was a young Virginia officer named George Washington. He was defeated, as was General Edward Braddock the following year.

The Seven Years' War between France and England broke out in 1756 and its North American extension got a name of its own—the French and Indian War. The conflict, which ended with the Treaty of Paris in 1763, was disastrous for France, although Louis XV's negotiators thought they got the better of the British by giving up Canada—"a few acres of snow," in Voltaire's phrase—and keeping the Caribbean island possessions with their sugar and coffee. Forgotten was Canada's fabulous fur trade, which fell into British hands.

The American War of Independence ended twenty years later with another Paris peace treaty. Besides acknowledging the independence of the thirteen colonies and the settlement of boundaries, William Petty Fitzmaurice, earl of Sherbourne (and a friend of Benjamin Franklin), conceded the right of American fishermen to dry and cure fish on British coasts. The American negotiators—Franklin, John Jay, John Adams, and Henry Laurens—in turn gave in to British demands that creditors on either side should meet no lawful impediment to collecting their debts. This provision went a long way to explain Thomas Jefferson's visceral hatred of Britain. Jefferson, who was President Washington's ambassador to France from 1785 to the outbreak of the French Revolution in 1789, belonged to Virginia's landed gentry (he owned eleven thousand acres), but he was deep in debt to English and Scottish banks. The effects of wartime inflation, the decline of productivity of his lands during his ten-year absence from Monticello, and his inability to live within a budget would keep him in debt to the end of his life. Not that his case was exceptional. Residents of the Old Dominion owed £2.3 million to English and Scottish creditors and Virginia's leading families were also the most prominent names on British merchants' list of thirty thousand delinquent debtors. As Jefferson explained to a French admirer, the debts of Virginia's planters were "hereditary from father to son for so many generations, so that the planters were a species of property, annexed to certain mercantile houses in London." This debtor's resentment became a tenet of Jefferson's policy as president. "Americans," Alexis de Tocqueville quoted Jefferson as saying, "should never be in a position to ask for special treatments of foreign nations so as never to have to return favors."

John Jacob was not to meet Jefferson until 1803, but the young fur trader was keenly interested in the part of the peace treaty by which Britain ceded territories stretching west of the thirteen states to the Mississippi. A series of Orders in Council in 1783 had excluded American vessels from Canada and the British West Indies except to trade in American products. Peace had reopened U.S.-Canadian trade, but the British government had no intention of giving up the lucrative fur trade carried out in the ill-defined territories bordering the Great Lakes.

Maps were one thing; reality on the ground was something else. West of the Mississippi, French Louisiana supposedly occupied an area double the size of the thirteen states, stretching from the Gulf of Mexico to central Canada. Beyond Louisiana, two-thirds of the rest of the continent was nominally Spanish territory. In a vast no-white-man's-land north of a line from modern-day Nebraska to California, a polyglot throng of trappers and fur traders was reaching the foothills of the Rockies. Ships from various countries plied the northern coast of the Pacific to trade for sea otter pelts, which commanded exorbitant prices in China. Robert Gray, an American captain, discovered and mapped the mouth of the Columbia River while George Vancouver, who had accompanied James Cook on his second and third voyages of discovery, charted and named Puget Sound and Georgia Strait. Alexander Mackenzie reached the Pacific at Dean Channel, on today's British Columbia coast, almost midway between Vancouver and Juneau, Alaska.

—m—

Trade—and its regulation—occupied the minds of government leaders on both sides of the Atlantic. Spain enforced a law that channeled all trade between its New World possessions and Europe through Spanish ports. The outbreak of the French Revolution, however, changed the chessboard. For a time British intellectuals responded warmly to the cry of *liberté, égalité, fraternité,* but the tumultuous events in Paris that led to the beheading of Louis XVI and *la terreur* cooled the democratic ardor. Feeling itself surrounded by hostile monarchies bent on strangling the republic to prevent its ideas from spreading, France declared war on England. What immediately hurt John Jacob in the pocketbook was the British decision to copy the Spanish trade restrictions, and forbid direct transit of goods between Canada and the United States. Montreal consignments for New York had to be routed via London.

In response to these limits on his actions, John Jacob began to seriously court politicians. He knew many of them from Tontine's, from Mrs. Keese's parlor, and from Masonic lodge meetings. From the state legislator and sugar importer James Roosevelt, the great-grandfather of President Franklin D. Roosevelt, he bought for $25,000 a tract of rural Manhattan in what is today an area bounded by 5th Avenue, the East River, 10th Street, and 125th Street, about 120 city blocks. Roosevelt had wanted to farm the land, but after cutting the timber he found the soil too poor and rocky.

Like his father, Isaac, James Roosevelt was a Federalist. Federalists were in control of Congress, but in New York Aaron Burr had introduced the drill and machinery of a political party to secure a majority for Republican candidates. Federalists liked to portray their opponents as parochial traditionalists who failed to grasp the revolutionary character of the Constitution. Jeffersonian Republicans returned the compliment by accusing the Federalists of wanting to concentrate power in their own hands. Fear of the revolutionary *terreur* spreading across the Atlantic infected the political discourse. By 1796, when Federalist candidate John Adams won the presidency over Jefferson by a small margin, he appeared everywhere in military uniform, a sword at his waist. In Congress his jingoist Federalists portrayed Jefferson's Republicans as Jacobins ready to import the guillotine to resolve political quarrels (Republicans called the Federalists worshipers of the British crown), and passed the Sedition Act.

Based on a British alien law suspending the writ of habeas corpus, the Sedition Act made it a crime to publish or print any false, scandalous, and malicious writings against the government or to stir up sedition or opposition to any lawful act. The new law was used to prosecute Matthew Lyon, a Republican congressman, for an article he published in the *Vermont Journal*, and Benjamin Franklin Bache, a grandson of the founding father and the editor of the anti-Federalist *Philadelphia Aurora*. Burr, Jefferson, and Madison were appalled and sought remedy in state courts. Aliens, they said, were under the jurisdiction of the states, not of the federal government. The Constitution, moreover, reserved to every "person," not just every citizen, the right to a jury trial.

None of the three alien and sedition laws of 1798 affected Astor, although retaliatory British measures would hurt him once he became a shipowner. Still, the passions provoked by the Sedition Act made him realize the importance of politics. His natural inclination was to stay above the partisan fray, but once he made up his mind to court politicians he did so with calculated impartiality. Republicans and Federalists were the same to him—equally confusing. Governor Clinton and the advocates of state sovereignty had set up a tax system that enabled New York to retire much of its debt. Nationalists like Alexander Hamilton, on the other hand, wanted to curb the power of the states to regulate the economy. Commerce was the engine of all great social changes, Hamilton wrote in the *Continentalist* and *Federalist* essays, but it was an engine that was geared to avoid "jealousy" between states. The country, he asserted, needed a strong central government to tune and regulate commerce. Anti-federalists in New York City suspected that behind the noble rhetoric of nation building was a ploy to restrain men like them. Like Astor, many of the city's merchants were busy reestablishing overseas trade and most of them believed the state was better suited to protect their interests than nationalists in Congress.

John Jacob was introduced to politics by a business acquaintance of his. James "Commodore" Nicholson not only had extensive commercial interests, he was also a leader of the anti-Federalist forces in New York City, on intimate terms with the Clintons and the Livingstons.

The Nicholson family had settled in Maryland early in the century. As a youth, James had gone to sea. During the Revolutionary War, he had commanded three vessels. A resolution passed by Congress in 1776 had placed his name first among the twenty-four captains in the American naval service, giving friends the excuse of calling him "Commodore." His wife, Frances, was the only child of Thomas Witter, a prosperous Bermuda-born merchant in New York. The Nicholsons had five children, four daughters and a son. Two of the girls were married: Catherine was the wife of Colonel William Few, the first U.S. senator from Georgia, and Frances was the wife of Joshua Seney, a congressman from Maryland. A fellow immigrant who was courting the Nicholsons' third daughter, Hannah, was to become John Jacob's lifelong friend, adviser, and go-between in dealings with the future administrations of Jefferson, Madison, and Monroe.

Albert Gallatin was two years older that J. J. and, like the ancestral Astors, his Swiss-French family had roots in Protestant Savoy. But with that the two young men's resemblance ended. Gallatin was born in Geneva into one of the city's leading families. His parents had died when he was nine, and Catherine Pictet, a distant maiden aunt of ample means, had brought him up and given him the best education the town of enterprising merchants and skillful watchmakers could bestow. A restless and romantic youth, the nineteen-year-old Gallatin had sneaked off to America without telling his foster mother and spent time in Maine and Boston before seeking to settle in western Pennsylvania. Mademoiselle Pictet had forgiven her foster son. On his twenty-fifth birthday, he had come into a substantial legacy that allowed him to marry, buy virgin land in Fayette County overlooking the Monongahela River, and, in short order, to become a delegate to a convention in Harrisburg that tried, unsuccessfully, to dilute the centralizing features of the new federal Constitution. Like Sarah Todd Astor, Sophia Allegre was the daughter of a widowed Richmond, Virginia, boardinghouse owner. After the wedding in Richmond in June 1789, Gallatin took his bride to Friendship Hill, as he called his Pennsylvania land. The following October Sophia fell ill and died. The bride of five months was buried in an unmarked grave at the top of Friendship Hill.

The young widower thought of going back to Switzerland. Mademoiselle Pictet, however, discouraged his return, writing that the revolution in France made "Genevans feel uncertain about their own governance." In due course, politics kept Gallatin in America. The people of Fayette County chose Gallatin as their delegate to a state constitutional convention. A year later they elected him their representative to the lower house of the Pennsylvania legislature. Reelected without opposition, he proved himself a skillful politician and a forceful proponent of democratic beliefs cherished on the Pennsylvania frontier. He had a talent for public finance. Despite his French accent, his gift for laying out issues with implacable logic impressed his colleagues, who made him a member of the state ways and means committee. In 1793, he was elected to the U.S. Senate. He became a friend of Alexander James Dallas, a tall, courtly Scot born in Jamaica who would become President Madison's secretary of the treasury.

Dallas had gained influence in the Democratic-Republican Party, and when he and his wife went to New York on a pleasure trip, they invited Gallatin, Hannah Nicholson, and several other young ladies to share a boat ride up the Hudson River to Albany and the Mohawk Falls. Miss Nicholson was twenty-seven and no beauty. Nor was Gallatin. In notes for a portrait he painted of Gallatin a decade later, the painter William Dunlap noted that his sitter had "dark hair, course and bushy, yellow complexion, long nose, hideous mouth and teeth." Hannah and Albert were married at New York's Dutch Reformed Church on November 11, 1793. The marriage was destined to be long and happy.

The newlyweds traveled to Philadelphia, where the U.S. Senate convened three weeks later. A few minutes after Gallatin took the oath of office, John Adams, presiding over the Senate, read a petition from nineteen residents of York, Pennsylvania, protesting Gallatin's election on the ground that he had not been a citizen for the required time. The charge was partisan and instigated by Federalists. Adams referred the petition to a committee headed by Federalists. Albert told Hannah that the Federalists were "moving heaven and earth" to preserve their slender Senate majority and that a tie was possible. The February 28, 1794, vote along party lines was fourteen to twelve against Albert. For a time, the Gallatins retired to Friendship Hill, but politics pulled Albert back to Philadelphia and New York, where, shortly after Hannah gave birth to their son, James, they became friends of the Astors, themselves the parents of six-year-old Magdalen, three-year-old John Jacob Jr., and one-year-old William Backhouse.

John Jacob and Gallatin forged a closeness that would help save the U.S. government from insolvency fifteen years later. In 1795, however, they were on opposite sides of their adopted country's relations with the European powers. The United States was officially neutral. Americans generally identified with the sister republic in France and the government in London managed to alienate pro-British sympathies by ordering the Royal Navy to seize American ships headed for French ports. In April 1793, the House of Representatives debated whether to embargo trade with Britain. Fearing a new war with the former colonial power, President Washington sent John Jay—an aristocratic New Yorker, member of the Federalist Party, diplomat, jurist, active participant in the formation of the United States, member of Franklin's negotiating team in 1783, and Supreme Court justice—to London to seek an accommodation.

Astor was keenly interested in the outcome of Jay's negotiations with Lord William Grenville, the British foreign minister, especially in provisions dealing with the border between the United States and British North America that for all practical purposes was nonexistent west of the Great Lakes. In return for evacuating Britain's western forts, Grenville insisted that Canadian fur traders be permitted to continue to trade with Indians in the territories ceded to the United States ten years earlier. For Astor, this meant the Northwest Company would continue to have limitless access to the richest sources west of the Great Lakes. More to his liking was the provision that, once ratified by both countries, Britain would lift its restrictions of direct trade between Canada and the United States.

The agreement Jay brought home averted war and redressed a number of American grievances. The commercial clauses granted the United States trading privileges in England but offered only limited concessions in the British West Indies. By allowing certain British maritime practices such as the confiscation of French property on U.S. vessels, the treaty acquiesced in the fact that Britain was the world's supreme sea power. France interpreted the Anglo-American accord as a violation of its own 1778 commercial treaty with the American republic. From Philadelphia, Madison sent word to Jefferson at Monticello that Federalists with inside information "do not assume an air of triumph," from which "it is inferred that the bargain is much less in our favor than ought to be expected." Jefferson and Madison denounced the treaty as a surrender to England and called Jay a "damned arch-traitor." In New York and Philadelphia, mobs burned Jay in effigy and stoned Federalist leader Alexander Hamilton. With the exception of an article dealing with the West Indian trade, the Senate nevertheless approved the treaty, and after ratifications were exchanged in London, President Washington proclaimed it the law of the land.

5

---m---

Rounding Out the Century

In the fall of 1794, John Jacob left Sarah, seven months pregnant, and sailed for Europe. The object of the voyage was to sell a large quantity of prime pelts, buy goods for the Indian trade, restock the music business, and develop commercial relationships with fur merchants in Rotterdam, Paris, and Leipzig. In London he was treated as an important merchant. He established friendly relations with Northwest agents, giving him yet another perspective on the company's breadth. He spent time with brother George before his affairs took him to Paris, where the Revolution was devouring its own and Maximilien de Robespierre himself was guillotined. Jean L'Herbette became Astor's Parisian representative. L'Herbette's son was not keen on being drafted into the revolutionary armies, and Astor assisted the young man in fleeing to America. From home, John Jacob received a letter from Sarah. A daughter had been born January 11, 1795. Sarah had christened the girl Dorothea, after the childless wife of J. J.'s brother Henry.

From Paris, J. J. hurried on to the Leipzig Fair. While in Germany, he visited Walldorf, where his father was a sprightly presence. Ann Eve, a twenty-four-year-old half sister, decided to follow her sisters Catherine and Elisabeth to New York, and planned to travel back with J. J. Back in London from Germany, he ordered a piano from Tschudi and Broadwood in Great Pulteney Street, the famous English piano manufacturer where George had once worked. In a note (no doubt dictated to someone in the City Coffee House since it was letter-perfect), he specified the instrument he wanted:

> City Coffee House, Cheapside, 14 March 1795
> To Messrs J. Broadwood
> Gentlemen. Please to make me one of the best grand pianofortes you can. I rely on your honors to let it be a good one. I wish to have it plain in every respect and the case of hornbeam wood. The pedals may be screwed fast when done. Call on Mr. George Astor for the payment. I shall wish to have it shipped in July or August by the ship *Hope* for New York or any other good ship, to be sent John J. Astor.
> I am, Gentlemen, with respects, yours,
> John Jacob Astor

As France broke off relations with the United States over the Jay Treaty, John Jacob, Ann Eve, and the piano arrived safely in New York. Little Dorothea was healthy; her father's business less so. J. J. had spent heavily in London and was short of funds. However, to take advantage of the Jay Treaty provisions allowing direct U.S.-Canadian trade, he rushed up to Montreal. To get funds or at least short-term credit, he wrote to his friend Peter Smith in Utica.

Peter had married Elizabeth Livingston, a descendant of Scottish-born Robert Livingston, landowner, politician, and merchant who had settled in Albany in 1674 and bought Indian claims to large tracts of land along the Hudson River until his estate included 160,000 acres. Elizabeth had made Peter give up shopkeeping for the life of a country gentleman. Their son, Gerrit Smith, would become a reformer and a philanthropist and, after seeing an antislavery meeting in Utica broken up by a mob in 1835, an abolitionist.

John Jacob wrote to Peter Smith:

> I Can not Describe to you an Black & white how much I am in
> want of Cash theare for If you Can Sent me any it will oblige
> me mush be the Sum ever so Smale. I am mush pressd for
> maney. I am told your making a grate fourtune & very fast
> which gives me mush Pleasure.

In Montreal, he stayed with Alexander Henry and
quickly learned the fur trade was in disarray, spooked by
the uncertainty of what the Jay Treaty would mean to the
Northwesters. The fine print revealed that the Northwest
owners had time to adjust since the provisions of the treaty
would not go into effect for another year. If there was a
downside to the accord for Astor it was, of course, that it
left the Northwest Company as powerful as ever. What had
to be counted as an upside was the fact that it no longer
mattered *where* in North America pelts came from.

At heavy discounts, he bought a sizable stock of furs in
Montreal with credit extended to him by Peter Smith. New
York City's population had doubled in ten years, and money,
it was said, was coming in over the bar at Sandy Hook with
almost every tide. And what pelts he couldn't sell on the
home market he could now export to wherever he chose.

Reflecting his rising status, Astor commissioned the
artist Gilbert Stuart to paint his portrait. After a career in
fashionable London doing portraits of nobility, gentry, and
fellow painters Reynolds, Gainsborough, and Copley, Stuart
had returned to his native America in 1792 with the avowed
intention of painting George Washington. He traveled to
Philadelphia, where George Washington twice posed for
him. Stuart copied the second portrait over a hundred times.
He had great social gifts and opened a painting room on
the southwest corner of Fifth and Chestnut Streets. The
aspiring elite flocked to Stuart's studio. Astor, however, was
less than happy with the portrait he commissioned. Stuart
was desperate for money and obliged with a second portrait.
This three-quarter-profile painting bore a resemblance to
the Washington portraits. It shows Astor as a princely figure
with refined looks that challenge contemporary descriptions
of him as a man of dour mien and boorish manners.

John Jacob Astor: portrait by Gilbert Stuart

Like his fellow New York merchants, J. J. was opposed to the "quasi war" with France. President John Adams sent three envoys to Paris to reestablish relations. As a prerequisite for normalization, the revolutionary Directoire demanded money. The envoys refused. When their letters home were published, the Federalists rode a storm of cries for war with France. Treaties with France were suspended and American frigates were authorized to capture French vessels guilty of depredations on American commerce. Fresh from his military victories in Italy, Napoleon Bonaparte staged a coup d'état in 1799 and renewed the peace with the United States.

It was only thirty-three years earlier that Nouvelle France had become British. Since then the thirteen colonies had rebelled. In the midst of their war of independence, the mutinous Americans had asked the left-behind French under British rule to join their fight. It hadn't happened because the British government promised the Quebecois they could retain their Catholicism and their language if they stayed loyal to the Crown. Britain had recognized the new United States in 1783, but successive governors-in-chief of Canada kept a vigilant eye on possible subversives or outsiders who might incite Canada's French-speakers to rebel. And indeed, Pierre Auguste Adet, revolutionary France's ambassador to the United States, was supporting David McLane, who was later executed for an attempt at insurrection in Quebec.

On August 31, 1797, governor-in-chief of Canada Robert Prescott drew the attention of the British envoy to the United States, Robert Liston, to the strange comings and goings of one fur dealer and importer named Jacob Oster. "A German person Jacob Oster," wrote Prescott, "has imported in the last ship from London 6,000 stand of arms and 100 casks of gunpowder . . . he frequently visits Canada . . . deals largely in furs, and is at present ('tis said) in that country." The British envoy sent Prescott's letter to Timothy Pickering, the U.S. secretary of state. On October 6, Pickering sent on the query to Joshua Sands, collector of the Port of New York, with a request for an investigation. A few days later, Sands forwarded his answer, which, through the channels, went back to Pickering, who wrote to Ambassador Liston that "it appears that Mr. Oster has imported no arms, and only a small quantity of gunpowder, in the usual course of his trade, and that the powder chiefly remains on hand."

The answer was less than forthcoming. But had Ambassador Liston perused the classifieds in the *New York Gazette and General Advertiser,* he would have found that John Jacob Astor had added firearms to his flutes and furs business. Fourteen thousand pounds of English gunpowder were offered for sale. Other ads offered "ten tons of the best english FF gun powder . . . at the Rate of Fifty Cents p lb wight delivered along with beaver, raccoon, muskrats, dressed and raw cooney skins, Camels and Germs hare wool." Under the heading ARMS AND AMMUNITION John Jacob offered an arsenal

of military supplies in the November 15, 1798, issue of the
Gazette:

> 24 CANNONS, 4 pounders, 1240 4 pound round shot, 20
> barrels of Cannon Powder, 600 quarter casks of fine Musket
> do. of superior quality, 300 half casks do, 90 whole casks do,
> 12 Muskets with Bayonets, 14 Swords.

The weapons business was little more than a
distraction—some of Astor's arms purportedly found their
way into the hands of Latin American *libertadores* fighting
Spain. Francisco de Miranda was supposed to be one of the
recipients of weapons, although his unsuccessful attempt
at overthrowing the Spanish regime in Venezuela didn't
happen until 1806. Whatever Governor-in-Chief Prescott's
suspicions, Astor was too astute to risk his commanding
position in Montreal for the meager profit of gunrunning
to hotheads bent on insurrection.

Trading pelts remained Astor's basic activity. He sent his
own representatives to the Great Lakes, but they made little
headway against the established and well-organized Northwesters. Gallatin weighed in. Perhaps Canadian dealers, he
said, had "a most dangerous influence over our Indians."
During the waning months of John Adams's presidency, it
was suggested that the United States try to regulate the fur
trade by establishing nonprofit government trading posts
where the sale of liquor to Indians would be forbidden. Not
what John Jacob had in mind. Firewater was the chief bargaining chip in dealing with Indians.

As Horatio (later Lord) Nelson destroyed a French fleet
at the battle of the Nile, J. J. once more sailed to London with
a shipment of furs. After disposing of his cargo and scouring
the city for premium import goods, he again visited brother
George and broadened his contacts among city merchants.

Back in New York in 1799, he closed the books on the
century. He was not yet thirty-seven, and after fifteen years
in the New World, his net worth was something more than
$100,000.

6

—ᴍ—

China Profits

It was on a sweltering September day in 1793 that ninety Europeans had been allowed to travel to Emperor Qianlong's summer retreat north of Beijing. The rulers of the world's largest and oldest empire had never dealt with other governments on the basis of equality and regarded all foreign envoys as bearers of tribute. Lord George Macartney, who headed the delegation, hoped to negotiate the first Western trade agreement with the octogenarian emperor Qianlong. To further their cause, the Westerners brought with them industrial marvels—modern firearms and saddles, chiming clocks and porcelain, crystal chandeliers, astronomical instruments, and a hot-air balloon complete with pilot. Qianlong was shrewd enough not to be impressed. "We possess all things," he noted in his official reply. "I set no value in objects strange or ingenious, and have no use for your country's manufactures." The Russians received better treatment than other foreigners, perhaps because they had long contacts with the peoples of Asia and the Chinese understood better how to deal with them. But by the time Qianlong died six years after Lord Macartney's visit, the frenzied energy of the industrializing West was shattering

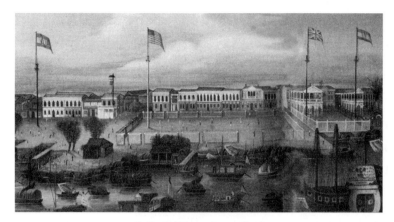

Canton factories, 1840

China's self-satisfaction. The Portuguese had obtained a toehold at Macao at the mouth of the Zhu Jiang, or Pearl River. French, Dutch, British, and American ships were to be found in the Macao harbor or carrying their goods upriver to Guangzhou, or as Westerners spelled the city, Canton.

The hazards of transatlantic commerce were among the reasons Astor turned his attention toward the China trade. To ease his way into the Asian trade, John Jacob bought consignments of tea and silk from other merchants and looked into the workings of the Canton market. Tea was both expensive and popular in New York. At $1.50 to $2.00 a pound, tea was ten times costlier than sugar ($0.16). By the pound, rice sold for $0.07, tobacco for $0.15, while salt was $4.00 a barrel.

Astor discussed the China trade with his brothers-in-law and other captains he met in South Street. Stewart Dean, a relative of Sarah's, was one of the first American captains to visit the Pearl River. When no captaincy was on offer, Dean worked for John Jacob as his representative in Albany.

Astor saw his chance at trying his hand at the China trade in 1800 when Dean became the master of the *Severn*, bound for Canton. Together with three other New York merchants, John Jacob loaded the ship with 30,573 sealskins, 1,023 beaver skins, 321 fox pelts, 103 otter skins, textiles, and scarlet-dyed cochineals and North American ginseng roots (in demand in China as an aphrodisiac). Just over a year later, the *Severn* was back, laden with silks, satins, nankeens, taffetas, fans, nutmegs, cloves, porcelain, and choice souchong teas, all of which the partners sold to retailers or reexported to Europe.

Foreign traders were eager to buy and sell on their own terms in Canton, but imperial edicts forced them to deal only with an officially designated group of merchants. Other irritants included the absence of fixed tariff charges, venal officials, the government's unwillingness to allow interaction on the basis of equality, and the bizarre prohibition against the Chinese teaching foreigners their language. Still, John Jacob quickly discovered that trading with China was better than buying and selling pelts. How much better? By May 1804, he was the sole owner of the *Severn*. Two other vessels, the *Magdalen,* named after his mother and eldest daughter, and the *Beaver,* were built to his specifications.

A round-trip from New York to Canton to New York took the better part of a year. American sea captains, most of them from Boston, had plied the China trade for twenty years. They knew the Roaring Forties, those westerlies that made the waters off Argentina the world's stormiest seas year-round. They knew how treacherous rounding the Horn could be, and they knew how to catch the trade winds for crossing the Pacific (with stopovers in Hawaii to take on freshwater). One of those wily sea dogs taught John Jacob a costly lesson. Astor hired John Cowman, a master mariner, as the captain of the *Magdalen,* who told the owner that the insurance company insisted the ship be equipped with a chronometer. A chronometer cost $500, and John Jacob maintained it was not the owner's but the captain's responsibility to obtain the navigating equipment. Neither man would yield. When Astor refused to pay, Cowman walked off the ship.

It took Astor one week to find another captain, and Cowman a month to find another vessel. Although Cowman sailed for China six weeks after the *Magdalen,* his knowledge of the sea-lanes down and around Cape Horn and across the Pacific was such that he was back in New York with a cargo of tea only one week after the *Magdalen*. Waiting for tea prices to rise, John Jacob kept his tea onboard. Cowman and his ship's owner, on the other hand, hurried his tea to auction. The resulting tea glut and falling prices cost John Jacob $70,000. When he saw Cowman on Broadway, he ran up to the captain, admitted he should have paid for the chronometer, and hired him on the spot. It was the nearest J. J. came to an apology.

Captain Frederick de Peyster was another China hand Astor had to thank. The death in Canton of John Jacob's agent Nicholas G. Ogden, a brother of John Jacob's fellow merchant in New York, Samuel Gouverneur Ogden, tied up nearly $750,000 worth of Astor goods in Wampoa warehouses. The situation became desperate when Chinese officials refused to let the merchandise leave the warehouse. Only de Peyster's energetic intervention and bribes got the goods on board Astor's ship.

While his friends were aghast and his rivals smirked, he invested nearly $300,000 of his China profits in Manhattan real estate between 1803 and 1806. New York was a city of 60,000, with few advantages over Philadelphia, Boston, Baltimore, or Charleston. Even though he had no idea that the raw land he bought beyond the city limits would pour millions into the coffers of his descendants, he would live to regret he hadn't bought the whole of upper Manhattan.

For Sarah and himself, he paid $27,000 for the spacious home of Rufus King, first U.S. senator from New York, ambassador to England, and Federalist candidate for vice president in 1804 and 1808. The new home was at 233 Broadway, on the block above Vesey Street opposite today's city hall. Besides rooms for the children, the residence featured a paneled dining room and a series of drawing rooms that opened on to one another. The property came with servants' quarters and stables. Sarah, now a mother of four small children, and John Jacob decided they could afford to have her give up supervising the sales of pianos, flutes, and clarinets. The profits were no longer worth it and the music business was sold to two German immigrant brothers.

Dinner guests invited to 233 Broadway included Sarah's nephew Henry Brevoort, a young man about town, who introduced John Jacob to Peter Irving, the publisher of the new *Morning Chronicle,* a paper that opposed the Federalists and supported Aaron Burr. Perhaps of more interest to J. J. and his expanding maritime interests, the *Morning Chronicle* also backed the rights of U.S. citizens to use the Mississippi and the port of New Orleans for trade. Indeed, it called for the United States to take control of Florida and New Orleans by force. Henry also introduced J. J. to Peter Irving's brother, Washington. The twenty-year-old Washington Irving was in law school but paid more attention to politics, poetry, balls, and the theater than to law books. His brother's newspaper allowed him to write articles praising Burr and reviews that panned the balls, plays, and concerts he attended.

J. J. liked to escape the city's unswept and unsewered streets by having a horse saddled and riding out the road along the Hudson. The path took him through King's Farm, stretching up along the west side of Broadway from Fulton Street to Duane Street and the Palisades, which marked the northern city limits. After the English conquest of Niew Amsterdam in 1664, the estate had become the property of the duke of York and, upon his ascension to the throne, named King's Farm. When seven of the eight heirs to Widow Annetje Jans sold their parcels, the property was enlarged northward to today's Christopher Street. For a rent of three shillings, Governor Lord Cornbury granted the title to King's Farm to Trinity Church in 1705 although Widow Jans's eighth heir was not satisfied and continued litigation. In 1803, Aaron Burr, the attractive and vivacious vice president, was the catalyst in getting John Jacob involved in the rights to King's Farm and the handsome Richmond Hill residence built on it. Although J. J. could never own the property, it would become the cornerstone of his real estate wealth.

Burr was, by the lights of his contemporaries, the most mysterious and sparkling member of the Revolutionary generation. John Adams believed Burr was the only man who could edge out Alexander Hamilton to become an American Napoleon. "He was dashing and brilliant in the Hamiltonian style, and his singular advantage over Hamilton, and indeed all competitors, was a total disregard for any moral or political principle that obscured his path to power," Jefferson biographer Joseph J. Ellis would write. Burr loved fine houses, costly furnishings, the best of wines and the best of books, and could not resist the lures of Richmond Hill, the place of his first meeting with George Washington. The origins of Richmond Hill went back to 1767 when Abraham Mortier, paymaster general to the British forces in North America, acquired from Trinity Church a ninety-nine-year lease, at the ridiculously low rent of $269 a year, on a tract of land along the Hudson, south of what is now Greenwich Village. Here, on a small hill overlooking the river, Mortier erected a mansion "with a lofty portico supported by Ionic columns, the front walls decorated with pilasters of the same order." When the federal government moved to Philadelphia in 1790, Burr got his chance to live in Richmond Hill.

To look into the affairs of Trinity Church, the New York legislature appointed a committee headed by Burr. Attorney Burr emerged from the appointment in command of a substantial part of the 465-acre Trinity lease, good for sixty-nine years at the same $269 a year Mortier had paid. The lease included Richmond Hill, where Burr entertained grandly. Since his wife, Theodosia, had died, their daughter, also named Theodosia, was Richmond Hill's hostess. She shared her father's whimsy and his pleasure in the fads and foibles of the world. Hamilton, Jefferson, and Madison dined at Burr's table and slept in the White Room or the Blue Room or the Little Bedroom West. The turmoil in France sent many glittering personalities to the New World, and practically all of them appeared on Burr's guest list. The most gifted visitor was Charles-Maurice de Talleyrand-Périgord, the cunning diplomat, politician, and ultimate survivor who during his life advised *l'ancien régime,* the revolutionaries,

Napoleon, France's enemies, and the restoration of the monarchy. Clubfooted by birth, his first career was ecclesiastic and he became bishop of Autun until revolutionary opportunities made him break with the Church. A ladies man like Burr, his illegitimate offspring included a son by the wife of the painter Eugène Delacroix. Also at Burr's table was Napoleon's youngest brother, Jérôme Bonaparte, whose American wife, Elizabeth Patterson Bonaparte, was to become a friend of John Jacob.

Playing the lord of Richmond Hill cost more than Burr could manage even at the height of his earning power as an attorney. In 1785, he negotiated the first of several loans that wrapped him in a tangle of debt from which he would never escape. Four years later, he launched a company whose business was the improvement of the city's water supply. In view of recent epidemics attributed to insalubrious water, the city approved the necessary charter, authorizing $2 million in capital, and providing that any surplus capital not needed for the project could be used "in any way not inconsistent with the laws and Constitution of the United States, or the State of New York." Burr and his backers used the surplus capital in the banking business. There was nothing the city fathers could do since they had written the charter themselves, but from then on chartering banks became an important part of the state legislature sessions.

In 1800, Burr was named the vice presidential candidate on the Republican ticket headed by Thomas Jefferson. Using his city hall connections, Burr carried his state and helped clinch the election for the party. Hamilton took defeat badly. When the electoral college deadlocked and the election was thrown into the House of Representatives, Hamilton intrigued to secure Burr's defeat, saying Burr was the most unfit man in the United States for the office. Jefferson was elected president. Burr became vice president. Two years later, Burr turned to Astor. For $62,500 John Jacob obliged by taking the Trinity leasehold on 241 lots off Burr's hands. The land lay between today's Spring and West Houston, Varick and Greenwich Streets. Included in the purchase was Richmond Hill. Even if he couldn't imitate Burr and launch a water company, Astor applied for water rights at nominal prices so he could fill in the land, subdivide the tide-washed stretch of the Hudson between Christopher and Houston Streets, and later build docks.

In 1804, Burr's friends in the New York legislature nominated him for the governorship of the state. Again Hamilton and his allies brought about Burr's defeat. In June, the month before the two men met at Weehawken, New Jersey, and fought a duel in which Hamilton was killed, Astor took over the rest of Burr's Trinity lease.

The duel ended Burr's political life, although he immediately went to Washington to preside over the impeachment trial of Justice Samuel Case and was received by Madison and Gallatin. With warrants out for his arrest in both New York and New Jersey, he headed west. As war was expected to break out between the United States and Spain over Louisiana and Florida boundary disputes, Burr and General James Wilkinson planned an invasion of Mexico with the object of setting up a nation-state with New Orleans as its capital and Burr as its benevolent philosopher-king. After his arrest on charges of treason, an aroused Jefferson was willing to violate basic constitutional principles to get Burr convicted. The trial was Chief Justice John Marshall's finest hour. The Constitution, he ruled, defined treason as levying war against the United States or giving aid and comfort to its enemies. For a conviction, there must be an overt act to which at least two witnesses could testify. Since the prosecution could produce no witnesses and Burr's plot had been nipped before he had time to commit a treasonable act, he was acquitted. By issuing a subpoena for Jefferson's records, Marshall also established that no president was above the law.

Astor would be 103 when the Trinity Church leasehold expired on May 1, 1866. In 1804, that meant he had 62 years to go. We do not know whether this gave him the idea of simply subleasing the property to others. Up to now he had sold real estate acquisitions as soon as a sale promised a profit. He did not begin to record the amounts paid to him for leases until 1806. On his ledgers for that year, income from leases amounted to $10,000, compared to more than $180,000 for property sold outright; that is, his returns on land sales were eighteen times larger than his income from leases. Yet the Trinity deal forced him to guess that the one to eighteen disadvantage of leasing over selling could be reversed. His and his descendants' immense wealth were contained in this hunch.

His intuition proved immediately to be right. Builders saw quick profits in erecting cheap tenements to house the onslaught of immigrants. And he was accommodating. How many lots for how years would you like? He signed subleases for fifty-seven, fifty-six, fifty-two, or forty-seven years. A lease to a single lot for fifty years went for $500. Builders were sure they could recoup long before the fifty years were up. There were minor catches, of course. John Jacob made the lessee agree to pay all taxes, duties, and assessments, except the annual $269 to Trinity Church, for which he was responsible. A lessee was allowed to remove any buildings within a certain brief period before or after the expiration of the lease. In some cases when the lessee couldn't pay, Astor granted a mortgage, payable with interest, usually 6 percent, and with the provision that in case of default on principal or interest, the property might be sold at auction.

John Jacob and Sarah were happy in their spacious house at 233 Broadway. Instead of moving on up, they leased the pseudo-Greek Richmond Hill mansion to Governor Clinton. Like Burr, Clinton found politics an expensive pastime, and in the summer of 1805 sold to Astor for $75,000 a half interest in Greenwich Village, north of the city. Clinton and Astor planned to divide the property according to streets to be laid out by them. However, before the partners could complete the project, commissioners appointed by the New York legislature had laid out new streets, which cut up the lots differently. Four years after Clinton died in 1812, his son-in-law Edmond C. ("Citizen") Genet mortgaged part of the Clinton lots to Astor. Other Clinton heirs sold out to Astor, whose real estate transactions with Burr, Clinton, and the Trinity Church accounted for over $715,000.

During the twenty years Astor had been a resident of New York, Manhattan's population had doubled and the city had advanced nearly a mile up the island. He could see no reason why New York shouldn't double again and advance another mile during the next twenty years. Acting on this reasoning, he began buying land and lots just beyond the city limits. An anecdote reported by Kenneth Porter in *John Jacob Astor, Business Man* shows J. J. at his logical best. In 1810, he sold a lot in the vicinity of Wall Street, which he had purchased in 1802, for $8,000. After papers were signed, the buyer seemed disposed to chuckle. "Why, Mr. Astor," he said, "in a few years this lot will be worth $12,000." "Very true," replied Astor, "but now you shall see what I will do with this money. With $8,000 I buy eighty lots above Canal Street. By the time your lot is worth $12,000, my eighty lots will be worth $80,000."

Burr was astonished by Astor's profits. He had gone to Europe to try and enlist Napoleon's help in his scheme to conquer Florida. Failing in this, he had lived abroad in penury for four years. In response to his daughter's entreaties, he returned to America in 1812, but the ship bringing Theodosia to meet him in New York was lost at sea. Bereft and lonely, he reopened his law office. One of his first clients was Astor.

7

Realpolitik

If megalomania barely tainted John Jacob and Sarah, the *folies des grandeurs* infected Napoleon. It would have been an extraordinary feat for even a ruler born to the purple to bring most of Europe under his thrall. Napoleon was a commoner, one of the eight children of a provincial Corsican lawyer. Six years younger than J. J., he was born in Ajaccio shortly after the French crown had purchased the turbulent island from the Republic of Genoa. At fifteen, he entered the prestigious Ecole Militaire in Paris. Most cadets took four years to graduate, but after one year Napoleon was a second lieutenant in the artillery.

The French Revolution, which began in 1789, favored opportunists. The beleaguered new republic was at war with most of Europe, and needed all the soldiers it could get. Defecting royalists had allowed the British to occupy the Mediterranean naval port of Toulon in 1793. With backing from Maximilien Robespierre, the then Captain Bonaparte forced his superiors to adopt his plan of using artillery to dislodge the fleet. Newly promoted to major, he carried it out and Toulon was back in republican hands in forty-eight hours.

He seized his next chance in 1795 when rioting and near-rebellion threatened to storm the Tuileries palace in Paris. Bonaparte assembled some artillery and coolly scattered the rioters. More than two hundred lay dead on the streets, but Napoleon's future was assured. Before the end of the year he was a divisional general in charge of the Army of the Interior. He also acquired Joséphine de Beauharnais, the widow of a guillotined aristocrat. They married although Josephine's lawyer warned her that all Napoleon owned was his army overcoat and his sword. The wedding night was inauspicious. While making love, the general was bitten on the leg by his bride's pug lapdog. Soon they were both openly unfaithful.

Not yet twenty-seven, he set off with a small staff to take the revolution to Italy. The Austrian Hapsburg monarchy not only controlled northern Italy and the Netherlands, but also claimed allegiance from the many small German states in between. By concentrating his modest but fast-moving troops against a succession of single points in the Austrians' extended lineup, Bonaparte defeated a series of enemy commanders until, by April 1797, he had driven the Austrians from northern Italy and stood only 120 kilometers from Vienna.

Margrave Karl Friedrich of Baden had tried to form an alliance with neighboring states against the threat of revolutionary France, but in 1797, Astor's homeland came under Napoleon's sway. As a result of territorial treaties from 1803 to 1810, Baden became a satellite of France. Being on the side of Napoleon, however, had its compensations for the margrave. Besides assuming the title of grand duke, Karl Friedrich saw his territories enlarged. Baden received not only parts of the bishoprics of Constance, Basel, Strasbourg, and Speyer, where John Jacob had embarked for London, but also the greater part of the Palatinate east of the Rhine.

Wars cost money. Was Monsieur Jefferson interested in buying Louisiana?

The offer did not come as a total surprise to the Jefferson administration. Occupied in the name of France by Cavalier de La Salle in 1682, Louisiana had been ceded to Spain and Great Britain in the Seven Years' War. In 1800, the Spanish part reverted to Napoleonic France (eight years later Bonaparte made his brother Joseph king of Spain). Austria sued for peace after a French victory in February 1801, effectively ending the land war in Europe. The sea war with Britain finished shortly after Prime Minister William Pitt failed to hold together a coalition with Naples, Austria, Russia, and the Ottoman Empire. Exhausted by almost a decade of fruitless struggle, a new British government was happy to sign a peace treaty.

Napoleon might be the ruler of much of Europe and since 1800 of Louisiana, but in faraway New Orleans, a Spanish intendant was still in charge of the harbor. In 1802, he abruptly forbade Americans to deposit merchandise in the port, as had long been their custom. Kentuckians and Tennesseeans—and New York's *Morning Chronicle*—were outraged. Jefferson feared hotheads in the two states would take it upon themselves to declare war on the Louisiana authorities. James Ross, a Federalist senator from Pennsylvania, proposed the government raise an army of fifty thousand men to take New Orleans by force. Jefferson feared the Federalists had found an election issue.

Treasury Secretary Albert Gallatin and Secretary of State James Madison hit on the idea of *buying* New Orleans or the province of West Florida. Jefferson was all for it and dispatched James Monroe, U.S. minister to England, to Paris to negotiate. Talleyrand, now Napoleon's crafty foreign minister, was more favorable to a deal than the Americans had hoped. And with good reason. Napoleon and his foreign minister were convinced the British would soon seize New Orleans and the rest of the territory anyway. On April 30, 1803, Napoleon authorized the signing of a treaty ceding to the United States not only New Orleans and part of Florida, but the whole vast territory of Louisiana. The price: $15 million. "I can give you no directions," Talleyrand said after the signing, "you have made a noble bargain for yourselves, and I suppose you will make the most of it." He was referring to the imprecise and therefore contentious borders of Louisiana.

Jefferson announced the purchase on Independence Day, 1803. Fifteen million dollars was double the federal budget. Many, especially in New England, thought the deal absurd. "We are to give money, of which we have too little for land, of which we already have too much," a Boston newspaper wrote.

—⁓—

The fur trade had made Astor look west. He had been farther west than most, visiting the trading center at Fort Williams on the far shore of Lake Superior in 1788. His main competitor in the fur trade with China was not the Northwest Company, however, but Russian trappers and traders working from the Pacific side of the continent. Besides being a continent closer to Canton, the Russians had the advantage of the rich resources of Alaska and the Pacific Northwest. Fur trading was a state monopoly in Russia. The czar acquired all the sable, ermine, seal, and otter pelts that fetched nearly their weight in gold in Canton. After discovering (and keeping secret) the breeding islands of the sea otter and nearly exterminating the animals, Russian hunters had invaded the Alaska coast for the northern fur seal.

President Jefferson also felt a need to explore the trans-Mississippi region and discover the most direct water route, if any existed, to the Pacific. While ambassador to France twenty years earlier, he had met John Ledyard, a Connecticut Yankee who dreamed of achieving wealth and fame by being the first to cross the continent. Unlike Mackenzie, who crossed Canada east to west, Ledyard planned to go through Russia to Alaska, then walk the Pacific Coast to the Mississippi, taking with him only two hunting dogs, a peace pipe, and a hatchet to chop firewood. Jefferson lent his name and some money to the venture, and Ledyard set out. The exploration ended abruptly when Catherine the Great had him arrested in Siberia.

As Washington's secretary of state, Jefferson had contracted the French botanist André Michaux to "seek for and pursue that route which shall form the shortest and most convenient communication between the higher parts of the Missouri and the Pacific Ocean." The American Philosophical Society raised only $128.50. Washington donated $25.00 and Jefferson $12.50. Michaux never made it past the Ohio River.

Now that he was president, Jefferson decided to try once more. "The river Missouri & the Indians inhabiting it, are not as well known as is rendered desirable," he wrote to Congress. "It is however understood that the country on that river is inhabited by numerous tribes who furnish great supplies of furs." To win support for the expedition he stressed its potential commercial benefits, and Congress duly appropriated $2,500. To the ambassadors of France, Spain, and Britain, whose territories the expedition would cross, the president emphasized its scientific purpose. Distrustful of American motives, the Spanish ambassador declined to issue safe conducts, but the British and French embassies wrote out passports. Jefferson simply ignored the Spanish objections.

To head the expedition, he appointed Captain Meriwether Lewis, a young Virginian who had served as his secretary. "Captain Lewis is brave, prudent, habituated to the woods, & familiar with Indian manners & character," the president wrote to Dr. Benjamin Rush, the Philadelphia physician and educator. "He is not regularly educated but he possesses a great mass of accurate observations on all the subjects of nature which present themselves."

Lewis in turn brought his friend William Clark on board, and in the spring of 1804 the first American expedition to try to reach the Pacific Ocean set out—"under a jentle brease," Clark wrote—from Camp Dubois, on the Illinois side of the Mississippi, upstream from St. Louis. The crew included soldiers from New Hampshire, Pennsylvania, and Kentucky, Canadian voyageurs, several sons of white fathers and Indian mothers, a slave named York, and eventually a Shoshone Indian woman who brought along her infant son. They reached the mouth of the Columbia River a year later. As nobody back East heard from them for two years, they were forgotten, rumored to have been killed or captured by the Spaniards as slave labor in Mexican silver mines. But in September 1806, they reappeared in their longboats at St. Louis, to learn that Jefferson had been reelected, that Aaron Burr and Alexander Hamilton had fought a duel and that Hamilton was dead, and that the country was edging toward war with England and Spain.

Peace between England and France had been little more than a truce. The British grew deeply suspicious of Napoleon's actions. Much of France's new energy seemed devoted to shipbuilding—not only men-of-war, but flat-bottomed invasion barges. Napoleon annexed the Italian state of Piedmont and sent his forces to impose a new government on the Swiss Confederation. Worse perhaps was his determination to turn Europe into a vast market reserved for French goods. This was intolerable for an island nation that thrived on commerce. On the pretext that France had not yet complied fully with certain provisions of the treaty they had signed fifteen months earlier, Britain declared war in May 1803. To supplement his war chest, Napoleon sold Louisiana to the United States two months later.

The Louisiana Purchase offered new opportunities to fur traders. The Canadian Mackinac Company was in the best position to start the race west. But this was not 1787, when a young German immigrant had tramped to Montreal to gape at the might of the city's furriers. This was 1803. Astor far outdistanced the Canadian pelt merchants in financial heft and in influence in the London market and, when the time was ripe, in Washington politics. If any fur trader should win this tempting prize, he decided, it should be him.

8

—ᗰ—

Punqua Wingchong

Napoleon resolved to starve his enemy into submission by imposing an embargo that closed all ports from the Mediterranean to the Baltic to British ships. Britain countered with a blockade of the whole continent of Europe, and both sides issued warnings to neutral nations that any trade with the other would be regarded as collaboration. The Royal Navy bombarded Copenhagen in 1801 because Denmark had the audacity to form a league with Russia, Prussia, and Sweden to resist a British claim to the right of search at sea. After the battle of Trafalgar four years later, the Royal Navy was no longer challenged by the French fleet, but successive governments in London kept up an unending vigilance. One of John Jacob's vessels was boarded and searched by British navy personnel in Canton. Another of his ships carrying silk to Livorno, Italy, was intercepted and seized by a French man-of-war.

For neutral nations, boarding and searching, and eventually confiscating, ships on the high seas amounted to lawlessness. During the War of Independence, American privateers had been busy plundering British merchantmen. Now, the shoe was on the other foot. President Jefferson believed a grander principle than maritime hijacking was at stake. The United States was a land of immigrants and American leaders were anxious to establish people's right to divest themselves of past allegiances by naturalization. As a nation at war, Britain claimed all Englishmen, even if they had taken out American citizenship, must join the fight for God and Country. While the U.S. government admitted it was difficult to distinguish native-born Americans from British subjects, some British naval officers considered all seamen who spoke English to be British subjects, unless they could produce proof they were native-born Americans. The government estimated that since 1803 the number of Americans dragooned into British naval service to be over four thousand, while admitting that the British had discharged about a third of the men.

A brazen case of so-called impressment of seamen happened on June 22, 1807, when the British ship *Leopard* fired on the U.S. frigate *Chesapeake*. After three Americans were killed and eighteen wounded, the *Chesapeake* hauled down its flag. The British commander came on board and seized four crew members as deserters. The *Chesapeake* incident provoked intense anger. In New York with his wife, Gallatin told his brother-in-law James Witter Nicholson and Astor that Secretary of State Madison was for accommodating George Canning, Britain's ambitious new foreign secretary, by forbidding the continued service on American vessels of British sailors employed less than two years. Nearly a quarter of the seamen in American service were Englishmen, however, and Gallatin and Astor calculated such a policy would result in the loss of nine thousand able-bodied seamen. Their estimate gave Jefferson pause.

By early August, Gallatin noted that anti-British feelings seemed to have evaporated, at least among New York City's businessmen. Back in Washington, however, Jefferson was reviving his old illusion that American exports were more important to Europe and Great Britain than the profits from their sale and transportation were to the United States. If the United States embargoed itself—that is, refused to sell to *anybody*—the government in London would come to its senses. The idea seemed to have originated with Secretary of State Madison, but it echoed Jefferson's moralistic vision of severing all connections with the aggressive and corrupt nations of Europe.

Astor was appalled. The act would wreck the American economy, have no effect on England and France, and, contrary to the Jeffersonian principle of limited government, make the federal government into a coercive power. Every coastal sloop would have to be intercepted at sea and forced to prove that its cargo of turnips and carrots was destined for Portland, Maine, and not Halifax, Nova Scotia.

Egged on by Astor, Gallatin criticized the proposed legislation. Enforcement was impossible because the proposed law was full of inconsistencies and ambiguities. Jefferson, however, turned a deaf ear to these protests. Since American exports exceeded $100 million a year, neither France nor Britain, he reasoned, could afford to go without American goods.

Six months to the day after the *Chesapeake* incident, Congress passed, virtually without debate, the Embargo Act of 1807 forbidding American citizens to trade with *any* foreign port. The act banned the departure of all vessels, American or foreign, from American harbors for foreign ports. There was one exception. Foreign vessels were permitted to leave "in ballast"—that is, to load gravel, sand, iron, or lead to ensure their stability at high seas—but not to carry cargo. The provision was inserted at Gallatin's suggestion because "they are so few as to be of no object to us, and we may thereby prevent a similar detention of our vessels abroad, or at least a pretense for it."

Cutting off one's nose to spite one's face seemed a poor way for a government to do business. As waterfronts were littered with idle ships, out-of-work sailors, and frustrated merchants and shipowners, the embargo provoked a howl of anger. John Lambert, a shrewd observer of the New York scene, noted in his diary on April 13, 1808:

> The embargo had now continued upward of three months, and the salutary check, which Congress imagined it would have upon the conduct of the belligerent powers, was ex-

tremely doubtful while the ruination of the commerce of
the United States appeared certain if such destructive measures were persisted in. Already had 120 failures taken place
among the merchants and traders, to the amount of more
than 5,000,000 dollars, and there were 500 vessels in the
harbor, which were lying up useless, and rotting for want
of employment. Thousands of sailors were either destitute
of bread wandering about the country, or had entered the
British service. The merchants had shut up their counting
houses and discharged their clerks.

As John Jacob had predicted, port officials found it impossible to decide whether a vessel loaded with flour, corn,
rice, and rye was taking its cargo to another American port,
as its owners declared, or to a foreign port to be sold at large
profits. As Gallatin had foretold, Congress would have to
give the executive the most arbitrary powers so that "not a
single vessel shall be permitted to move without the special
permission of the Executive . . . the collectors [shall] be invested with a general power of seizing property anywhere
without being liable to personal suits."

Jefferson announced his retirement and for most of the
remaining year of his term, as his biographer Joseph J.
Ellis would write, "surrendered all essential decisions to
Madison and Gallatin, thereby creating a sense of drift
in American policy at the very moment when the unpopular and cumbersome embargo required executive leadership." There was loose talk, even in Democratic-Republican
circles, of Pontius Pilate washing his hands of unpleas-
ant responsibilities. Federalists gleefully recalled how Jefferson had fled British soldiers during his final days as
governor in Revolutionary Virginia. In an off-guard moment six months later, Jefferson admitted to Gallatin that
the consequences of the embargo law were more than he
had bargained for. The embargo "is certainly the most
embarrassing we have ever had to execute," he wrote to
Gallatin.

We do not know whether, through Gallatin, Astor knew
of the president's cooling ardor. What we do know is that
J. J. schemed to become the first shipowner to break the
embargo and profit from it.

—◇◇◇—

In mid July 1808, Jefferson received a letter from U.S. senator Samuel Latham Mitchell of New York urging him to allow Punqua Wingchong, a supposedly highborn mandarin stranded by the embargo in New York, to return to Canton. The president was well disposed toward Mitchell, who, in addition to his political duties, was also a professor of natural history at the College of Physicians and Surgeons in New York City. Wrote Senator Mitchell:

> Punqua Wingchong, a Chinese merchant, will be the bearer of this note of introduction. He came to New York about nine months ago, on business of a commercial nature, and has resided during that time, partly here and partly in Nantuck[et]. Having completed the object of his visit to the United States, he is desirous of returning to Canton, where the affairs of his family and particularly the funeral obsequies of his grandfather, require his solemn attention.
>
> This stranger is represented to me as a man of respectability and good standing in his own Country; and is consequently entitled to a corresponding regard and treatment in ours.
>
> The chief object of his visit to Washington is to solicit the means of departure in some way or other, to China, but he feels at the same time a strong desire to see the Chief executive officer of the United States.

Jefferson had already left the capital for his estate at Monticello, and did not meet Punqua. Although the president was studiously avoiding opinions on the country's chief problems, the philosopher-president saw diplomatic advantages in acceding to the request. In New York, China traders smelled a rat. They called Punqua "a Chinaman picked up in a park" or "an Indian dressed up in silk and adorned with a peacock fan." Merchants along Broadway, Wall, and Pearl Streets and at Tontine's listened with incredulity to reports that the *Beaver* was being loaded for a China voyage. To be disguised as a fake voyage to New Orleans? Or did Astor think he could run his ship past the navy blockade at Sandy Hook? Unless the winds were exceptionally favorable, could a heavy-laden East Indiaman hope to outrun a frigate?

Jefferson gave written permission for Punqua to commission a vessel in New York for his homeward voyage. The ship Punqua chose was the *Beaver.* Despite a new roar of indignation and letters of protest that made local representatives of the federal government feel awkward, the *Beaver* sailed on August 17, 1808, for the Pearl River. New York's *Commercial Advertiser* attacked Jefferson. John Jacob answered that if the newspaper were fair and not influenced by other merchants' jealousy, its editor would realize no misrepresentation had taken place. The *Beaver* didn't sail empty, of course. Grocers were clamoring for tea, and souchong fetched the price once asked for imperial gunpowder. When the ship returned in the fall of 1809—the first ship to come to New York in more than a year—the gossip at Tontine's had it that her round-trip had made her owner $200,000.

After John Jacob hoodwinked Jefferson into giving him this temporary monopoly on the China trade, he and his twenty-year-old daughter Magdalen journeyed to Montreal. Their host, an English merchant, recorded in his diary how Alexander Henry, Astor's old friend and shareholder of the Northwest Company, gave a ball at which "the sprightly dance was kept up till past twelve, chiefly country dancing but some reels and one cotillion in compliment to Miss Astor."

9

—⚏—

Family

If Astor's first aim was to become rich and independent, his second ambition was to do as much for each of his children as he did for himself. If his business manners were cold, reticent, and austere, his attitude toward his family was caring. Even distant kin could count on his kindness. His enemies included those who in his winning he defeated, people who were envious and jealous, and people who in his personality, his methods, ambition, and growing influence saw a threat to their own power. He felt no compassion toward the larger community or for the country that gave him so much. He had done it all himself. He might be a butcher's son, but he scorned Thomas Jefferson's ideals of equality for white men. He stood outside the narrow circle of landed families who controlled New York politics, but like them he believed only members of the gentry and self-made men were capable of discerning the common good. Like most Americans of his temperament and class, he favored Great Britain against the rabble of the Place de la Révolution and understood the French people's enthusiasm for the man on the white horse, Napoleon Bonaparte. The American Revolution had been a palace revolt, an uprising of upper-class men against the king. "There was not, and never had been, a single one of the Revolutionary leaders, not even the most radical of all, Sam Adams himself, who believed in the people," historian James Truslow Adams would write. "What they believed in . . . in varying degrees, was the people who had money, talents or social position." Astor wholeheartedly approved such sentiments, even if this view contained a measure of self-delusion and hypocrisy. Just as Jefferson liked to insinuate that Virginia slave owners like himself were moving inexorably toward emancipation, so Astor believed that for now there could be no equality between a merchant or a trader and a man of no property. Liberty, he believed, gave a man of humble birth a chance to advance himself, but to give the common worker a voice in political affairs was wrong and fraught with danger. A majority of politicians shared this view and carefully designed state constitutions to keep the control of at least one house of the legislatures "in the hands of property."

This idea was also rooted in the Illuminati free thought movement of John Jacob's youth. Members of the secret society, founded in Bavaria by a professor of canon law and a former Jesuit, called themselves "Perfectibilists" and, as a vehicle for enlightenment, believed in compassionate despotism by notables. Although their number never exceeded two thousand, they gained a commanding position in various Masonic lodges and attracted Goethe and the reigning dukes of Gotha and Weimar. Die Illuminaten kept internal discipline by spying on each other and, as a consequence, suffered internal dissension. By the time John Jacob was in London, the Bavarian government had banned the movement as a threat to Catholicism. In America, Thomas Jefferson, Albert Gallatin, George Clinton, and Astor were rumored to be Illuminati.

—∾∾—

A dark cloud over John Jacob and Sarah's family life was their first son's mental state. Little John Jacob would fly into rages or sink into lethargy for months. Doctors were unable to diagnose or treat the condition that left him alternating between phases of lucidity and torpor. Almost normal at times, he usually existed in a state of mental inactivity. A friend of the family wrote that the boy had periods of restored mentality when he wrote poetry. His room was in the back of the house at 233 Broadway where no one could see him, although street urchins climbed the garden wall hoping to catch a glimpse of "the mad Mr. Astor." His parents could and did afford the best medical knowledge, but mental illness was shameful and visitors were not permitted to see him. For years his father insisted the other children treat the boy as normal, but that failed. Sarah prayed for him and John Jacob professed to believe a miracle was possible, but to the end of his existence (he lived to be seventy-eight), John Jacob II was lodged in a mansion of his own, attended by physicians, a tutor, and a staff to make his life as agreeable and isolated as possible.

With concern, John Jacob and Sarah watched the growth of William Backhouse—Sarah cuddled the second son, J. J. said. However, there was every indication that the boy was normal. So was his sister, Dorothea. John Jacob and Sarah's third son, born in 1797, had died shortly before his second birthday.

BROAD WAY FROM THE BOWLING GREEN, 1828

Broadway in 1828

A letter dated December 7, 1799, and addressed to someone named Peter (Smith?) gives us a glimpse of John Jacob's feelings:

> Dear Peter
> I Recie' Several Letters from you that of the 11 ulto is the Last you might will esspected Some from me for you ought to have had tham but youil esuse me when I tell you that on my Return from Canada I found my family at Albany and my 3 Children Ill one of whom I lost a fine Little boy 23 Months old Died 14 Days ago. In this Situation I could not think mush of business.

Magdalen was a vivacious but not particularly pretty girl, spoiled by her parents and, as an adolescent, introduced everywhere. William Backhouse grew up a quiet boy, studious and favored by his mother. Dorothea was named for the aunt who had married J. J.'s brother Henry Astor. The youngest daughter, Eliza, born in 1801, was a frail child.

Sarah was the steady hand in the children's upbringing. Her tastes were simple and God-fearing. William grew up burdened with a sense of responsibility and a liking for the drudgery of detail. The girls' education followed the precepts of the day. Their father spoiled them a bit. Their mother taught them to be kind and loving.

To escape the city heat and the dreaded infections that drove the genteel classes out of the city each summer, Sarah insisted the children spend time in the country. To accommodate her wish, John Jacob bought Hellgate, a country estate near what is now Eighty-eighth Street. Hellgate—pious tongues pronounced it "Hurlgate"—had grounds that sloped down toward the East River, above Blackwell's Island (now Roosevelt Island) and below Wards Island. J. J. loved Hellgate for the view. Whether ships were descending from the Harlem River or coming up the East River, they had to make sharp maneuvers at half sail right in front of his windows.

John Jacob was proud of the homes he provided his wife and children and seemed to have found pleasure in hoodwinking people into believing he was a man of modest means. The only man in the United States who had more

Hellgate

money than him was the childless, French-born Philadelphia banker Stephen Girard. Thirteen years older than John
Jacob, Girard was a native of Bordeaux who had gone to
sea as a cabin boy at fourteen and ten years later was the
captain of a vessel plying the American coastal trade. His
fleet was a rival to Astor's merchantmen, but the two men
were personal friends. Girard said of Astor that he had
"passed through every stage of mercantile life, from small
toy-seller to respectable fur dealer, then to the immense
China merchant, cracking his half million cargoes of teas
as you would a bale of goods." Banking was Girard's second
vocation, but he lived like a miser without kith and kin.
An anecdote recalls Girard telling Astor: "I am surprised
that a man having so much property as yourself should be
so anxious to increase it." To which John Jacob answered,
"You cannot be so much surprised at my course as I am by
your remark, coming as it does from a man who has a much
greater fortune than I have, and seems much more desirous
to enlarge it." Girard got the last word: "Oh yes, but you
forget that I have no children to be spoiled by it."

When Dorothea was seventeen, her parents let her travel
to Washington to be the houseguest of Albert and Han-

nah Gallatin. Hannah, whom Washington Irving called "the most stylish woman in the drawing room," dabbled successfully in matchmaking. She had brought her younger sister Maria to Washington, where in the whirlwind of parties, fishing club fetes for ladies, turtle feasts, plays, and "routs," Maria had met, and later married, Congressman John Montgomery of Maryland. Gallatin sometimes got into the matchmaking act. He hinted broadly to Jonathan Roberts, a bachelor congressman from Pennsylvania, that his attentions would be welcome at the home of General William Van Ness, where pretty Sarah Smith, daughter of New York senator John Smith, was visiting.

For Dolly Astor, the atmosphere at the Gallatins was new, liberated, and intoxicating. At one of Hannah's social events, Dolly met Colonel Walter Langdon, an impoverished but dashing New Englander five years her senior. Seeing the effect the colonel had on Dolly, Albert wrote a quick note to John Jacob, telling him he "had better send for his daughter to come home . . . as Col. Langdon has every recommendation except wealth, being a member of a large family." Before the families could act, the young couple eloped. Hannah and Albert were apologetic; John Jacob furious. The newlyweds settled in New York, but it took years before Astor forgave them. Family legend would have it that seven years later J. J. happened to drop in at a children's party in the home of a friend. A pretty six-year-old girl caught his eye and when he asked her her name, she answered, "My name is Sarah Sherburne Langdon." With emotion in his voice, he said, "For your sake, I shall have to forgive your mother and father."

Britain's war with Napoleon spilled over into the Caribbean. To prevent the Danish colonies in the Lesser Antilles from falling into French hands, the British West Indies fleet took control of St. Croix, St. Thomas, and St. John—the Virgin Islands Denmark would sell to the United States in 1917 for $25 million. Taking control meant ousting Adrian Bentzon, the governor of St. Croix. Bentzon found himself in New York out of a job and attracted to Magdalen Astor. A match had advantages for both parties. The Dane would marry money and the German immigrant's daughter would join the diplomatic community. The wedding took place on September 14, 1807.

Since Governor Clinton was no longer Astor's tenant at Richmond Hill, John Jacob offered the residence to his daughter and new son-in-law. The writer Gulian C. Verplanck, who had dined with Burr and John Quincy Adams at Richmond Hill, came to dinner and thought "Counselor Bentzon" maintained the hospitable traditions of the house. Bentzon was "a man who had traveled in every part of the world, knew everything and talked all languages." Confusing his host's nationality (easy enough since Norway was part of the Danish realm until 1814), Verplanck wrote:

> I recollect dining there in company with thirteen gentlemen, none of whom I ever saw before, but all pleasant fellows, all men of education and of some note—Counselor a Norwegian, I the only American, the rest of every different nation in Europe, and no two of the same, and all of us talking French together.

Astor found his cosmopolitan son-in-law to be a valuable asset when it came to negotiating with governments. A fortune in furs was piling up in his warehouses. Could he possibly find a way of skirting Jefferson's silly embargo? Bentzon knew Andrei Dashkov, the new Russian ambassador, and quickly forwarded an invitation to meet with Astor.

—⋙—

In the middle of the previous century, Vitus Bering, a Danish navigator in the czar's employ, had carried the Russian flag from Siberia to North America. Later, the czar "by right of possession" had conferred upon the Russian-American Company a hunting and commercial monopoly. In 1799, the company founded New Archangel, an island settlement at today's Sitka, Alaska, and pursued a precarious existence based on fur trade with the not always friendly Indians. No precise border marked off Russian sovereignty. The Russian-American Company's monopoly was extended by its charter as far south as fifty-five degrees north longitude, or midway down today's British Columbia coast. This brought Russia into conflict with unmarked Spanish pretensions resting on voyages as far as Mount St. Elias (today's southern Alaska) and British assertions of sovereignty over the same coast going back at least to the maritime exploring of Captains Cook (1778) and Vancouver (1792) and the overland journey of Mackenzie in 1793.

Ambassador Dashkov arrived in Washington with instructions to protest the practices of American traders on the Alaska coast. He made a formal demand that no trader be allowed to sell Indians firearms and munitions for pelts. If the American government would agree to this, the czar would come to see the occasional errant American trader on the Alaskan coast in a friendlier light. An agreement would help secure the safety of American citizens in such cases and in general would strengthen relations between the two countries.

At the meeting with Ambassador Dashkov, Astor listened with apparent sympathy to the plight of the Russian-American Company. Perhaps, he suggested, he could help. In exchange for the right to trade in the Russian territory and its waters, he would be willing to guarantee to supply the Russian settlements. He would also promise not to trade with Indians near the Russian outposts.

Dashkov was sympathetic. What Astor should do, the ambassador suggested, was send a supply ship to New Archangel, and coordinate with Alaska governor Alexander Baranov for dependable repeat voyages to restock the colony. Events overtook them both. Madison was elected president, with 122 electoral votes, over his Federalist opponent, Charles C. Pinckney, who received 47 votes. Still, the discontent with Jefferson's embargo translated into Federalist gains in Congress. Taking office, Madison repealed the embargo.

Astor wasted no time disposing of the fortune in furs that had piled up during the embargo. He bought the brig *Sylph* and sent her to Canton under the command of Edward Daniel. Her valuable cargo included $92,000 in specie and thousands of otter, fox, and beaver skins, cotton, ginseng, and cochineals. Under the command of Captain Cowman of the chronometer incident, the Astor brig *Fox* sailed for Calcutta. Cowman again set a record, making the round-trip in seven months and fifteen days. With Captain Richard Marner on the quarterdeck, the *Beaver,* of Punqua fame, sailed for Canton with an immense cargo of cotton, furs, and currency. Astor's ship *Huntress*, cleared for an unspecified destination in the "S Seas," vanished. She limped into port several years later, having escaped unidentified captors.

Inevitably, Astor had both admirers and imitators. The devotees included Joseph A. Scoville, an astute financial observer who wrote under the name Walter Barrett and realized how Astor had taken advantage of the government's poor business legislation. To assist American shipowners competing with British, French, Dutch, Spanish, and Scandinavian outfitters—and their powerful financiers like the Baring brothers and the Rothschilds—the Treasury allowed importers engaged in the China trade to delay remitting duties collected on a cargo for eighteen months. Astor thought he would be a fool if he didn't take advantage of the government's inept attempt to bolster American flag carriers. Scoville calculated that with the enormous cargoes of tea Astor was importing, the government in effect gave J. J. interest-free loans of over $5 million for a year and a half. But at least Astor paid the collected duties when the eighteen months were up. John H. Smith was a midget Astor who went into the China trade with only a few thousand dollars, overextended himself, and kept the import duties he collected for the year and a half. When John H. Smith & Sons failed, the shipping firm owed the Treasury $3 million, a sum that was never paid. Because the defaulters were bankrupt, none was prosecuted. The government's loss on import duties between 1789 and 1823, Arthur Howden Smith calculated a century later, was $250 million, or $50 billion in today's money.

10

—ɷ—

The Good Ship Enterprise

The land west of the Mississippi had never been charted and therefore had no defined borders. California was a Spanish possession, and Russian traders had their foothold on the coast of Alaska. In between, the Northwest Company and its subsidiary, Mackinac, dominated the fur trade carried out with Indians. Since John Jacob had traveled with a Northwest crew from Montreal to the far end of the Great Lakes in 1788, the Canadians had established trading posts farther and farther west; so far west, in fact, they had problems hauling out supplies and bringing back furs in one year. Even if crews set out with the first thaw, the turnaround was so far west that autumn turned into another winter before they could get back to the Grand Portage depot on Lake Superior, let alone back to Montreal. Why didn't they think of hauling cargo *west* to the Pacific? Because, as British subjects, they were not allowed to trade with Canton. Since 1670, that privilege belonged, by royal charter, to the East India Company.

The Northwesters were nevertheless determined to hunt and trade on the western slopes of the Rocky Mountains and perhaps reach the Pacific. In 1800, Northwest president William McGillivray, his brother Duncan, and the explorer-trader David Thompson had made plans to find a way across the Rockies, perhaps by way of the headwaters of the North or South Saskatchewan. Thompson was a legend. Because of his knack for mathematics, talent for drawing, and interest in geography, this orphan from the lower depths of London had been recruited at fourteen by the Hudson's Bay Company. By day he traded and traveled. At night he took out his sextant to make observations of altitudes to determine where he was. Indians called him the "star-man." In 1796, he had journeyed four thousand miles to the Mississippi headwaters and in the course of twenty-eight years in North America would plot and map almost 2 million square miles of territory. He had taken a métis woman as his wife in the manner dictated by Indian custom, and brought her, and later their young children, on several expeditions. His and Duncan McGillivray's 1801 trek to the Pacific had ended in failure as McGillivray was crippled, an Indian guide lost his way in a minor river valley, and the onslaught of winter forced them to turn back and abandon the mission. Since then, Simon Fraser had supervised the installation of several fur trading posts along the river that was to bear his name and followed it down to the Strait of Georgia.

No royal privilege forbade Americans from trading from the West Coast. If that was possible, Astor reasoned, who needed voyageurs, Montreal, Grand Portage, or such alternatives as shipping furs down the Mississippi from St. Louis? For that matter, who needed war-ravaged Europe, where Napoleon was at the height of his power?

—⟪⟫—

The year Astor had reached Montreal and made his first important fur trades, a group of Boston merchants raised $49,000 to outfit the ship *Columbia,* John Kendrick master, and the sloop *Lady Washington,* Robert Gray master, to sail for Nootka Sound on the island of Vancouver. No more was heard from the expedition until the *Columbia* sailed into Boston harbor in 1790, the first American vessel to circumnavigate the globe. Although a Spanish flotilla under Estevan José Martínez had seized two British vessels at Nootka, Captain Gray reported he and Kendrick had wintered there, unharmed by Martinez. In the spring of 1789, Gray had reached China with a cargo of furs in the *Columbia,* formerly under Kendrick, while Kendrick had remained on the Northwest Coast with the *Lady Washington* to establish a trading port.

On the *Columbia*'s second voyage, Gray was off the Oregon coast when, at latitude 46° 19', he saw "a spacious harbour abreast of the Ship" and entered the river that he named after his ship. In the meantime, Kendrick had run the miniature *Lady Washington* to Hawaii and then, with a first cargo of sandalwood, to Canton. The Chinese loved the fragrant wood and sandalwood became a part of every transpacific cargo. Hawaiian kings ordered their people to cut the trees. Entire forests were decimated. By 1827, thirty years after the start of the sandalwood boom, it was rarer in Hawaii than in China.

The Northwest trade, as it was called, had expanded in fits and starts. After the success of *Lady Washington* and *Columbia,* a dozen Boston skippers thought nothing of logging forty thousand miles, running south with the trade winds, beating around the Horn, and heading north the length of South America, up the North American coast to the foggy waters of the Georgia Strait and Puget Sound.

Astor bought the *Enterprise,* a brand-new ship built in Philadelphia, to try his hand at the inter-Pacific trade. The new ship would sail to the North Pacific coast and, as Ambassador Andrei Dashkov suggested, supply the Russians in Alaska. It would buy pelts from them and from Indians along the coast and head for Canton, unload, and return to Alaska with Chinese supplies. No need to sail back to New York at all. A second Astor vessel could follow eight to ten months later, rendezvous with the *Enterprise,* resupply her with whatever she needed from New York, and pick up her strongbox of earnings.

To command the *Enterprise,* Astor hired John Ebbets, a Boston veteran of both the China and the Northwest Coast trade. Six years earlier Ebbets had won the gratitude of Governor Alexander Baranov for rescuing a number of his men during a bloody Indian uprising in New Archangel. The captain, John Jacob said, "enjoyed both the esteem and confidence of the Indians and had long been known to Mr. Baranov, who had seen proof of his trustworthiness in many a business transaction."

The *Enterprise* left New York on November 15, 1808, laden with dry goods, hardware, gin, molasses, rum, tobacco, powder, and other merchandise. Ebbets had two sets of instructions—one for his eyes only, the other to show to Governor Baranov in New Archangel. The directives asked Ebbets to stop at California ports. Did Astor believe turmoil in Spain and Mexico spelled opportunities in far-off California? Six months before the *Enterprise* left New York, Napoleon had imposed his brother Joseph as king of Spain, provoking demands for self-government in Mexico. Ebbets followed Astor's instructions. We do not know whether the captain reported back that the political upheavals in distant Madrid and Mexico City caused little stir among the less than eight thousand Spaniards in California. While the *Enterprise* dropped anchor at Monterey, south of San Francisco, revolution broke out in Mexico. California remained loyal to Spain.

Next Ebbets was to stop at the Indian village of Neweetee on the southern tip of Vancouver Island—today's Victoria, British Columbia—and "prepare the Indians for a friendly reception to some white men who would come to stay with them." The second, confidential set of instructions asked the captain to observe in minute detail the circumstances of the Russian colony, note the extent of its trade, its strength, defenses, and Governor Baranov's powers. He was to leave a letter containing the information he had gathered under a marked tree at Neweetee. The next Astor ship would pick up the letter.

Ebbets followed the orders, touched at several West Coast ports, and, on June 11, 1810, arrived in Neweetee. He bought some furs here and proceeded to New Archangel where he was greeted with open arms. Astor had provided copies in French of his letters to the governor, but not in Russian. Baranov could not read French and it was only when the Russian sloop of war *Diana* arrived a few days later that they found a translator. Unfortunately, Astor's secret instructions were among the papers Ebbets handed to the multilingual Captain V. M. Golovnin for translation. Observe in minute detail the circumstances of the colony, note the extent of its trade, its strength, defenses, and Baranov's powers. Was there any other word for it? Ebbets was a spy. The way Golovnin read the private instructions could only mean the United States was weighing the odds and costs of grabbing Russian America. He suggested Baranov submit the matter to St. Petersburg.

New Archangel was a fort high on a rocky promontory, impregnable to Indian attack, as it mounted a hundred guns. In *Astoria,* Washington Irving informs us that the Russian contingent consisted of sixty men and that many Indian hunters of the Kodiak tribe "were continually coming and going, or lounging and loitering about the fort like so many hounds round a sportsman's hunting quarters." Historians disagree on who Baranov was. Irving describes the governor as "a rough, rugged, hospitable, hard-drinking, old Russian, somewhat of a soldier, somewhat of a trader, above all, a boon companion of the old roistering school." Later authors either call him another hard-nosed Astor or a bureaucrat hating the godforsaken outcropping of an island (later named after him) and counting the days until retirement. In *The Westward Crossings: Balboa, Mackenzie, Lewis and Clark,* Jeanette Mirsky would write: "Here were two audacious schemers, vastly different, who for a while joined hands to achieve the daring, gigantic desires that each independently nursed: Astor to capture the fur market of the world and dominate a large part of the world's commerce; Baranov to extend Russian influence so that the North Pacific Ocean would become a Russian sea." John Terrell, on the other hand, describes Baranov in *Furs by Astor* as being "weary of his job, tired of life in a remote and unimportant outpost. In all probability he didn't really give a damn what happened to Russian America, and it would have been all right with him if it were given back to the Indians. All he wanted was to be relieved, and return to the comforts and civilization of Saint Petersburg."

Ebbets could only curse his own stupidity, hunker down—fleeing was out of the question with Golovnin's warship in the harbor—and hope for the best. Luck was with him. Governor Baranov liked him and no doubt liked the distraction the arrival of the Americans offered. What also played in Ebbets's favor was that the governor had recently applied for permission to retire, and did not wish to become involved in a contretemps that might lengthen his stay. The question of Russian America was the subject of talks in St. Petersburg between U.S. ambassador John Quincy Adams and Chancellor Count Rumiantzov. Adams had orders from President Madison not to sign anything that might amount to formal recognition of Russian sovereignty over a vast and unbounded area of North America. Count Rumiantzov held out a carrot that would legalize what Astor was trying to do. If the United States would sign a convention recognizing the Russian territories, the St. Petersburg government would turn over to American neutral ships the transpacific carrying trade between the Russian-American Company's settlements and Canton.

Both sides were cagey. Adams asked the chancellor to point out the southern boundary of Russian territory on the Northwest Coast. This would require some consideration, Rumiantzov replied, insofar as Russian maps included the whole of Nootka Sound on Vancouver Island and the coastline of the future state of Washington to the mouth of the Columbia. In a follow-up session Adams pressed the question of Russia's boundary lines. He was told the government of Czar Alexander I wanted to defer the question to some future time. Meanwhile, American ships would be free to trade with Russian settlements. In a letter to Secretary of State Robert Smith, Adams quoted Rumiantzov as saying, "Our attachment to the United States is obstinate, more obstinate than you are aware of."

Governor Baranov and Captains Ebbets and Golovnin knew nothing of this, of course. Baranov, however, showed a generous measure of the obstinate attachment to the United States that the czar's chancellor impressed upon Adams. He was willing to interpret Astor's secret instructions to Ebbets as little more than a routine request for a commercial assessment of a new prospect. Still, cutting a deal with Ebbets proved difficult because Astor had failed to list prices for which the goods in the hold of the *Enterprise* were to be sold. Baranov would have to judge for himself whether it was more advantageous to trade with Astor or depend on passing traders.

Baranov had never forgotten how Ebbets rescued a number of Russians some years earlier, and his affection for the American helped him overcome his scruples. He purchased part of the *Enterprise* cargo for $27,000, payable in furs. He also arranged for Ebbets to carry 6,600 sealskins, 3,000 sea otter skins, and other Russian furs on consignment to Canton, where the captain would sell them for specific Chinese goods. Ebbets's commission would be 5 percent of the sale plus $18,000 for freight. Baranov also gave Ebbets a list of prices at which he was willing to take goods. If Astor approved these figures, he could send another ship to New Archangel and repeat the transaction.

Ebbets sailed in August. Since he still had cargo to sell, he stopped to trade at various places along the coast. At Neweetee he placed a letter under the designated tree, and in October headed for the Pearl River.

While Ebbets was selling furs in Canton, making a $20,000 profit on the small quantity of Astor's furs and more than $74,000 for Baranov's pelts, the *Beaver* reached Canton. It brought no word for Ebbets from Astor. Ebbets deducted his 5 percent commission and $6,000 for freight and invested this money with his profits in Chinese merchandise that was loaded onto the *Beaver* and sent to New York.

Ebbets was back in New Archangel the following June. Baranov was still the governor and was delighted with the profits Ebbets had made, and with the sugar, millet meal, nankeens, teas, silks, and chinaware the captain came back with. Baranov paid Ebbets the remaining freight charges, amounting to $12,000, and bought $35,000 worth of European goods, which Ebbets had obtained from the *Beaver*. Both the freight charges and purchases were paid in furs, meaning Ebbets sailed once more for China, this time carrying $48,000 worth of sea otter and seal skins.

—ᴥ—

In New York, John Jacob went on the assumption that Ebbets's venture was a success. In Washington, Count Frederic Petrovich Pahlen replaced Dashkov as Russia's minister, and Astor decided to send his son-in-law to meet the new ambassador. St. Petersburg was not pleased, Adrian Bentzon was told. American adventurers continued in the North Pacific. Bentzon gave the new ambassador a polite civics lesson on the limits of government power in a democracy. Private enterprise was more powerful than authorities under the American system, meaning the U.S. government could never give Russia the satisfaction it demanded, whereas a plan such as Astor favored might succeed.

Count Pahlen advised Bentzon that a final decision would be made in St. Petersburg, and suggested Astor send an agent with a detailed plan, to which he would attach his own recommendation. Count Rumiantzov, Pahlen implied, had no love for the British and might be open to ideas that would lower British influence in the North Pacific.

By appealing to Treasury Secretary Gallatin, Astor got the stateroom on board the official frigate *John Adams* for his son-in-law and for his daughter, who suddenly wanted to see foreign shores. Adrian and Magdalen reached St. Petersburg in the spring of 1811 and were courteously received. Astor's suggested terms were accepted with one exception. The Russian-American Company's control would be inviolate, said Count Rumiantzov. Bentzon yielded and a four-year agreement was signed, saying the czar's monopoly and Astor's American Fur Company were to act in concert against interlopers, assist each other, and not sell arms and ammunitions to Indians. The American Fur Company was to have exclusive rights to supply the Russian ports, receive peltries in payment, haul furs to Canton, sell them on commission, and bring back the proceeds minus agreed-upon freight charges. Astor took the word "interlopers" to mean his redoubtable rivals—Hudson's Bay and the Northwest Fur Company. Little love was lost between the two Canadian companies. Territorial claims had never cramped the Northwesters' style. For decades they had hunted and traded in regions that were, by act of Parliament, the legal territory of the Hudson's Bay Company.

11

—∿—

A Perfect Triangle

In the spring of 1808, when the idea of becoming the partner of Czar Alexander's Alaskan monopoly had not yet taken shape in Astor's mind, he had convinced himself that what he needed was his own New Archangel. Trading with the Russians depended on the goodwill of Czar Alexander I, a benevolent, myopic, and slightly mad half-German giant with red blond hair. It also depended on the dexterity of diplomats, maybe even on peace in Europe. Napoleon had defeated a Prussian-Russian coalition at Friedland in 1807 and forced the czar into a secret Franco-Russian alliance against Britain.

Why not build a line of trading posts up the Missouri, across the Rockies, and along the Columbia River to the Pacific? Here, at the mouth of the river that Captain Robert Gray had claimed for the United States in 1792 and thirteen years later Meriwether Lewis and William Clark had visited, he could set up a trading center, modestly named after himself. His ships would carry furs from the Astoria depot on the mouth of the Columbia to China, return to New York with teas, silks, and other rich Asiatic merchandise, be outbound again with "bells and blankets, knives, tobacco and rum" for barter with Indians, and, laden with pelts, again head for the Pearl River. He would do what the American government was not strong enough to do—conquer for himself the riches of an immense land few white men had ever seen.

Sailing up the Columbia River was not easy. Captain Gray had described how sandbars and breakers forced him to anchor at a respectful distance from the shore and lower a well-manned boat to row in. The Indians had never seen a ship or a white man. They were sure the *Columbia* was a monster from the deep, and the men in the rowboat cannibals sent by the gods to ravage the country and devour the inhabitants. Gray charted the estuary, lifted anchor, and at sea met Captain Vancouver. The two conferred and Gray gave Vancouver his chart. Vancouver also anchored offshore and sent his lieutenant, a man named Broughton, up the river. The lieutenant and crew rowed up some one hundred miles until in the southern distance they saw a snowcapped mount that Broughton named Mount Hood.

So was the river American or British? Since nations laid claims based on who was first, and Captain Gray and the *Columbia* had indeed been first, the river and its shores were American. Negotiations in London in 1807 to replace the Jay Treaty strengthened the American claim. Compared with the vexatious issue of impressment, defining the boundary west of the Great Lakes was relatively easy. Jefferson's envoy, James Monroe, agreed with Lords Auckland and Holland to accept the 49th parallel as the boundary between British America and the United States. The new border was no more than a diplomats' line on ill-defined maps. What Monroe, Auckland, and Holland couldn't know, for example, was that the Columbia was the largest river flowing into the Pacific from North America, and that it crossed the line on their maps. The source of the 1,214-mile river was near the crest of the Rockies. The first 460 miles of its course were north of the 49th parallel, while latitude 46° 19' established the mouth of the river to be in what was designated as future U.S. territory.

If there was one thing that stirred Jefferson's visionary energies at the end of his eight-year term it was the West. He had sent Meriwether Lewis and the Corps of Discovery west to explore unknown lands. His instructions had been explicit. Lewis was to "explore the Missouri river, and such principal streams of it, as, by its course and communication with the Pacific ocean . . . may offer the most direct and practicable water communication across the continent for the purposes of commerce."

In 1805, a year after the expedition's departure, Jefferson had taken delivery of some of the findings that Lewis had sent back from a winter camp: charts and journals, seeds, animal droppings, reports on Indian peoples, a live prairie dog. The president took the Indian corn and planted it in his garden, and pored over the expedition's painstakingly drawn maps. He brushed aside doubts that Federalists, and even members of his own party, entertained about the country's ability to assimilate the vast Louisiana Territory. The West, he believed, would release new national energies, even if it meant breaking the United States in two. "Whether we remain in one confederacy, or form into Atlantic and Mississippi confederacies, I believe not very important to the happiness of either part," he had written to the British philosopher Joseph Priestley in 1802. "Those of the western confederacy will be as much our children and descendants as those of the eastern, and I feel myself as much identified with that country, in future time, as with this."

Lewis, Clark, and the Corps of Discovery expedition members had returned as national heroes. Congress had awarded the men double pay and 320 acres of land for their services; Lewis and Clark each got 1,600 acres. A statue was made of Lewis and placed in Philadelphia's Independence Hall. We do not know what was actually said when Lewis reported to Jefferson in the White House, but the president later wrote that he spread Lewis's maps out on the floor and "examined these sheets myself minutely."

Lewis knew what Astor only suspected. The rivers out West, he said in an early written account to Jefferson, "abound more in beaver and common otter than any other streams on earth." News of the marvels to be found in the Rocky Mountains and beyond filled newspapers. The *Philadelphia Register* and the *Boston Columbian Sentinel* reported that winters were very mild on the Pacific. Other papers gave other details: an Indian on the far side of the Rockies was considered poor if he didn't own three hundred horses; sheep in the mountains weighed eighty pounds.

The first book appeared in 1807. *A Journal of the Voyage and Travels of a Corps of Discovery under the Command of Capt. Lewis and Capt. Clark* was an illustrated eyewitness account of the expedition. Its author, Sergeant Patrick Gass, knew how to be dramatic. "We were to pass through a country possessed by numerous, powerful and

Oct. 1, 1806.

By the last Mails.

MARYLAND.   BALTIMORE, OCT. 29, 1806.

A LETTER from *St. Louis (Upper Louisiana)*, dated *Sept.* 23, 1806, announces the arrival of Captains LEWIS and CLARK, from their expedition into the interior.—They went to the *Pacific Ocean ;* have brought some of the natives and curiosities of the countries through which they passed, and only lost one man. They left the *Pacific Ocean* 23d March, 1806, where they arrived in November, 1805 ;—and where some American vessels had been just before.—They state the Indians to be as numerous on the *Columbia* river, which empties into the *Pacific,* as the whites in any part of the U.S. They brought a family of the Mandan indians with them. The winter was very mild on the *Pacific.—* They have kept an ample journal of their tour ; which will be published, and must afford much intelligence. —————

News of Lewis and Clark

warlike nations of savages, of gigantic stature, fierce, treacherous and cruel; and particularly hostile to white men," he wrote.*

Jefferson's mission statement to Lewis and Clark had been specific. Their exploration was "for the purposes of commerce," music to Astor's ears Still, John Jacob thought it prudent to couch his ambitions in patriotic language. He traveled to Washington and, helped by Albert Gallatin, told the government his aim was to wrest the fur monopoly from the Northwest and Mackinac companies. Besides talking about "extending the American domain" and "adding new states to the Union," he suggested Native Americans could also profit. If the government would grant him an exclusive charter, he would be in a position "to prevent irresponsible fly-by-night traders whose only interest was in quick killings from gaining a foothold." The venture, he said in a letter to Jefferson, would be "of such magnitude that it would require a greater capital than any individual or unincorporated association could well furnish."

Jefferson asked his secretary of war, General Henry Dearborn, to look into Astor's reputation. Dearborn in turn wrote DeWitt Clinton, Governor George Clinton's nephew and, since 1803, mayor of New York City. John Jacob had known Clinton since they had been admitted to the Masonic lodge back in 1790. After receiving Clinton's reply, Dearborn advised the president that the mayor of New York "speaks well of Astor as a man of large property and fair character, and well acquainted with the fur and peltry business." Meriwether Lewis had become governor of the Louisiana Terri-

---

*Lewis promised a three-volume account but died in 1809 without having written a word, and Clark was so conscious of his lack of formal education that he hired an editor to help him, only to see two publishers go bankrupt. It would take almost a hundred years before the complete journals of Lewis and Clark were published in 1904. Gass was the last survivor. He was sixty when he married a twenty-year-old and sired six children. He was ninety when he volunteered to fight in the Civil War. He lived to see the completion of the transcontinental railway in 1869, dying the following year a few months short of his hundredth birthday.

tory and Jefferson wrote him recommending Astor. Lewis in turn informed fur traders in St. Louis. They received the news of a formidable competitor ready to muscle in with less than enthusiasm.

John Jacob had his own man in St. Louis. Charles Gratiot, who had met Astor in Montreal, offered his services, but John Jacob considered Gratiot a lightweight. After the New York legislature obliged J. J. by approving the incorporation of the American Fur Company on April 6, 1808, he traveled north to directly cut the Montreal fur kings in on the deal. Two years later, Northwest president William McGillivray came to New York to offer Astor a share of the Mackinac Company, established on Michilimackinac Island, which J. J. had visited twenty-two years earlier.

Why this sudden cooperation? As in most strategic plays, the alliance ratified the reality on the ground. Astor had reached such economic mass that accommodation was in his rivals' best interests. His business sense, his capital, his trade with China, and his intimacy with cabinet members in Washington made him too formidable to take on in open combat. His American Fur Company might be the bitter rival of the Northwest Company out West, but a takeover of the Mackinac Company would make him an ally on the Great Lakes. To put pressure on McGillivray to accept his terms, J. J. let it be known he was expanding his Great Lakes trade by hiring new agents and importing sizable quantities of goods from England to be used specifically in the area. On January 28, 1811, McGillivray and Astor signed the agreement that gave birth to the Southwest Fur Company. Leaving boundaries deliberately vague, the new Canadian-American organization was to operate for the most part on what Astor had just told Jefferson might be future U.S. domain. The new company agreed not to poach on Northwest posts in parts of Lake Huron, but the agreement emphatically spelled out that these territorial limitations did not cover "any Countries beyond the ridge of the Rockey [sic] Mountains nor the river Missouri nor to the North West Coast or in the Pacific Ocean."

—◆—

Astor's moves were watched with increasing hostility not only in Montreal but in the roiling Upper Louisiana boomtown of St. Louis. The settlement on the confluence of the Mississippi and the Missouri was base camp to a polyglot crowd of Kentucky and Virginia hunters, Mississippi boatmen, Canadian voyageurs, soldiers, adventurers, and Indians of various tribes. Billiard parlors, saloons, and whorehouses competed with the outfitters for the dollars the trappers obtained for their skins when they returned from the wilds. John Jacob was too powerful to fear the underfinanced St. Louis traders who shipped out via the Mississippi and New Orleans. He would know how to play them against each other, how to side with one outfit or another, and how to switch sides if any one of them became dominant.

He had first become aware of the St. Louis traders in 1799, when, on behalf of a London fur house, he had tried to collect money from Gratiot and Pierre Chouteau Jr., the nephew of René Auguste Chouteau, who with the New Orleans merchant Pierre Laclède had been a founder of St. Louis. Instead of pressing strongly for payment, Astor had suggested it might be in the interest of Gratiot and Chouteau to ship their merchandise directly to him in New York. He had contacts throughout Europe, he wrote them, and could sell their pelts at top prices. Chouteau had ignored the offer, but Gratiot wrote back that he would be happy to do business with Astor. He had forwarded a note for £1,000, payable to Astor in April 1804, and asked J. J. to secure debentures on trade goods sent by land across the Mississippi. He also suggested Astor look into shipping St. Louis furs to Europe via New Orleans. No deal had been worked out, but J. J. and Gratiot had met in Philadelphia. When Gratiot's £1,000 note became due and he was unable to honor it, J. J. had not demanded a settlement. Gratiot was deeply appreciative and wrote a friend, "I am indebted to Mr. Jacob Astor who has treated me with great indulgence. I wish to satisfy him with all the means in my power."

Three years before Astor's patriotic charm offensive in Washington, Chouteau had sent his son, also named Pierre, to Washington on a similar errand. The Louisiana Purchase had thrown doubt on the Chouteaus' profitable monopoly on trade with the Osages on the Arkansas River (worth $20,000 a year). Chouteau Jr. had obtained an audience with Jefferson and Gallatin and boldly asked for exclusive rights to all the profits of trade with Indians in all of the Louisiana Territory. Gallatin was familiar with his friend Astor's pushy demands, but Chouteau's brazen request left him breathless. Jefferson wondered whether Chouteau would be "useful or dangerous," and referred the request to Secretary of War Dearborn, who turned it down, but in time granted the Chouteaus, père et fils, licenses to trade extensively along the Missouri.

A third personage, less wealthy than the Chouteaus but bolder, more cunning, and an enigma even to his associates, was Manuel Lisa, the only Louisiana Spaniard prominent in the St. Louis trade. "In boldness of enterprise, persistency of purpose, and in restless energy, he was a fair representative of the Spaniard of the days of Cortez," General Hiram Chittenden would write in his authoritative *American Fur Trade of the Far West*. "He was a man of great ability, a masterly judge of men, thoroughly experienced in the Indian trade and native customs, intensely active in his work, yet a perfect enigma of character which his contemporaries were never able to solve." The kind of men he drew to him included his second in command, George Drouillard. This half Shawnee's skills at sign language had made him the interpreter on the Lewis and Clark expedition. As Astor incorporated the American Fur Company in New York, Lisa organized the Missouri Fur Company in St. Louis, a move duly noted by John Jacob.

Four years before J. J. sent his daughter and son-in-law to St. Petersburg to beguile the czar's minister, Lisa, Drouillard, and a formidable team of voyageurs had left St. Louis in a keelboat heavily loaded with goods destined for barter. Their goal was to trade at the headwaters of the Missouri, a journey of more than two thousand miles through unfriendly Indian country. They were at the mouth of the Platte River in today's South Dakota when they saw a lone white man come down the Missouri in a canoe. The traveler was John Colter, who had also been a member of the Lewis and Clark expedition. On the Corps of Discovery's return trip, Colter had told Lewis he would be lonely in St. Louis and wanted to begin a new life in the West. Lewis had released Colter from the expedition and allowed him to join two American trappers on their way to Yellowstone to hunt for beaver. People shook their heads in disbelief when he told them he had seen geysers and smoking cones in the Yellowstone River country.

Lisa immediately saw the value of a man who had been to the Pacific. He persuaded Colter to turn around and come with him and his team up the Missouri to the Yellowstone River. They continued up the Yellowstone to the confluence of the Bighorn River, where they built the first trading post in today's Montana, variously called Fort Lisa, Fort Manuel, or Manuel's Fort. Colter had been here before and advised Lisa to trade with the Crow Indians to the south because the Blackfeet to the north were not to be trusted.

The Blackfeet were the strongest and most aggressive military power in the northwestern plains. The Blackfoot nation included three closely related and allied Algonquian-speaking tribes: the Blackfeet proper—the name apparently derived from their tradition of using ashes to stain their moccasins—the Piegans, and the Bloods. Originally from Saskatchewan, they were a nomadic people who, in the mid-eighteenth century, had drifted west in search of buffalo and lived and hunted on a territory the size of France and Spain combined, covering modern-day Alberta and Montana. They were expert horseback riders and fierce warriors feared by other Native American groups. Except for raising tobacco, they did no farming. Colter's advice and Lisa's decision to trade with the Crows was their biggest mistake. The Blackfeet never forgave Lisa— and by extension any white man reaching the upper Missouri waterways—for preferring to trade with their bitterest foe. Lisa and crew realized as much and after successfully trading with the Crows, prudently headed back down the Missouri in the spring of 1808, their keelboat low in the water with furs.

Lisa's chief rivals in St. Louis were a pair of Scots, Ramsay Crooks and Robert McClellan (sometimes spelled McLellan). Crooks had arrived from Scotland at the age of sixteen in 1803, and at once entered the service of the Montreal fur traders. He went to Michilimackinac as a clerk. At nineteen, he pushed on to St. Louis, where he teamed up with the older McClellan, a daring hunter who had distinguished himself in the early Indian wars under General Anthony Wayne in Ohio. Financed by the Chouteaus, Crooks, McClellan, and eighty men set out for the upper Missouri in 1808. They were near the confluence of the Cheyenne River in today's South Dakota when they were met by a war party of six hundred Sioux. The Sioux chief barred Crooks and McClellan from traveling any farther, but offered to trade with them. Making a virtue of necessity, the partners began setting up a trading post. In their talk with the chief, they realized Lisa had bribed the Sioux to prevent them from continuing. As soon as the last Indian left for home to fetch his furs, Crooks, McClellan, and their men fled down the river. In St. Louis, they swore revenge.

—∞—

In Washington, meanwhile, everything was going right for John Jacob. Jefferson called Astor "a most excellent man," and had no doubts the Astoria enterprise would succeed. In a letter to Astor that Washington Irving later found in J. J.'s papers and quoted in *Astoria: Adventure in the Pacific Northwest,* Jefferson wrote:

> I remember well having invited your proposition on this subject [extending American trade and influence to the West Coast] and encouraged it with the assurance of every facility and protection which the government could properly afford. I considered as a great public acquisition the commencement of a settlement on that point of the western coast of America, and look forward with gratification to the time when its descendants should have spread themselves through the whole length of that coast, covering it with free and independent Americans, unconnected with us but by the ties of blood and interest, and enjoying like us the rights of self-government.

Jefferson didn't quite grasp Astor's strategy. Whereas John Jacob didn't care whether the new empire was American or Canadian as long as he himself was in charge and pocketed the profits, the president was under the impression that several American companies would engage in the trade. Four friends—James Fairlee, William Edgar, William Denning, and Edward Laight—provided window dressing for J. J. as commissioners of the American Fur Company. "The four commissioners were paid for the use of their names, either with cash or a share or two of stock," John Upton Terrell would write in *Furs by Astor.* "They had no more authority, no more voice in the affairs of the company, than did the Indians it intended to rob."

In Astor's mind, it was a major undertaking to send not one but two expeditions to the entrance of the Columbia. One would be seaborne, sailing from New York via Cape Horn, the other would go overland from St. Louis, and more or less follow the Lewis and Clark trail. Because his financial exposure over the next years might reach $400,000, he took on partners. Because he distrusted both these partners and the people he hired to lead the two-pronged mission, he divided the expedition leaderships, with disastrous results.

The partners were Scots from Montreal: Alexander McKay, Duncan McDougal, David Stuart, and the latter's nephew, Robert Stuart, who were to sail to the future Astoria. McKay had been part of Alexander Mackenzie's team on the 1793 cross-Canada expedition. McDougal's uncle Angus Shaw was a principal partner of the Northwest Company. The elder Stuart was a Northwest veteran, as was Donald McKenzie, who was to join the overland party. To ensure their loyalty, Astor made them minority partners in the enterprise.

McKenzie had worked ten years for the Northwest Company and should have been the logical choice to lead the riverborne expedition. In selecting Wilson Price Hunt, a scrupulously respectable merchant from New Jersey with business interests in St. Louis, over McKenzie, J. J. chose expedience over experience. Perhaps because he had hoodwinked Jefferson into the Punqua exception to the embargo,

Astor thought it politically expedient to have an American in charge. Perhaps to compensate for Hunt's lack of knowledge of frontier life, J. J. negotiated a contract with Ramsay Crooks and Robert McClellan, the St. Louis partners who had been stopped by the Sioux and wanted to get back at Lisa, and an associate of theirs, Joseph Miller. A native of Baltimore, Miller was a former army officer who had resigned over a refusal to grant him a furlough. His education and his experience as a trapper and Indian trader made him a valuable addition to the overland party.

Long work sessions in Astor's new office at 69 Pine Street set out the interest of each of these men. Bankrolled by John Jacob to the tune of $400,000—he would later claim the undertaking cost him $1 million—they set up the Pacific Fur Company. In return for providing vessels, goods, provisions, arms, ammunitions, and all other requisites for the enterprise, Astor retained management of all the new company's activities. A hundred shares were issued. J. J. got fifty and retained the privilege of making his shares over to the American Fur Company under certain conditions. Fifteen shares were reserved for the use of the company. McKay, McKenzie, McDougal, David Stuart, Hunt, and Crooks received five shares each, and McClellan and Miller got two and a half shares each. After five years, it was agreed, all losses and profits would be apportioned on the basis of the number of shares held by each partner.

Was Astor Machiavellian enough to suggest McKay and McDougal debrief British ambassador Francis Jackson before the departure? Did the two partners decide on their own to play both sides? There are indications that J. J. had his doubts about his partners' allegiance because he suggested they become American citizens. Neither the partners nor the clerks they hired voiced objections. Taking out citizenship, however, was no longer a simple matter of swearing that one had resided in the United States for five years. War hysteria and a fear of foreigners had provoked Congress to pass the Naturalization, Alien, and Sedition Acts of 1798, which extended from five to fourteen years the time "necessary for an alien to reside here before he can be admitted a citizen."

Citizenship would not be of much help to the seaborne partners since only native-born Americans were exempt from impressment should a Royal Navy man-of-war stop them on the high seas. Astor, however, was told his Scottish and Canadian minority partners had followed his suggestion. Only years later did he find out that they had not become citizens. We do know that they appraised British ambassador Jackson of the Pacific Fur Company plans because Jackson expressed "surprise and admiration . . . that a private individual should have conceived and set on foot at his own risk and expense, so great an enterprise."

Early in 1810, Wilson Price Hunt left for Montreal to prepare the overland expedition. In July, Astor celebrated his forty-seventh birthday, and less than two months later saw the sea mission off with the departure of the *Tonquin,* a ship mounting twelve guns and carrying a crew of twenty-one. He had spared no expense outfitting the three-hundred-ton ship. She carried a capacity cargo of merchandise, stores, equipment, and ammunition for the establishment of the permanent post on the Columbia.

News of the Astor expedition to the Pacific was received with apprehension in Montreal, where the significance of the enormous undertaking was readily understood. Hunt was appalled at the surly resentment he encountered, resentment that translated into denying him and McKenzie the first pick of voyageurs. Agents of the Northwest Company persuaded some of the best boatmen to beg off. Money, however, spoke loud enough to recruit a party of thirty men, and on July 5, 1810, they slid their huge birch canoes into the St. Lawrence above the Lachine Falls. Hunt had met Canadian boatmen in St. Louis. As he had never been in charge of a group of voyageurs, the men took advantage of his inexperience. Several times a day they sought to land, build a fire, brew tea, smoke, talk, and sing. It took seventeen days to reach Michilimackinac. Here, Ramsey Crooks joined them.

Crooks told Hunt the story of his encounter with the Sioux. A force of thirty men, he said, would be too small to

Wilson Price Hunt

scare off attackers. Thirty men, in fact, were few enough to encourage an attack. With his help, a few more men were hired at Michilimackinac, but the recruiting proved even more difficult than in Montreal. Hunt offered advances on wages, which were squandered overnight. Some men suddenly remembered previous commitments, which could only be discharged for "reasonable considerations." Hunt paid the "considerations." Others owed bills for goods and liquor, which had to be settled before they were free to leave. Hunt paid one man's court fine. On August 17, partners and crew pushed on to Green Bay, continued up the Fox River and overland to the Wisconsin, joined the Mississippi at Prairie du Chien, and in early September arrived at St. Louis.

Hunt was anxious to push on. The reason was Manuel Lisa, who was not about to relinquish any part of his business to the Astor money and to his enemies Ramsay Crooks and Robert McClellan. When Hunt tried to recruit boatmen, they told him Lisa had already hired them for the next spring.

Why didn't Astor merge with or buy out Lisa's outfit? Teamwork was what the expedition he alone was financing demanded. John Jacob wanted disciplined men who had come up through Northwest's long apprenticeships, men who knew how to follow orders and endure hardship. Writing in the 1920s, biographer Arthur D. Howden Smith would sense a streak of anti-Americanism in Astor's choice of former Northwest Company men while conveniently forgetting that Lisa's partners were also mainly Canadians. "Possibly, he thought Canadians would be easier to work with," Smith would write. "And he seems always to have been contemptuous of the American trappers who were the pathfinders of the West. They were a turbulent, lawless lot, more individualistic than the French Canadians; but their individualism made for initiative, and as a rule five of them were worth more than ten of the Canadians and half-breeds."

This reading of who was worth more than whom runs counter to Washington Irving's observations in his opening chapter of *Astoria*:

The adroit and buoyant Frenchman and the cool and calculating Briton . . . penetrated, in defiance of difficulties and dangers, to the heart of savage countries, laying open the hidden secrets of the wilderness; leading the way to remote regions of beauty and fertility that might have remained unexplored for ages, and beckoning after them the slow and pausing steps of agriculture and civilization. It was the fur trade, in fact, which gave early sustenance and vitality to the great Canadian provinces. Being destitute of the precious metals, at that time the leading object of American enterprise, they were long neglected by the parent country. The

French adventurers, however, who had settled on the banks of the St. Lawrence, soon found that in the rich peltries of the interior, they had sources of wealth that might almost rival the mines of Mexico and Peru.

Crooks had helped with the recruiting at Michilimackinac. In St. Louis, Joseph Miller saved the day. Miller was popular with the local traders and another thirty voyageurs were hired and supplies loaded onto new keelboats. Hunt was afraid that if they waited in St. Louis until spring, his sixty-man crew would melt away. On October 21, they set off. They paddled, poled, and hauled their boats up the Missouri. The progress was slow. As the channel frequently shifted with bends and sandbanks, the boatmen had to steer the keelboat in zigzags. Crew members often had to jump into the water at shallows and wade along with towlines. Also delaying the advance were floating trees, driftwood, and, even more dangerous, submerged trees that threatened to impale the canoes, which went ahead of the keelboats to probe the river. Irving again:

> On these occasions it was that the merits of the Canadian voyageurs came into full action. Patient of toil, not to be disheartened by impediments and disappointments, fertile in expedients, and versed in every mode of humouring and conquering the wayward current, they would ply every exertion, sometimes in the boat, sometimes on shore, sometimes in the water, however cold; always alert, always in good humour; and, should they at any time flag or grow weary, one of their popular boat-songs, chanted by a veteran oarsman, and responded to in chorus, acted as a never-failing restorative.

They were near today's Kansas-Nebraska state line in mid-November when the Missouri began to freeze over. On the eastern bank of the river they began to build log and earth shelters for winter quarters. The prospect of four months of idleness brought out simmering conflicts among the partners. McKenzie regarded Hunt as a rank amateur, and Hunt suspected the Northwest veteran of divided loyalties. Many felt that if McKenzie had been in charge from the time the expedition was launched in Montreal they wouldn't be wintering 450 miles from St. Louis, but at the headwaters of the Columbia River.

Partner Robert McClellan and a strapping Virginian named John Day, who lived and dressed like an Indian, rode into the camp. McClellan carried letters from Astor. One of them ordered Hunt to assume full command of the expedition. When McKenzie was shown the letter, he considered it a personal affront and a violation of his agreement with Astor. Hunt decided to return to St. Louis so he could hire more men and send dispatches to Astor on the progress and condition of the company. In his absence, he divided the command of the camp between McKenzie and Joseph Miller. The two didn't get on well. Traveling by horseback, Hunt reached St. Louis on January 20, 1811.

Recruiting proved difficult. Nearly every voyageur for hire was either already with Hunt up the river or signed up for Lisa's expedition slated to get under way at the first thaw. Again, Hunt was forced to pay out substantial advances to secure recruits. Luck and money, however, gave him Pierre Dorion, a half French, half Indian interpreter of Sioux languages whose father had filled the same function for Lewis and Clark. The previous year, young Dorion had been Lisa's interpreter. Lisa now tried to lure Dorion over to his team, forcing Hunt to outbid Lisa until Dorion's wages for the expedition reached $300. Hunt also allowed John Bradbury and Thomas Nuttall, two British naturalists who had come out to collect American wilderness plants, to join the expedition as far as the friendly Mandans who lived on the confluence of the Missouri and Knife Rivers, north of today's Bismarck, North Dakota. Bradbury and Nuttall were eccentric amateur explorers and scientific researchers with a knack for wandering into dangers that seasoned trappers would avoid, only to extricate themselves—or get extricated. When suddenly surrounded by three hundred Arikara in present-day South Dakota, Nuttall turned to one of the partners and said, "Sir, don't you think these Indians much fatter, and more robust than those of yesterday?" The pair were a source of amusement for the French-Canadians, who called Nuttall *"le fou"* ("the crazy one").

Hunt was about to leave in a new keelboat with Bradbury, Nuttall, Dorion, and his new workforce when five
American hunters from the winter encampment showed up,
saying they had been ill-treated by McKenzie and Miller and
had fled in the dead of night. The deserters told their tale
to the new recruits with the result that they, too, refused to
embark. Hunt managed to change the mind of one hunter.
But Dorion had a new demand. He wanted his Sioux squaw
and two children to come with him.

On March 19, Hunt, Dorian, his wife and children, the
one returning hunter, and Bradbury and Nuttall left St.
Louis. On the third day of their push upriver past St.
Charles, they stopped at an old French encampment called
Charette and were met by Daniel Boone. The legendary
frontiersman was seventy-seven—Washington Irving would
say he was in his eighty-fifth year. He was still leading a
hunter's life and, to prove it, brought some sixty beaver skins
to the riverbank.

By mid-March, the Hunt party reached the army post at
Fort Osage, forty miles below today's Kansas City, where
Crooks and several men were waiting, and where Pierre
Dorion picked up rumors of war between the Osages and
the Ioways. A war party three hundred strong was supposed
to be roaming the countryside. Hunt, Crooks, and company
spent three days at the fort as guests of a Lieutenant Brown-
son and witnessed the Osage warriors return with seven
Ioway scalps impaled on poles. In Irving's retelling, the
triumphant scalp dance so intoxicated Dorion's wife that
she wanted to stay. When everybody was ready to push
off into the spring runoff, Pierre summarily reembarked
his squaw and, before anyone could interfere, gave her a
thrashing.

Bodies of drowned buffalo floated past them with flocks
of turkey buzzards feeding on the carcasses. Bradbury was
delighted to see snakes emerging from hibernation and
collected a number of them. The party arrived at the winter
encampment on April 17, 1811. Although they didn't know
it, the mouth of the Columbia River was still three thousand
miles away.

Map of the Oregon Territory, 1855

12

—ᴍ—

Outbound

The seaborne expedition battled the gales of the south Atlantic and near mutiny. The skipper of the *Tonquin* was Lieutenant Jonathan Thorn, on loan from the U.S. Navy. Political considerations were behind Astor's choice of Thorn. Republicans—all under forty and most from the western states or the western parts of the older states—were angrier at Britain than at France. To these men, who voted Henry Clay of Kentucky the new House Speaker, their barely settled regions already seemed overcrowded. To get more land, they were ready to drive the British from all of North America. At Tippecanoe Creek, in the future state of Indiana, the U.S. Army defeated an uprising of an Indian confederacy, which western hotheads in Congress mistakenly believed was inspired by the British. The tall, lordly Clay remarked that he was tired of seeing his country tied "eternally to the tail of the British kite."

Astor liked his ships to make money and his instructions to Captain Thorn were therefore twofold. The prime mission of the *Tonquin* was to land the partners, their men, and their equipment at the mouth of the Columbia River. While they built the trading fort, however, Thorn was to turn himself into a trader, sail north toward New Archangel, and barter utensils for pelts from Indians along the coast. Thorn was a veteran of the war with Tripoli and, Astor reasoned, should the *Tonquin* run into an armed privateer or a British man-of-war, who better to have on the bridge than Thorn? As the master of the *Tonquin,* Thorn proved to be typical of naval officers of his day: brave, simpleminded, tyrannical, and inflexible.

Anxious to establish his authority the first night out, Captain Thorn ordered "lights out" at eight o'clock. McDougal, McKay, and the Stuarts were incensed. As partners of the Pacific Fur Company, which was financing the voyage, including the captain's salary, they were onboard *their* ship and entitled to turn out the lights whenever they pleased.

Everything about the landlubbers infuriated Thorn. Seeing the elder Stuart, thirteen voyageurs, and five mechanics sitting on the deck laughing and gossiping while passing a pipe in the manner of the Indians made him struggle with his temper. The simplest things annoyed him. Gabriel Franchère, a young Montrealer with deep blue eyes and a funny tuft of hair, was determined to keep a journal of the adventure. Two other clerks also scribbling diaries were Ross Cox and Alexander Ross, the latter a young Scotsman who had come to Canada in 1804 and after several years of fortune hunting had eagerly enlisted as a clerk. When Captain Thorn saw these young men sitting on deck writing their impressions, he couldn't help denouncing them in a letter to Astor. "The collecting of materials for long histories of their voyage and travels appeared to engross most of their attention." There was more, Thorn wrote. "They were determined to have it said they had been in Africa, and therefore insisted on my stopping at the Cape de Verde. Next they said the ship should stop on the coast of Patagonia, for they must see the large and uncommon inhabitants of that place. Then they must go to the island where Robinson Crusoe had so long lived. And lastly, they were determined to see the handsome inhabitants of Easter Island." When storms tossed the *Tonquin,* he cursed his passengers for staying below deck. Seeing them crawl up on deck to vomit over the side was such a sight he put it in his log. They appeared, he wrote, "like spectres from the hatchways, in capotes and blankets, with dirty nightcaps, shivering about the deck, and ever and anon crawling to the sides of the vessel, and offering up their tributes to the windward."

At the Falklands, where the *Tonquin* took on freshwater, Thorn tried to leave without his passengers. When the signal to return to the ship rang out, McKay, David Stuart, and five clerks, including Franchère, were apparently too slow for Thorn. Furious, he ordered sails raised. The members of the shore party couldn't believe their eyes. They climbed into their boat and rowed after the ship, slowly sinking behind. On board, young Robert Stuart got a gun and charged up to the bridge. Twenty-six years later, here is Washington Irving's description of what happened next:

> Fortunately for all parties the wind just then came ahead, and the boat was enabled to reach the ship, otherwise disastrous circumstances might have ensued. We can hardly believe that the captain really intended to carry his threat into full effect, and rather think he meant to let the laggards off for a long pull and a hearty fright. He declared, however, in his letter to Mr. Astor, that he was serious in his threats, and there is no knowing how far such an iron man may push his notions of authority. "Had the wind," writes he "(unfortunately) not hauled ahead soon after leaving the harbour's mouth, I should positively have left them; and indeed I cannot but think it an unfortunate circumstance for you that it so happened, for the first loss in this stance would, in my opinion, have proved the best, as they seem to have no idea of the value of property, nor any apparent regard for your interest, although interwoven with their own."

As they rounded the Horn on Christmas Day and plowed across the Pacific to reach Hawaii—or Owhyee, as Ross spelled Captain James Cook's Sandwich Islands in his diary—there was virtually no communication between passengers and crew. On February 13, 1911, they anchored at Karakkooa Bay within a mile of where Captain Cook had been killed in a scuffle with Hawaiians thirty-two years earlier. Thorn acted ever more high-handedly. Two sailors

ENTRANCE OF THE COLUMBIA RIVER.
Ship Tonquin, crossing the bar, 25th March, 1811

The *Tonquin* crosses the bar at the Columbia River.

who overstayed their Hawaiian shore leave by fifteen minutes were flogged and put in irons. A third crew member
who remained ashore overnight was beaten unconscious and
thrown overboard to drown, only to be rescued by Hawaiians
and left behind.

Thorn's scorn for the partners grew and his notion of
his duty hardened. The last leg of the voyage was the
worst. When McDougal, McKay, and the Stuarts began
to distribute arms to the men, a normal precaution since
they planned their landfall on a possibly hostile coast,
Thorn's suspicion of imminent mutiny reached a point where
the relationship between him and the Scots was beyond
repair.

The *Tonquin* arrived off the Columbia River sandbar in
foul weather on March 22, 1811. The mouth of the river was
four miles wide. A bay and a spit of land named Cape Disappointment formed the northern shore. Prudently, Thorn
anchored eight miles off the sandbar. Over the objections of
his first mate, he ordered a whaleboat lowered. The boat
and five-man crew, including the first mate, careered in
choppy seas toward the coast and were never seen again.
The weather moderated, but Thorn lost a second boat and

three more men, and narrowly avoided losing the *Tonquin* herself, before he managed to enter the bay behind Cape Disappointment.

Thorn couldn't wait to unload his passengers, cargo, and primary responsibilities. McDougal, who now considered himself the head of the expedition, reconnoitered both shores with David Stuart. On the north shore several miles upriver from the *Tonquin*'s anchorage, they saw a village. Captain Thorn, meanwhile, found a little cove on the southern shore twelve miles from the open sea, and began unloading equipment. He had had enough of what he called the partners' "sporting excursions." The site he chose was a grassy elevation on the headland north of where Lewis and Clark had wintered in 1805–1806. The location commanded a stunning view of the wide estuary, the sandbar, and thundering breakers. To the south the short Klaskanine River emptied into the bay, which, to the north and west, was framed by the right bank of the Columbia and, in the distance, Cape Disappointment.

All hands set to work cutting down trees, clearing thickets, and marking out the sites for log buildings. Some found driftwood and hauled it up to the construction site. On the beach, ship carpenters laid the keel of a coastal schooner with planks carried aboard the *Tonquin*. The vessel, christened the *Dolly* after Astor's daughter, was never strong enough for the roaring surf and was used only on the river. Captain Thorn was anxious to leave on the second part of his mission—to cruise northward along the coast and barter pelts. The partners decided one of them should embark with Captain Thorn and gain knowledge of Indians farther up the coast. McKay volunteered. On June 5, he and a crew of twenty-three were back on board the *Tonquin* when Thorn ordered the anchor lifted.

The Astorians, as McDougal and his men called themselves, had been on shore only a short time when a large sea canoe came toward them from the opposite bank. Paddled by ten men, it ferried the one-eyed Chief Comcomly (Conconully, or "white salmon," in some transliterations) and one of his favorite women across the estuary. Comcomly brought a hundred fresh salmon, each weighing from five to eighteen pounds.

McDougal, who in the absence of McKay considered himself Astor's proxy, established friendly contacts with them. They were Chinooks. Alexander Henry, a nephew of the Northwest partner Astor had met in Montreal back in 1787, called the Chinooks "a very filthy race, so surrounded by fish offals and excrements that it demands the utmost precaution in walking to avoid them." They were friendly enough, however, and came to barter sturgeon, salmon, geese, ducks, mats, and berries for nails and axes. One of them carried a musket of Russian manufacture.

The Astorians were finishing their fort when an Indian came down the river in a canoe with word that a party of thirty white men had appeared at the second rapids and were building houses there. If they were building log cabins, they couldn't be the Hunt party, but Northwest men trying to seize the upper part of the river. McDougal sent a party to investigate. About two hundred miles up, the party members climbed the first rapids on foot, but could find no Indians to tell them of white men felling trees and building log cabins. The party returned to Astoria, where two Indian

ASTORIA, AS IT WAS IN 1813.

Astoria in 1813

women came to the river. They had seen white men building a trading post on the Spokane River. On July 15, David Stuart and eight men were ready to set out to investigate when a canoe with nine white men came downriver. Franchère was there to chronicle the arrival: "Toward midday we saw a large canoe with a flag displayed at her stern rounding the point we called Tongue Point. The flag she bore was the British, and her crew was composed of eight Canadian boatmen or voyageurs. A well-dressed man, who appeared to be the commander, was the first to leap ashore."

He introduced himself as David Thompson, explorer, trader, and partner of the Northwest Company. He didn't mention that he had tried to reach the Pacific in 1801, but explained he and his men were on their way back to Montreal. Coming down the Columbia from the Spokane, he had heard from Indians of a ship's arrival. The presence of seals playing in the river had told him he was very near salt water.

As a Northwest veteran himself, McDougal thought it best to be hospitable. David Stuart was sure Thompson was a spy and balked at McDougal's suggestion that they give the Thompson party provisions for their journey back across the Rockies. McDougal overruled Stuart, and in addition to supplies handed Thompson a letter and asked him to forward it to Astor. The letter announced their safe arrival, and that they had not yet heard from Hunt. With that, Thompson embarked for the return trip back East. Three weeks later when Stuart went upriver, he and his men found Union Jacks planted at river junctions, proclaiming possession of the country for Great Britain and the Northwest Company. A July 9, 1911, entry in Thompson's own diary confirmed this:

$1/2$ a mile to the Junction of the Shawpatin [Snake] River with this the Columbia, here I erected a small Pole, with a half Sheet of Paper well tied about it, with these words on it—Know hereby that this country is claimed by Great Britain as part of its Territories, & that the N.W. Company of Merchants from Canada, finding the Factory for this people inconvenient for them, do hereby intend to erect the Factory in this Place for the Commerce of the Country around.

Down at Astoria, McDougal and his men did not know of Thompson's claims. They could only conclude that he had come downriver to see whether an American settlement was under construction.

Historians poring over Thompson's foolscap sheets in his handwriting could only wonder. An 1810 entry in his *Discoveries from the East Side of the Rocky Mountains to the Pacific Ocean* reads:

> April 15. Set off to recross the Mountains with the furs &c to Lac la Pluie [Rainy Lake on today's Ontario-Minnesota border nine hundred miles to the east], where we arrived July 22nd, 1810. Mr. Astor, having engaged some of the clerks of the N. W. Co'y, formed a company and sent a vessel around Cape Horn to the Columbia. Everything was changed. I was now obliged to take 4 canoes and to proceed to the mouth of the Columbia to oppose them. Accordingly I set off from Lac la Pluie.

James K. Smith, Thompson's biographer, would write that there was no proof Thompson was told to fight the Astorians. "However, an order to go and *oppose* them would be a typical and unexceptional Northwest company order: meet competition head on and outsell or undersell it." That Thompson did try. On his return journey up the Columbia, he handed out gifts of tobacco and assured many tribes he would be back to trade with them. By mid-August he was at the Spokane and again asked Indians to bring in good furs because he was off to the mountains for a supply of trade goods. At Kettle Falls, in the northeast corner of today's Washington State, he sent word to a subordinate to keep the Flatheads and their allies supplied with ammunition. The Flatheads and Thompson's enemies to the east were the Piegans, with whom American Fur agents would also be in trouble.

—⁕—

The *Tonquin*, meanwhile, sailed north. In a bay, Captain Thorn picked up an Indian named Lamazee from a fishing canoe. The man spoke some English. He had made two voyages along the coast and knew something of the languages of the various tribes. In a few days Thorn, McKay, and crew reached Vancouver Island and, against the advice of Lamazee, dropped anchor. Washington Irving would place the anchorage in the bay on the Juan de Fuca Strait where Victoria, the capital of British Columbia, is today. Canadian historians, however, now believe the *Tonquin* anchored in the Templar Channel at Clayoquot Sound four hundred miles to the northwest on the rugged west coast of Vancouver Island. Though not as well known as the more northerly Nootka Sound, where Captain Cook had been the first white man to step ashore in 1778, Clayoquot (also spelled Klooquat and Klaoquaht and meaning either "a different people" or "a different place") was an established trading station. The natives were supposed to have been a peaceful tribe renowned for their finely crafted canoes. For unexplained reasons, they had become savage and unpredictable. Lamazee knew as much and warned Thorn and McKay that although the locals might be accustomed to trading, they were deceitful and treacherous.

Soon a number of Indians brought their canoes alongside the *Tonquin,* holding up sea otter skins and gesturing that their pelts were for sale. It was too late in the day to trade, but through Lamazee it was agreed that six Indians would come aboard as hostages while McKay and a few men went ashore to pay their respects to Wicananish, the chief of the surrounding territory. Wicananish greeted McKay with professions of friendship and prevailed upon him to spend the night in the village.

Thorn knew nothing of Indian customs. Before McKay returned the next morning, the captain told his men to spread a display of wares on the deck—blankets, clothes, knives, beads, and cooking utensils—ordered boarding nets lowered over the side, and allowed the Indians, who had surrounded the *Tonquin* in their canoes, to come aboard. The visitors included a son of Wicananish and an old chief named Nookamis. With years of experience with New England and Russian traders, Nookamis drove a hard bargain, and his fellow vendors took their cue from him. Lamazee translated for Nookamis: the price the captain offered for an otter skin was scornfully low. Thorn lost his temper, kicked the laid-out furs, flung one skin in Nookamis's face, and ordered the Indians off his ship.

McKay returned to the *Tonquin*. Lamazee not only told him what had happened but begged him to prevail on the captain to set sail. Thorn refused. The *Tonquin* was armed with cannons and had enough firepower to repel naked savages. The next morning, twenty canoes came alongside. Indians pointed to their furs. They gestured that they had changed their minds and were ready to do business.

Before leaving New York, Astor had told Thorn to be courteous and kind in his dealings with Indians, but never to admit more than a few on board at a time. As the Indians were unarmed, the ship's officer allowed them aboard. Within an hour, two hundred were on deck. They agreed to exchange their beautiful skins for knives, which Thorn allowed to be distributed to them.

Suddenly fearful, he ordered the crew to weigh anchor. Too late. The Indians' smiles turned to war cries. McKay, who was seated on the taffrail, sprang to his feet but was instantly knocked down with a war club and flung backward into the sea, where women in canoes killed him. Thorn, who had come on deck unarmed, was bludgeoned to death. Sixteen crew members were slaughtered.

Lamazee, who didn't take part in the fight, got into a canoe and headed for land, later to escape and give an eyewitness account. Five crew members, including the badly wounded ship's clerk, James Lewis, managed to barricade themselves in a cabin and to hold off their assailants with musket fire. They decided they could sneak off in a rowboat during the night. Lewis was too seriously wounded to make it. His four shipmates slipped away in the darkness.

At dawn, Lewis crept out on the deck and found the ship deserted. Indians again approached, perhaps with the intention of looting the *Tonquin*. Lewis motioned them to come aboard. He went below and waited until several hundred were swarming over the deck, then set fire to the powder magazine, killing himself and a number of Indians on deck.

"Arms, legs and mutilated bodies were blown into the air and dreadful havoc was made in the surrounding canoes," Washington Irving would write in *Astoria*. "The ship had disappeared but the bay was covered with fragments of the wreck, with shattered canoes, and Indians swimming for their lives or struggling in the agonies of death."*

On shore, surviving warriors sat mute while their women lamented. What had gone wrong? The captain had insulted their leader. They had avenged the insult and now their victory had turned to defeat. The wails turned into fury at the sight of Lewis's four shipmates, who were brought captive into the village. Lamazee was allowed to interview the four before they were killed.

Irving doesn't tell us how the news reached Astoria, but that the Astorians were distressed when they heard. Stuart and eight men were upriver—540 miles upriver at the junction of the Okanogan, McDougal would later learn—and the handful of Astorians felt exposed. The ship that had brought them was no more and they were surrounded by tribes who, when *they* learned what had happened, might try to extract revenge. McDougal got an idea how to neutralize, if not win over, the local Chinooks. As smallpox had ravaged the Columbia River Indians the year before, he invited Comcomly and the chiefs of the various nearby tribes to meet with him. When he had their attention, he showed them a bottle and told them it contained the germs of the dreaded disease. If he uncorked the bottle they would all be stricken. The ploy worked. The chiefs promised peace, and kept their word.

*The *Tonquin* is periodically the object of diving expeditions, but despite the use of sonar equipment and magnetometers, the wreck so far has not been found.

13

—ɯɯ—

The Hunt Journey

As Wilson Price Hunt and the sixty-man overland expedition left the winter quarters on the future Kansas-Nebraska state line for the dreaded trek through Sioux territory, Manuel Lisa, with a handpicked crew of twenty rested men, set out from St. Louis in hot pursuit. Hunt was nineteen days and 240 miles ahead, but if anybody was going to open trade to the Pacific, Lisa was determined to be part of it. He urged his crew forward with curses, whiskey, and promises as he steered the heavy keelboat into the raging spring runoff.

When Hunt reached the Omaha villages on May 10, Lisa was 150 miles behind. Nine days later, Lisa passed the Omahas, and realized he could not catch Hunt before Sioux country. He sent a messenger overland asking Hunt to wait for him. The courier reached Hunt at the mouth of the Niobrara River in today's northeastern Nebraska. Crooks and McClellan had been victims of Lisa's tricks and warned Hunt that all the Spaniard was up to was to pull ahead of them so he could bribe the Sioux into making trouble for the Astor party. Hunt sent back a reply that he would wait. As soon as the messenger was out of sight, Hunt redoubled his effort to stay ahead of the Missouri Fur Company. In *Furs by Astor,* John Upton Terrell would call Hunt's message a ploy totally unjustified by trade rivalry. Crooks and McClellan's accusation that all Lisa wanted was to get ahead and bribe the Sioux to instigate obstruction had no merit. Terrell would write: "Lisa had only 20 men with him, not enough to guarantee his safety in the Sioux country. Hunt had more than three times that number. Moreover, Lisa knew that Hunt was going straight through to the Columbia, and did not intend to trade east of the Rocky Mountains."

When Lisa and his men reached the Niobrara, they were only sixty miles behind. They averaged eighteen miles a day and during one twenty-four-hour period covered seventy-five miles. Each day the ashes of Hunt's campfires told Lisa he was gaining.

The Astorians were having breakfast on May 26 when they saw two white men in one canoe and a single man in a second boat coming downriver. They were Kentucky hunters on their way home after trapping in the Rocky Mountains for Lisa's Missouri Fur Company. The leader was a man in his sixties, Edward Robinson, who had once been scalped and wore a scarf around his head. His companions were John Hoback and Jacob Rezner—younger, experienced mountain men. The Kentuckians were so impressed by Hunt's well-armed and well-equipped sixty traders, trappers, hunters, and voyageurs that they signed on. The admiration was mutual. Hunt counted himself lucky to engage a trio who knew the Rockies.

On May 30, Sioux warriors stopped the Hunt party. The Astorians threatened gunfire and were allowed to pass. Two days later, Lisa and his smaller crew were also allowed to pass. On the morning of June 2, when Sioux again threatened Hunt, Lisa's boat came in sight. For a while the two parties roared ahead along opposite riverbanks, separated by mutual antagonism. To avoid the fierce Sioux Tetons, Hunt headed directly for the so-called Mandan villages on the confluence of the Missouri and Knife Rivers.

The Mandans were a sedentary people who lived in five large, permanent villages. Just under five thousand in number, they formed a population greater than that of St. Louis or Washington, D.C. When Alexander Henry visited, he marveled at the size of their accommodations and spent two pages of his *Travels and Adventures in Canada and the Indian Territories* describing the construction of their teepees. They were bigger farmers than their neighbors and cultivated corn, squash, beans, tobacco, and sunflowers. They had helped the Corps of Discovery survive a difficult winter, and their chief, Sheheke, had accompanied Lewis and Clark east to meet their chief, President Jefferson. Lost to history is what, upon his return, Sheheke told his nation of the cities he saw and of the man who called himself the "great father." The Mandan villages were the end of the voyage for Bradbury and Nuttall. The two naturalists waited for a Missouri Fur Company team who took them back to St. Louis. Back in England, they wrote famous books about their voyage in America's Wild West.

The Astor party grew again as Alexander Carson and four experienced mountain men returning from the upper Missouri were persuaded to hire on for the trip to the Pacific.

Hunt had wanted to follow the Missouri and Yellowstone Rivers, but Robinson and Carson advised him against exposing the expedition to the implacable Blackfeet. The way to go was to abandon the rivers, veer southwest, and buy horses from the Arikara, the Plains Indians who were relatives of the Pawnee and the Wichitas. Inasmuch as no one knew exactly where, once across the Rockies, they would find the Columbia or one of its mountain tributaries, Hunt followed the advice. Buying horses from a left-handed chief and a second chief called Gray Eyes proved to be an elaborate exercise in etiquette and diplomacy. After smoking several peace pipes and gravely nodding to an assembly of braves, the left-handed dignitary doubted he could spare any horses. Gray Eyes, however, said that if they didn't have enough mounts in the village he knew where they could steal horses. The trade was as intricate as the negotiations. The Arikara were getting ready for war against the Sioux and the articles they demanded were guns, ammunition, tomahawks, and other weapons. While some young men put horses through their paces, showing off the animals' galloping speed to Hunt, Lisa, and their men, other youths rode off to steal horses from their enemy. The trade was interrupted when scouts, posted on a ridge, signaled that an army of four hundred Sioux was approaching. No battle ensued, either because it proved to be a false alarm or because, once discovered, the enemy retreated. The trading resumed. As soon as one horse was purchased, his tail was cropped to distinguish him from the tribes' mounts. In all, the Arikara sold Hunt eighty-two horses.

Lisa and his men were left behind and the trek across the prairies went well. Hunt, McKenzie, McKay, Crooks, Miller, and McClellan rode. So did Dorion, and a pony was assigned to his wife and two children. The rest of the party walked. They found plenty of buffalo and other game to eat. Pawnee Indians sold Hunt thirty-six more horses so each member of the party could get a turn riding. The Astorians skirted the Black Hills and on August 17 saw the crests of the Bighorn Mountains in a hazy distance. On September 9, they drank the icy waters of the Wind River in today's western Wyoming. They headed north, climbed to the 9,210-foot Union Pass, crossed the Continental Divide without knowing it, caught glimpses of the Tetons, and found the headwaters of the Green River. On September 24, a stream led them to a fine, gray-green mountain river that Hoback recognized as the Snake, a tributary of the Columbia. They were overjoyed, although they had no idea how far they were from the mouth of the Columbia. They followed the swift mountain river for three days. The banks were so close to the river they were forced to scramble up and down rugged outcroppings. Horses took dangerous spills; one plunged nearly two hundred feet with its heavy load, only to stand up, unharmed. As the river meandered among rocks and precipices, they were obliged to ford the roaring waters. Several men and horses were nearly swept away.

Winter was coming. They were high up in the mountains of today's Grand Teton National Park, but the country was rich in furs. Since they had failed to establish a single staging post, meaning that much of the purpose of the land route was all but lost, Hunt decided the Pacific Fur Company would finally establish a camp here. The team would split up. The Kentucky mountain men would form one party, Carson and four Canadian hunters would make up a second unit. The two groups would hunt through the winter and, in the spring, bring their fur harvest down to the Astoria that everybody by now hoped existed. But Robinson had a suggestion: Why didn't they all make for Fort Henry, the Missouri Fur Company's ultimate outpost which could be no more than a ridge or two away? Fort Henry—named after Lisa's partner Andrew Henry—was on a confluent of the Columbia, which might be easier to navigate than the Snake.

On the evening of October 8, after a cold day's ride through snow flurries, they arrived at Fort Henry. It was only last May that Robinson, Hoback, and Rezner had left the base for St. Louis, and they and the rest of the Hunt team happily took possession of the log huts. The camp would be perfect for storing the pelts the Robinson and Carson teams would collect.

The voyageurs, happier on water than on land, insisted the time had come to take to the rivers again. Hunt was indecisive. They had horses, after all. A majority, including McKenzie, sided with the voyageurs, and Hunt agreed to the construction of fifteen canoes from the abundance of birch trees. His inability to inspire confidence turned an expedition that was on the brink of failure into a caricature.

As the main party would leave their horses there, Hunt engaged two Snake Indians who came to the camp to take care of the animals until the Robinson and Carson hunting teams rendezvoused in early spring. The Snake flowed smooth and large, but the Indians shook their heads. The river was treacherous and impossible to travel by canoe. The Canadians laughed. What did mountain Indians know of water travel?

Tired of the bickering and lack of coordination among the partners, Joseph Miller opted to go with the trappers. He left the fort with four experienced hunters. Indians attacked the five men and robbed them of virtually all their possessions. Months of aimless wandering ended the following year. Only

Miller got back alive, as marauding Indians had killed his four companions.

For nine days Hunt's main party skillfully guided their canoes through torrents and rocky runs. Ramsay Crooks's canoe was torn apart. One of the voyageurs drowned. On the twelfth day, they found the upper reaches of the Snake River impassable. This meant abandoning the new canoes and continuing on foot, carrying whatever they could on their backs. They didn't know it, but they were still a thousand miles from the Pacific Ocean. Hunt argued that once past the obstruction nothing barred their way to the sea. McKenzie didn't agree. Behind the mountains might be other mountains or plains, desertlike expanses where they might starve or get lost. The way to proceed, he said, was to find the headwaters of the Columbia. Following the river, they'd always have water. They'd be able to catch fish and beaver and perhaps run into Indians from whom they could obtain provisions. On November 9, McKenzie and five men left the main body to find a route through the mountain passes. On the way they met two small scouting parties sent out by Hunt. The two groups banded together. Their sufferings in the wintry wastes were terrible, but nothing compared to those facing Hunt and his men.

After losing three more canoes, the main party was short of food and facing passes blocked by snow. Hunt divided his men into two groups, one led by himself, the other by Ramsay Crooks, each exploring the opposite banks of the upper Snake River. As the weather worsened and incessant rains turned to snow, they met only a few half-starved Indians. Mad with hunger, they were reduced to gnawing on boiled beaver pelts. Stretches of the river were so steep they had to abandon it and carry everything on their backs.

Pierre Dorion's wife, whose name we do not know, was pregnant. Despite carrying one child and leading the other by the hand, she bore the hardship without a murmur. Shoshone villagers bartered cured salmon and buffalo coats for tin kettles and even sold them a horse Hunt wanted as a packhorse. The men bought a second horse for Dorion's wife. Hunt used sign language and drew maps with sticks on the ground, but all he could learn from Indians was that the great river, the Columbia, was still far away. They were about to slaughter and eat the horse Dorion's wife was riding when they saw horses grazing near Shoshone dwellings. Too starved to try to bargain, they fell on the Shoshones, who fled in fright, and stole six of their horses, slaughtering one on the spot for food. On Christmas Eve, they loaded the five surviving Shoshone horses and abandoned the Snake. Dorion's wife gave birth. The rest of the team decided to push on and left Dorion with the horse to attend to his wife. Nobody expected to see her again, but a day later she rode into camp with the infant in her arms. She could not keep the baby warm. Within a week it was dead. Several men died; others became crazed with hunger, and wandered from the marching line, never to be seen again. Crooks and several others fell ill and were abandoned, to follow later if they survived.

On January 18, 1812, an emaciated and ragged band finally found a route into the lowlands of Umatilla Valley in the northeast corner of today's Oregon. Friendly Indians let them camp and recover their strength. Hunt hoped Crooks, John Day, and perhaps some of the other stragglers would find them. As none of those left behind appeared and their fate remained unknown, the party pushed on to the Columbia. They bought canoes. On February 15, after eleven months, Hunt, his men, and Dorion's wife and two children reached Astoria. McKenzie and his men had arrived a month earlier.

14

—ɯ—

No News

The pessimist in John Jacob counted the months; the optimist in him believed everything had gone as planned. The only way to know what was happening to the two-pronged venture, and whether Astoria existed at all, was to send a second ship after the *Tonquin*. For this he selected the *Beaver,* recently back from Canton. To command his favorite vessel he chose Cornelius Sowle, a veteran of the China trade. Captain Sowle was the opposite of brave Jonathan Thorn, an overcautious mariner. A new partner in Pacific Fur was to sail with him. He was John Clarke, another Northwest Company trader. On his mother's side, he was said to be a distant relative of John Jacob. His mother was a German whose maiden name had been Waldorf. George Ehninger and Ross Cox were making the voyage as clerks. Ehninger was John Jacob's nephew; Cox a Scot who forty years later would publish his eyewitness account and total up the cost in human lives of Astor's imperial undertaking.

Since Astor knew neither the fate of the overland expedition nor the tragic end of the *Tonquin,* his instructions to Sowle and Clarke were unavoidably tentative. Sowle and

Clarke were to stop at Hawaii and inquire about the fortunes of the *Tonquin*. If they could confirm that a settlement had been established at the mouth of the Columbia, they should hire as many Hawaiians as the *Beaver* could accommodate. Upon arrival at the Columbia, Sowle should exercise extreme caution. If Sowle saw a budding community, he should approach it pretending he was either a passing voyager or the master of a ship in distress, until he had made sure the post had not fallen into hostile hands. If Hunt, McKay, McKenzie, and the others greeted him, he should unload the part of the cargo destined for them, proceed to the Russian settlement at New Archangel, backtrack to Astoria, collect whatever stores of furs the Astorians had amassed since their arrival, and sail for Canton.

On October 10, 1811, the *Beaver* left New York freighted with cargo for the Columbia River outpost and supplies for New Archangel. Clarke's crew included five clerks, fifteen laborers, and six Canadian voyageurs. Two sailors were washed overboard and lost off Tierra del Fuego on Christmas Eve and a hunter died of scurvy, but otherwise, as Captain Sowle noted, the voyage was without incident. After hiring several Hawaiians at Oahu, the *Beaver* reached the Columbia sandbar on May 6, 1812.

Captain Sowle fired two signal guns. No one responded. The following morning, he ran his ship to within four miles of the shore and again fired signal guns. When no one responded, a boat was lowered to sound for a channel, but returned without success. Sowle was about to give up when Clarke said that if the *Tonquin* team and the overland party had perished, he and his clerks, voyageurs, and Hawaiians would establish Astoria.

The next morning, when Sowle ran the *Beaver* toward the shore for the third time and fired the signal gun, three guns were heard. He remained cautious. Maybe Indians had surprised the fort, massacred its residents, and were now firing greetings to lure him across the bar and seize his vessel. Through his telescope, he saw a white flag on Cape Disappointment. A bonfire blazed through the night.

When an Indian canoe was seen coming toward the *Beaver* the next morning, Sowle ordered all hands to be on the alert. Chief Comcomly stood tall and majestic while six of his men vigorously paddled the canoe through the surf. Behind them came a barge with McDougal, McClellan, and eight Canadians.

The reunion was joyous. Even Ramsay Crooks and John Day were there to tell their harrowing story of being robbed, stripped, and left for dead by one band of starving Indians, only to be rescued by friendly Walla Walla Indians. Still, the situation was far from promising. A number of the men were sick.

We do not know whether Astor had instructed Sowle and Clarke to get news to him or whether the erstwhile partners thought it astute to forward to J. J. their version of events. However, it was decided to send clerk John Reed to New York. The purpose, the partners told each other, was not only to bring Astor up to date but also to ask him for reinforcements and supplies. During the past year, the Kentuckians—old Robinson, Hoback, Rezner, and another man named Cass—had accumulated a rich cache of mountain furs. A party headed by Robert Stuart's uncle David had come down from the Okanogan with twenty-five hundred beaver skins and other pelts.

Hunting was expanded. Newcomer Clarke was to take his fresh crew of clerks, laborers, and Hawaiians to the Spokane and set up yet another outpost. McKenzie took a party to the Snake River country, where, it turned out, they found themselves among Indians who preferred to hunt buffalo rather than trap beaver. The clerks Ross, Cox, and Russell Farnham were sent to trade among the Flatheads. The term was loosely applied to Chinooks, Choctaw, and Salish who customarily practiced head-flattening by applying boards to toddlers. The flatter the forehead, the more aristocratic the person.

News of the *Tonquin* disaster was printed on the front page of the *New York Gazette and General Advertiser* on May 12, 1812. Astor refused to believe it, but five weeks later Captain Ebbets sailed the *Enterprise* into New York harbor and confirmed the news of the *Tonquin*'s fate. Ebbets's success at New Archangel and Canton and the ship's return with a small fortune in Chinese goods eased the pain of the

Tonquin's loss. The door was open to future New York–New Archangel–Canton triangular runs.

In Astoria, meanwhile, it was decided to have Robert Stuart lead the expedition back East. Stuart had not come over the mountains, but on the *Tonquin*. Still, his youth and vigor made him the natural choice. André Vallar and Francis LeClerc, voyageurs from Hunt's expedition, would be his and Reed's boatmen, guides, and hunters, and the Virginian John Day would accompany them as far as the Snake River, where Clerk Farnham was to retrieve the furs hidden by the Kentuckians. As the quintet prepared for the trek, McClellan and Crooks decided they wanted to return East. They resigned their partnership in Pacific Fur and signed papers surrendering their shares. By the time the Stuart canoes pushed off under a cannon salute from the fort on June 23, 1812, the party was a dozen men strong.

Indians attacked them at the Long Narrows, or The Dalles, as the French Canadians called the flat-stoned stretch, where canoes had to be unloaded and men had to carry the boats and their cargoes for a stretch. With too much to carry, they sought the assistance of Cathlasco Indians, who agreed to carry the goods for them on their horses. Reed was up front with the first load. As they passed through a rocky and intricate gorge, the Indians suddenly spurred their horses and galloped off. The rest of the convoy reached the end of the Long Narrows intact, but Reed was badly clubbed.* John Day went crazy, tried to kill himself, and was sent back with Indians who had traded with Astoria before. On August 20, the Stuart party met the hunters Joseph Miller, Hoback, Robinson, Rezner, and Cass and inventoried their carefully hidden hoard of mountain furs. They all traveled together for nine days to the Snake River lands of the Walla Wallas. Robinson, Hoback, and Rezner wanted to stay and hunt in the Rockies but Miller had had enough. He, too, signed over his stake in Pacific Fur Company and joined the Stuart party. Stuart bought twenty horses from the Walla Wallas.

*Today the Dalles National Scenic area near the John Day Dam.

The party crossed the Continental Divide and, in November, reached the Bighorn region. They were pitching camp for the winter when Crow Indians attacked them. Forced to flee, they traveled day and night for two weeks before they dared set up camp.

While the party wintered, unmolested, in today's Wyoming, John Jacob was trying to keep his adopted country out of another war with Britain. Rumors of war with England became persistent, but Astor hoped it could be avoided. "We are happey in the hope of Peace & have not the Smalest Idia of a war with England," he wrote to Gratiot in St. Louis.

His sentiment was not shared by hawkish new members of Congress, who said that if the price of peace were appeasement, they would have none of it. Freshly elected congressmen seemed hell-bent on what they regarded as a second war of independence, which would drive the last redcoats from the continent and bring Canada into the Union. The rallying cry was Britain's refusal to give up its self-proclaimed right to board American ships to check for Englishmen evading military service.

Astor sent missives through Albert Gallatin to the president, pleading with him not to get into war. Avoiding conflict was in John Jacob's interest, of course—war ruins commerce—but it was also in the interest of the secretary of the treasury. For the first time since Gallatin became responsible for the Treasury Department, the federal government was operating in the red. In the year ending September 30, 1809, the $1.3 million deficit was in part due to the Embargo Act and the resulting slowdown in customs receipts. In a letter to outgoing President Jefferson, Gallatin had written:

The reduction of the public debt was certainly the principal object in bringing me into office and our success in that respect has been due both to the joint and continued efforts of the several branches of government, and to the prosperous condition of the country. I am sensible that the work cannot progress under adverse circumstances. If the United States shall be forced into an actual war, all the resources of the country must certainly be called forth to make it efficient, and new loans will undoubtedly be wanted.

Ten years earlier, Gallatin had flayed the Federalists for borrowing money to meet normal defense requirements. Now, as Britain escalated the sea war against Napoleon, Gallatin was forced to eat crow. He recommended that the government be authorized to borrow a sum "not to exceed the amount of the public debt that it would pay off." Was he thinking of asking Astor to lend the Treasury money? John Jacob's commercial genius was recognized and feared on three continents. He was the undisputed leader of the world's fur trade, a shipping tycoon, owner of ever-bigger tracts of New York real estate, and a millionaire. The idea was premature, but it lingered in Gallatin's mind.

———m———

At Astoria, the partners agreed that Hunt should sail with Sowle to Alaska so he could observe and learn the coastal trade and meet the commander of the Russian post. In August, Hunt boarded the *Beaver*, leaving McDougal in charge of Astoria. At New Archangel, Captain Sowle exchanged provisions for fur. It took nearly a month to load the ship, but when the *Beaver* left, she had more than seventy-five thousand sealskins in her hold, worth $150,000 in Canton. A November storm blew the vessel off the coast and damaged it.

The absence of the *Beaver* and the departure on hunting expeditions to the Okanogan and the Spokane interior left Astoria low in manpower, a fact that was reflected in increasing insolence by local Chinooks. Among them were travelers from Vancouver Island who had not forgotten how victory had been snatched from them when the lone survivor of the massacre had blown himself and the *Tonquin* to smithereens. McDougal ordered Astoria reinforced with palisades and posted sentinels day and night. The Neweetees (or Clayoquots) returned home without attacking and McDougal became friendly enough with Chief Comcomly to propose that he marry the chief's daughter. The negotiations were protracted and worthy of an Old World dynastic merger. Comcomly vaunted his daughter as having the flattest and most aristocratic head in the tribe and said he would be flattered to have McDougal as a son-in-law. On July 20, a squadron of canoes crossed from the village of the Chinooks bearing the royal family and court. Here is how Washington Irving described the wedding twenty-four years later:

> A horse was in waiting to receive the princess, who was mounted behind one of the clerks and thus conveyed, coy but compliant, to the fortress. Here her expecting bridegroom received her with devout, though decent joy. Her bridal adornment, it is true, at first caused some little dismay, having painted and anointed herself for the occasion according to the Chinook toilet; by dint, however, of copious ablutions, she was freed from all adventitious tint and fragrance, and entered into the nuptial state the cleanest princess that had ever been known, of the somewhat unctuous tribe of the Chinooks. From that time forward, Comcomly was a daily visitor at the fort, and was admitted into the most intimate councils of his son-in-law.

At New Archangel, Captain Sowle told Hunt he had no intention of trying to run his damaged ship back to Astoria and cross the Columbia bar. Instead, he would go against Astor's orders and head directly for Hawaii, where the *Beaver* could be repaired. Hunt agreed there was no reason to risk shipwrecking the *Beaver* on the sandbar and losing seventy-five thousand sealskins. At Oahu, Hunt would wait for the next Astor ship, expected in the spring of 1813. If none showed up, he would charter the next available ship to take him back to Astoria.

In New York, Astor and fifty-five merchants appealed to President Madison not to blunder into war with Britain. Some believed the hawkish complexion of Congress after the 1810 election was pushing the reluctant president toward armed conflict, while others feared Madison was caught in his own bellicose rhetoric. When the New Yorkers' appeal seemed to fall on deaf ears in Washington, J. J. rushed to the capital.

15

—⚏—

Mr. Madison's War

Astor was between Philadelphia and Baltimore on
June 18, 1812, when he heard President Madison
and Secretary of State James Monroe had declared
war on England. Historians are divided on what Astor did
next, some maintaining he ordered his coachman to turn
around and head back to New York, others saying he reached
Washington in the evening of the nineteenth. What is not in
dispute is that he wrote urgent messages to John L'Herbette
and Thomas Clark, his agents in Michilimackinac and Niagara Falls. Back in 1795, Astor had helped L'Herbette
flee French military service. Clark was a Canadian. Now
Albert Gallatin allowed J. J. to include the letters to his
agents in a Treasury Department dispatch via courier to
General William Hull at Fort Detroit. Reuben Atwater, the
Treasury collector at Detroit, tried to forward Astor's letter
to L'Herbette, but the courier returned with news that the
British had captured Michilimackinac and that a relief force
sent north from Fort Dearborn (Chicago) had been massacred by Indians. The British commanders in Upper Canada
first learned of the outbreak of war when Clark told them
the contents of Astor's message to him. The "accounts of a

declaration of war," General Isaac Brock wrote to General Sir George Prevost, were "received first through a mercantile channel."

General Hull was furious and accused Gallatin of helping to get word to the British that war had been declared by sending a letter under government frank. But Gallatin and Monroe had bigger fish to fry than soothe a field commander. To Gallatin's horror, he realized Madison assumed the conflict would be primarily maritime. Yet the president did nothing to protect American vessels until Gallatin protested that ships were arriving each week from foreign ports with cargoes valued at $1.5 million. The U.S. Navy did not possess a single battleship and the entire fleet consisted of eight frigates and eight smaller seagoing warships. Madison ordered a patrol of the coast, but the government had made no naval preparations along the waterways bordering Canada—Lakes Champlain, Ontario, and Erie. As for the army, enlistments were slow. Congress had authorized a force of thirty-five thousand in the hope of taking Quebec City, but the regular army consisted of only seven thousand men.

Gallatin and Monroe were appalled by how unprepared the United States was for war. In July, General Hull decided to cross the Detroit River into Upper Canada. His men, many of whom came from the Ohio militia, were poorly equipped and, except for one small regiment, proved insubordinate and unreliable. The people of Upper Canada were impoverished and hostile. Hull fell back to Detroit, where General Brock forced him to surrender his thirteen hundred troops as prisoners of war. The United States thus lost control of the entire Great Lakes region, and British troops soon invaded northern Ohio. Farther east, American forces along the New York-Quebec border were routed. In December, Gallatin wrote to elder statesman Jefferson at Monticello that "the series of misfortunes experienced this year exceeds all anticipations made even by those who had least confidence in our inexperienced officers and undisciplined men."

John Jacob's first thoughts had been faraway Astoria. He could only wonder whether the allegiance of McDougal,

McKenzie, and the other Montrealers out there was to king
and country or to their own financial stake in the Pacific Fur
Company. The best he could do, he decided, was to be ahead
of them, Madison, the war hawks, and everybody else. Why
not send his own *British* ship to Astoria's rescue?

He wrote:

> As soon as war was Declard, I considerd Columbia in Danger
> if not Lost, but wishing to Safe it as much as I wishd to
> safe my Life it acurd to me that I aught to procure ane or
> two Confidential persons to go to england & there Pracure a
> neutral vessel put on board of her Arms munitions Blankets
> & Cleare for the Pacific but go Derict to Columbia for this
> purpose I placed 12000 £ Stg in the hands of the gentlemen
> who I send—a vessel was pracurd and Loaded but the Delay
> is beyond everything.

In a matter of months the hostilities unraveled his globe-
girdling commerce. Yet he was lucky. None of his ships was
captured. All arrived at their destinations "at a time when
foreign commerce was almost annihilated and tea doubled
in price, his gains were immense." His friend and fellow
shipowner Stephen Girard was less fortunate. Girard's ship
Montesquieu was captured and ransomed to the tune of
$180,000.

—⚬⚬⚬—

The winter of 1812–1813 was busy for Astor. When the
departure of the British rescue vessel was delayed "beyond
everything," he got word to Captain Sowle in Canton to sail
for Astoria with supplies and arms, but the captain had no
stomach for confronting the British fleet. Sowle stayed in
port. At Oahu, Hunt kept scanning the horizon for ships,
and learned of the war from the brig *Albatross* coming
from China. On his own, he chartered the *Albatross,* loaded
whatever supplies and equipment he could obtain in Hawaii,
and sailed for the Columbia.

The Astorians first heard war had broken out on January
13, 1813, when Donald McKenzie came down the Columbia.
He had been upriver at John Clarke's post on the Spokane

when a Northwest Company party led by John McTavish arrived with the news that the United States had declared war on Britain. McTavish's party numbered seventy and included the first white woman to reach the Northwest. Known only as Jane, she was a Portsmouth barmaid. McTavish told McKenzie and Clarke a British frigate would soon sail into the Columbia and train its guns on the outpost. Without consulting with Clarke, McKenzie had broken camp, returned to his own post on Snake River, cached his furs, and with his people descended to Astoria to tell that war had broken out.

As John Jacob had guessed, the news quickly provoked fissures. McKenzie had never forgotten the humiliation he had felt two winters earlier when Astor had chosen Hunt over him to lead the expedition. Now, he and fellow Scot McDougal theorized that even if no Royal Navy frigate would come over the bar and bombard them, the British fleet would interdict any and all Astor vessels coming to their rescue. Since no supplies had arrived since the *Beaver* a year before, the fort would have to be abandoned. Their excuse for not taking the other Astorians into their confidence was that such foreboding news might lower morale. On March 6, Astor's ship, the three-hundred-ton *Lark,* left New York with supplies for the Columbia settlement. Two weeks later, his informants in Montreal and London told him the Northwest Company regarded the war as an opportunity to snatch Astoria from him.

To get British naval backing for their planned attack on Astoria, the Northwesters exaggerated the scope and strength of the American outpost. They alluded to Astor's acquisition of the Mackinac Company and, as Washington Irving would write, expressed "their fears that, unless crushed in the bud, it would affect the downfall of their trade." Their presentation was placed in the hands of Foreign Secretary Viscount Castlereagh and the president of the British Board of Trade, but no official action was taken. In a second, more desperate appeal, the Northwesters said they were taking steps to establish a colony of their own on the Northwest coast and pleaded for naval escort. This time Castlereagh ordered the frigate *Phoebe* and several other navy ships to convoy the Northwesters' own vessel, the *Isaac Todd,* a twenty-gun ship, to the mouth of the Columbia to capture Astoria or, at a minimum, to set up a rival post.

News arrived in dribs and drabs and John Jacob's mood fluctuated with each piece of information. He was encouraged when the captain of a returning China clipper told him Hunt had chartered the *Albatross* and was on his way to Astoria. Finally, Robert Stuart, Ramsay Crooks, and the clerk John Reed reached New York and gave the first eyewitness account of the saga, from Stuart's outbound voyage aboard the *Tonquin* and Crooks's overland trek with Hunt to their own departure from the Columbia. John Jacob wasn't totally satisfied with the account Crooks and Stuart gave of themselves. Unlike Hunt, who was trying to salvage the greatest investment J. J. had ever made, the two Scots had thrown up their hands and headed east. What Crooks didn't say was that he had realized early on how Astoria was beyond salvation.

The looming loss rankled John Jacob. Contemporaries noted he was taciturn and full of anger and frustration. He dictated a letter to Gallatin that played up Astoria's strategic importance to the United States: "It is of great national importance and will prove a new source of wealth. There is no person who possesses the information which I do and there is yet but little known of the importance of it in Europe. But it soon will be, when we shall find it more and more difficult to accomplish an advantageous arrangement on that subject. The present is the time!"

He brooded over what might have been when the war brought new dangers and new opportunities.

—◊—

The nation that had been his for nearly thirty years might be at war with the country that had given him his first opportunities, but if flying a Union Jack and sailing with the Castlereagh flotilla was what it would take, well, so be it. At the same time as he told President Madison to send Gallatin to Europe to negotiate peace, he had agents in London buy the brig *Forester,* and outfit her with arms, ammunition, and provisions with which to fight the Northwest Company. To make sure nobody would suspect the *Forester,* he got former Russian ambassador Andrei Dashkov to explain to Admiral Sir John Borlase Warren that the Astor vessel was headed for New Archangel with badly needed supplies for the Russians in Alaska. The period following Napoleon's suicidal attack on Russia—and wintry retreat from Moscow—was no time for a British admiral to withhold an ally's request, and Warren issued Dashkov a laissez-passer. To make sure no American man-of-war would send the stealth ship to the bottom of the sea, John Jacob told Secretary of State Monroe his ship would have a passport from the Russian minister, but said nothing of the British permit. When the convoy cast off from Admiralty Quay and eased down the Thames, the *Forester* sailed right along.

It might all have worked had McDougal, McKenzie, and the other partners out in Astoria possessed a share of J. J.'s venal refusal to take sides. What he couldn't know was that McDougal and McKenzie had decided the war made their situation hopeless. The young American clerks and several of the voyageurs wanted to fight if and when the British frigate showed. They argued that the frigate could be defeated. First, the sandbar would prevent the man-of-war from running close enough to fire cannons at the fort. Second, if an invasion force was lowered into boats and the surf and rocks didn't capsize or smash their boats, Astoria's own guns could blow them out of the water. They were sixty Astorians inside a fortress, which they had reinforced. It was hard to say what the arrival of McTavish, his seventy men, and one white woman meant. Polite and fraternal, weren't they all Northwesters *au fond?* He didn't try to enter Astoria but camped under the fort's guns. Time, of course, was on McTavish's side. All he had to do was wait for the arrival of the *Phoebe* and reinforcements.

McKenzie returned to his Snake River cache to find it robbed. He sent one of his men to Spokane and Okanogan to tell Clarke and Stuart to join him at Walla Walla. After a great deal of trouble, he recovered most of his stolen pelts and made the rendezvous with Stuart and Clarke. They floated down the river together, arriving at Astoria on June

5. The mood was somber. McDougal and McKenzie were for selling out. Clarke and Stuart angrily disagreed.

In hindsight, McDougal's actions would be seen as gutless and duplicitous. However, he was without news and reinforcement from Astor and without news from Hunt. The *Lark* never reached them. As he would learn much later, the ship got safely around the Horn and had the Hawaiian Islands in sight when, on March 6, 1813, gales drove her ashore on Maui, where she capsized, with the loss of five men. For seventeen days the wreck drifted. Natives in canoes pillaged the cargo of pork, flour, rum, and other stores in the name of King Kamehameha. The shipwrecked crew pleaded with the Hawaiians to let them have their own clothes.

McTavish was not threatening to destroy the settlement, but offering to *buy* its stock of goods and furs. In the absence of Hunt, McDougal's powers were limited and specific and did not include permission to sell Astoria. However, even in Washington Irving's retelling of the events, no objections were raised. In the end, vehement pleas from McDougal carried the day.

On October 16, 1813, McDougal and the partners sold the fort's stores, guns, and furs to the Northwest Company for the best price they could get: thirty cents on the dollar. More than $200,000 worth of furs was relinquished for less than $80,000. The American contingent and a number of the Canadians viewed the sale with shame and resentment. They found McTavish's warning of naval action a ruse or an empty threat. Surely the Royal Navy would not open fire on a post that, in a large part, belonged to British subjects.

If the *Lark* had foundered in Hawaii, the captain of Astor's stealth ship decided not even to try. By the time the *Forester* arrived at Hawaii, its captain, William J. Pigot, knew Astoria had been sold. Deciding it was unwise to head for the Columbia, he slipped away from the British convoy and sailed north to New Archangel. There, he discovered that since Hawaii the British knew of the *Forester*'s true mission. Captain Pigot wintered in California, hiding from the Royal Navy.

In New York, John Jacob celebrated his fiftieth birthday on July 17 by contacting Gallatin and begging Secretary of

State Monroe to send a fast sloop of war to overtake the *Phoebe* at the mouth of Columbia. Monroe hesitated, granted Astor's request, only to change his mind and assign the brig for service on the Great Lakes. Lost, for lack of a frigate, was 614,000 square miles of the West—a domain larger than the thirteen original colonies.

—ᜍᜍ—

Astor made back every penny ten times over.

The military setbacks caused deep anxiety in Washington and popular cries for scapegoats. Charges of treachery flew all too easily as opponents and supporters of "Mr. Madison's war" clashed openly in Congress and on street corners. By mid-1813 the British naval blockade choked all major ports, although some ships managed to break out. The war and its commercial restrictions were extremely unpopular, especially in New England, where separatist sentiments seethed. John Jacob knew he was too powerful and too well connected to be in the crosshairs of congressional "War Hawks," and his only scrape with the law was in a court case two years after the war ended. In *John Jacob Astor, owner of the brig* Caledonia v. *United States,* he was fined. Early in 1813, he decided to heed Gallatin's appeal and help bankroll the war.

It is hard for twenty-first-century Americans accustomed to century-long government deficits to fathom the obsession of Madison and Gallatin with a national debt of $17 million in period money. Gallatin had been secretary of the treasury since the Jefferson administration and had worked passionately to wipe out the national debt (in 1801, the number of federal employees in Washington totaled 130). Public debt, he—and Jefferson—believed, led to corruption in government and to a spiraling evil of ruin. But now armies had to be paid, warships had to be built. At the outbreak of the hostilities, Gallatin had allowed John Jacob to use the Treasury's frank to dispatch instructions to his agents. After a desperate Congress authorized the sale of $16 million in government securities, Gallatin asked his friend to join the only man reputed to be richer than him, Philadelphia banker Stephen Girard, and loan the government $10 million.

The loan became the first bond syndicate in American history.

Dipping into his own strongbox and borrowing from banks on the strength of his collateral, John Jacob first bought $2 million worth of government paper. The rate was $88 for a $100 certificate yielding 6 percent interest. On August 15, 1814, Astor wrote to Girard in Philadelphia to suggest they each come up with $4 or $5 million more. In a postscript, he hinted at movements toward peace: "We have just now a prize Schooner arrived with English accounts of 8 July they state that g. Britain had appointed and Send 5 Commissianors to meet ours & that the Genral belive was Peace if you do leik to Loan to government 4 or 500M$ and will Loan it to me I will give you Stocks at Low Rate and my note with good name to make it perfectly safe to you. I want it not for MySelf but I wish to help the treasury at this particular moment."

The third investor was Alexander Dallas, the Jamaican-born lawyer and financier, who became secretary of the treasury in 1814 when Madison appointed Gallatin to the peace negotiation team. In his absence, Gallatin had David Parish, an influential German financier, who in two years made $2 million selling New World gold and silver for the Spanish government and invested in land in upstate New York, canvas smaller capitalists in New York, Philadelphia, and Baltimore. The full $16 million subscription was filled not a moment too soon, for the Treasury was empty and unable to pay the government's bills. After the British sacked Washington, the war loan sank to $75 and even lower. Astor did not sell. He bought government bonds dumped on the market. Years later the *New York Tribune* accused him of making even more money than his speculation showed. According to Horace Greeley, founder of the first weekly *New Yorker* and of the *Tribune,* Astor gave Gallatin notes worth fifty cents on the dollar and this "must have cleared more than a million dollars in hard money on every two millions of paper thus lent."

John Jacob's wealth and influence in the world of high finance meant that he could obtain a private audience with

President Madison. Not that he sought to meet the increasingly desperate president. Instead, he thumbed his nose at both sides by floating part of the war loan in London.

———∽∽∽———

Using tricks and deceptions, Astor kept buying furs in Canada. One shipment alone consisted of 20,000 marten, 46 bear, 18,000 muskrat, 526 fisher, 6,021 otter, 3,389 mink, 2,048 fox, 271 cat, and 6 wolf skins. He got his furs to London by convincing Jean-Victor Moreau, a French general who, with the rise of Napoleon, had fled his homeland and spent ten years in the United States, to offer his services to the British.

Keeping a cool head when others panicked gave J. J. the ship *Hannibal*. This ship was on the high seas with a particularly rich load of teas when the outbreak of war spooked her owner, who offered ship and cargo at an attractive price. J. J. bought the *Hannibal* and watched her sail unscathed into New York harbor. As he had done as a young man, he put the tea chests in warehouses and waited for the inevitable wartime shortage to collect immense profits.

With the connivance of son-in-law Bentzon and former ambassador Dashkov, he got the *Hannibal* through the British blockade. The czar was an ally of Britain, and the British navy off Sandy Hook could hardly block a vessel on the business of an ally, especially since Astor took the precaution of having the *Hannibal* fly a Russian flag. Besides Moreau, the *Hannibal* carried several hundred tons of furs. While Moreau was mortally wounded in the battle of Dresden, where Napoleon beat back a Russian-Austrian offensive, Astor sold his furs in London at top prices.

The authorities in Washington could not afford to be too critical of their lender of last resort. In a long letter to Secretary of State Monroe, Astor urged peace by sacrificing the main point for which the war had been declared—the right of the British to search American ships and seize English seamen:

New york, 22 July, 1814

Privert

Dear Sir

Senice I had the pleasure to See you at Washington I have recid a Letter from Gottenbourg and an other from London. Boath are from very Inteligent Merchants after Speeking on the Subjict of commerce thy bouth give it as thire apinion tha Great Britain will not make Peace with this country unless we acknowledge thea Right of theire coming an Board of aur Ships to take thire Seamen or Subjicts. The Englishman Says if your government or the publick mind is not prepard to Conseed this point the war will go on until thy are. It is to me Some what Singular that two merchants the ane in London & the other in Sweedne should at Same time write & express opinions so leik each other.

On Conversing with Some of our most Intelligent men in this part of the country I find it the prevailing opinion that we aught to canceed this point—I had the ather Day a long conversation with Mr. Ruffus King. When Specking an this Subjict I could Let great Britain have her men fram aur Ships but I Daubt whether aur commissnors have Such Power or even the Discrisson & if thy have whether thy will exursize it & take the Respancebelity on thamSelfs and the less So if g. B [Great Britain] Shauld Desire it in terms which might Leave a Reflection an the country but Says he if it can be Done in any mode to give it not a Disgracesfull apearanis I would acknowledge the Right to its fullest extend and the country will aprave of Such a treaty but if g. B. asks anything more I would befor war otherside for Peace which he exspects will be the Result of the present negociation it is his opinion that a Cal of Congress would at this time excite too mush alarm the more if for the purpose as is Sayd to have been asserted by Mr. Barker to aid the treasury it might Injure the Credit of the country more than Do it good it wauld be otherwise if Congress ware cald to Recive Some Important communication from the President. Mr. Judge Brackholst Livingston with whom I had yesterday a Long conversation is Disitedley of opinion that we aught to acknowledge the Right of the British to take there Subjicts from aur ships and he adds that as an Englishman he would carry on the war until we Did acknawledge this Right.

In a Canversation with Mr. Harsey of Delaware* I found him of the same apinion. In fact as I Sayd before this is the prevailing opinion in this part of the country and I think that anless we admit this right the war can not be mad Popular but if this point be yelded and g. B maks any father Demand she will unite us in the War When We Shall have everything to hope for the Honnor of the Cauntry—whether this question is to be Left to the Discression of aur commissnors may be very Important they may Refuise to take the Respuncebelity & it will becam a question whether the executive aught not to take this Responsibelity as otherwise it may be too tought as Schrincking from what may at this time be considrd as necessary to be boldly faced—I presume you are not to mind aponions in Matters of Which you can judge better than those who give tham Still I wish you to Knaw tham—I have at present 2 fine ships in this port I would Licke to employ ane of tham as Cartel hawer [however] I have no papers from the British Admiral if one could be employd without I wauld Licke it if government wish a fast Sailing vessel to go to a flag to Europe I can also furnish one.

I am with very great Respt
Dear Sir your most obd Sert
John Jacob Astor

The Hanebl James Munroe

A transcription in standard English follows.

New York, 22 July, 1814

Private
Dear Sir
Since I had the pleasure of seeing you at Washington I have received a letter from Gothenburg and another from London. Both are from very intelligent merchants. After speaking on the subject of commerce, they both give it as their opinion

---

*Nothing is known of Mr. Harsey of Delaware. Jacob Barker was a supporter of the government who had clashed with Astor over the war loans.

*that Great Britain will not make peace with this country
unless we acknowledge the right of their coming on board
our ships to take their seamen or subjects. The Englishman
says if our government or the public mind is not prepared to
concede this point, the war will go on until they are. It is to
me somewhat singular that two merchants, one in London
and the other in Sweden, should at the same time write and
express opinions so like each other.*

*In conversing with some of our most intelligent men
in this part of the country, I find it the prevailing opinion
that we ought to concede this point—I had the other day
a long conversation with Mr. Rufus King. When speaking
on this subject, I could [say], let Great Britain have her
men from our ships, but I doubt whether our commissioners
[peace negotiators] have such powers or even the discretion,
and if they have, whether they will exercise it and take the
responsibility on themselves, and the less so if Great Britain
should desire it on terms which might leave a reflection on the
country. But, he says, if it can be done in any mode without a
disgraceful appearance, I would acknowledge the right to its
fullest extent and the country will approve of such a treaty. But
if beyond peace, Great Britain asks anything more [prewar
demands?], which he [Rufus] expects will be the result of the
present negotiations, it is his opinion that calling Congress
into session would at this time excite too much alarm, the
more so if, for the purpose as it is said to have been asserted
by Mr. Barker to aid the Treasury, it might injure the credit
of the country and do more harm than good. It would be
otherwise if Congress were called to receive some important
communication from the President. Mr. Judge Brackholst
Livingston with whom I had yesterday a long conversation
is decidedly of the opinion that we ought to acknowledge the
right of the British to take their subjects from our ships. He
adds that as an Englishman he would carry on the war until
we did acknowledge this right.*

*In a conversation with Mr. Harsey of Delaware, I found
him of the same opinion. In fact, as I said before, this is
the prevailing opinion in this part of the country and I
think that unless we admit this right, the war cannot be
made popular. But if this point be yielded and G.B. makes
any further demand, she will unite us in the war where we
shall have everything to hope for the honor of the country.
Whether this question is to be left to the discretion of our*

commissioners may be very important [as] they may refuse to take responsibility and it will become a question whether the Executive ought not to take this responsibility as otherwise it may be too tough as shrinking from what may at this time be considered as necessary to be boldly faced. I presume you are not to mind opinions in matters of which you can judge better than those who have them. Still, I wish you to know them. I have at present two fine ships in this port I would like to employ one of them as cartel [?]. However, I have no papers from the British admiral. If one [ship] could be employed without [papers], I would like it if the government would wish a fast sailing vessel to go to Europe, I can also furnish one.

I am, with great respect, dear Sir, your most obedient servant.

John Jacob Astor
The Honorable James Monroe

This plodding and repetitive letter gives little sense of Astor's political shrewdness. After General John Armstrong resigned as secretary of war for his ineffectual conduct of the conflict, Astor again wrote to Monroe. Rufus King, whose home on Broadway J. J. had bought in 1804, was the twice-defeated Federalist candidate for vice president and current senator from New York planning to run against Monroe for the presidency. J. J.'s Machiavellian suggestion for eliminating King before the 1816 election was to appoint him ambassador somewhere: "Let Mr. King cam in to the Deportment of State the federals would be pleasd & aid in every Respect the Administration."

While the unpopular war played itself out, Astor looked out for his own interests. And that meant salvaging as much as possible of his stock in Canada. Hoping that Thomas Jefferson might use his personal prestige to help, he wrote to the former president. Jefferson's reply was polite, but its vagueness suggested he had not bothered to read J. J.'s letter. Gallatin was more obliging and issued letters authorizing Astor to travel to Canada for the purpose of recovering his property.

J. J. had no intention of going himself and in two of his partners in the Astoria venture found the men he needed.

Adversity had hardened Ramsay Crooks, and Astor appointed him manager of the American Fur Company. Robert Stuart sensed Astor didn't totally trust him. J. J. nevertheless made him the head of the Michilimackinac operation with instructions to report to Crooks. The journey back from Astoria had cemented a friendship between the two Scots that allowed Stuart to call Astor the "old cock" in a letter to Crooks: "You can very readily draw your own conclusions regarding [Astor's] views, which I really believe are as friendly toward us all as his own dear interest will permit, for of that, you are no doubt aware, he will never lose sight until some kind friend will put his or her fingers over his eyelids."

As the Admiralty could not spare enough ships from the war against Napoleon, naval control of Lake Erie passed to the United States. British supply lines were broken and American naval dominance of Lake Erie helped U.S. land forces to regain ground. Detroit was recaptured. The death of the Native American leader Tecumseh while fighting in the British ranks brought an end to Indian resistance in the region. The lines of engagement fluctuated with the fortunes of war and John Jacob dispatched Stuart and Crooks as stealth Britons or undercover Americans. Stuart was sent to British-occupied Michilimackinac and Crooks to the Canadian side of the border to collect payments from a number of independent traders who owed money to the American Fur Company. From Michilimackinac, Stuart shipped pelts to Montreal that Astor claimed he had acquired before the war. Here, J. J. had several agents, including George Astor, his nephew. The young man had come to New York from his native London shortly before the war and J. J. had agreed to teach him the fur trade. The place to start was Montreal, where George's British birth was no doubt an asset.

Along the ill-defined border, Crooks collected the debt in pelts and when in doubt about their provenance also shipped them to Montreal. From here the furs were smuggled into the United States on Lake Champlain, the long body of water between New York and Vermont whose northern tip is in Quebec. It was twenty-four years since young John Jacob had slept in front of Peter Sailly's open kitchen fire. Peter was still in Plattsburgh, New York, still the U.S.

customs agent. He knew the lake and agreed, for a price, to smuggle J. J.'s pelts out of Canada. Getting the furs to Rouses Point on the New York-Quebec border was one thing. Making them legal in the United States was another. Many of Astor's business records were destroyed after his death, perhaps deliberately, but it seems he had the U.S. government (Sailly) seize the pelts as contraband. Once the furs were in government custody, John Jacob put up bonds for their knockdown value, in effect buying them as seized government surplus. A fortune in pelts and trade goods reached his New York City warehouses and, because of wartime shortages, were sold at hefty profits.

—⁂—

Harbors were jammed with idle ships, their topmasts housed, their mastheads covered with tar barrels called "Madison's nightcaps" to protect them from rotting. The few that sailed were armed and carried letters of marque authorizing them to capture enemy merchantmen and commit acts that would otherwise be considered piracy. Perhaps because a ship of his had been the victim of piracy in the Mediterranean, Astor refused to take part in freebooting. The plunder of British merchantmen had been popular during the War of Independence, but public sentiment did not endorse this method of picking up a living on the high seas. Still, fifty-five privateers were outfitted from New York. John Jacob thought shipowners were foolish to risk their capital investment on privateering. He found the perilous game of running the British navel blockade much more thrilling and profitable.

His ship the *Flirt* left New Orleans for Bordeaux with cotton and furs, and succeeded in getting through the British blockade. His schooner the *Boxer* made profitable runs to Havana, New Orleans, and back to New York. He boasted that the *Boxer* was "often chased & outsailed all she met with." The *Boxer* stole out of New York harbor, loaded with furs and general freight, bound for Nantes. Outdistancing pursuing British warships, she reached her destination only to learn the war was over.

Ships were cheap. For $27,000 cash, he bought one of the

world's fastest sailing vessels. His choice was the 407-ton brig *Macedonean,* and he spent another $40,000 outfitting her. Through Gallatin, he learned the navy was sending men-of-war to the Pacific to attack British shipping. He arranged to have the *Macedonean* sail along as a "store ship." This meant it would have to carry some naval stores, but there was space enough for furs and ginseng. If she could make Canton before the war ended, John Jacob said, her round-trip "will clear $300,000." Under the command of Curtiss Blakeman, the *Macedonean* put to sea with the U.S. Navy frigate *President* and several other navy ships. After a bloody and desperate encounter with a British flotilla, the *President* was forced to surrender. With the Royal Navy in hopeless pursuit, the *Macedonean* vanished over the horizon, arriving in Canton after a fast 169-day voyage.

Finally, Astor heard from Captain Pigot and the *Forester.* After eluding the British and hiding out in California bays, Captain Pigot had again sailed north to New Archangel, and, in an about-face, sold his furs to the Russians at Okhotsk on a letter of credit. Under the command of a clerk, he sent the *Forester* to Hawaii to be sold, while he went overland to St. Petersburg to collect the money. The *Forester* was sold to King Kamehameha and paid for in sandalwood.

And there was more. The schooner *Powhattan* reached New York from the Mediterranean early in 1813, but his brig *Adolphus* was captured. The *Rockingham,* not owned by Astor but carrying his cargo, got through. John Jacob's nerve failed him in the case of his beloved *Enterprise.* He tried to get the ship out of New York under Russian colors and got former ambassador Dashkov to ask the British to "suffer the Enterprise to pass." This time, the Royal Navy refused. The *Enterprise* was unloaded and laid up.

The trickiest skullduggery involved flying different flags outbound and inbound. To make sure the *Hannibal,* carrying nearly a quarter million dollars' worth of cargo, would not be seized or sunk by *anybody,* John Jacob not only convinced Andrei Dashkov to get British permission for the Russian ship to sail to England, he confided to President Madison that he had managed to get permission to send a vessel to England for the Russians. The president asked that the

Hannibal carry diplomatic pouches. The diplomatic pouches missed the sailing of the *Hannibal* on July 22, 1813, but just before the gangway was lowered, Adrian Bentzon got on board. The listed value of the cargo of furs was $60,000, but actually worth three times as much. Also in the ship's holds was freight Astor was carrying for others. Because of the war, he had received an extraordinary $27,000 in freight charges. On approaching Europe, the *Hannibal* changed course and instead of heading for a British port sailed to Gothenburg, Sweden. Two months later the *New York Gazette* reported that the "Prussian ship *Hannibal,* Capt. Leisevitz, 50 days from Bremen with assorted cargo" had arrived. A Prussian ship? Napoleon's retreat from Moscow had freed Prussia to ally itself with Russia and declare war on France. In Germany, Bentzon therefore "sold" the *Hannibal* so that she might return under the colors of Britain's new coalition partner.

But not every transaction was profitable or the wartime currency transactions simple, as shown in Astor's letter to his nephew:

New york Septr 14, 1814

George Astor
Dear George.

I have received your letter of 26th Ult°. From Detroit, your voyage I expect will turn out unprofitable, for the great expense & delay attending it will I fear half consume the property however I am anxious the business wound up & to know the worst of it, the whole has been a scene of misfortune, disaster & disappointment, Muskrats are not in demand. I have a large quantity on hand & cannot get 30¢ for them, if you could dispose of some at Detroit or its vicinity for good bills on this or Philada, at about 31 or 32¢ I would recommend the sale or if you can get British army bills they would do as well as they are worth par here, but I am told there are many counterfeits, you can therefore only take them under good guarantee or indorse good bills on Montreal or Quebec are equally good or better, as to aur country Bank notes I do not think that it will do to take them if you have a large quantity of Muskrats & Mr. Crooks is with you perhaps it might do as well for him to take the whole & go with them

to Pittsburgh & dispose of them. . . . I pray you take care not
to expose the goods to damage or capture as I can less than
ever afford the loss.
        Yours &c J. J. A.

Everybody could see the beginning of the end of Napoleon and Astor saw profits in getting vessels to Europe. As
he wrote to Secretary of State Monroe on July 14, 1814, he
had "2 fine ships" he would like to dispatch to Europe. Was
Mr. Monroe interested in seeing the ships carry diplomatic
pouches? The State Department was so interested in book-
ing passages for government officials that Astor turned the
Fingal into an all-passenger vessel by hastily rigging cabins
in her cargo space. People who seemed to have no fear of
being captured and interned fought for accommodations and
paid $270 for passage.

Czar Alexander offered to mediate the British-American
conflict. The government in London was uncomfortable with
the czar's offer to intercede in what it considered a near-
domestic quarrel, and was surprised by Madison's quick
acceptance. The Anglo-American dispute was over maritime
law and neutral rights, and on that ground the position of
the Baltic powers had never been satisfactory to England.
Madison sent John Quincy Adams and Albert Gallatin to St.
Petersburg, where they cooled their heels. The czar was not
in St. Petersburg; he was with his army, fighting Napoleon.
Adams and Gallatin found that no steps had yet been taken
by England beyond the communication of a note, which
discouraged arbitration.

Astor got news of his brother George's death in December
1813. England's now decade-long war had hurt the musical
instrument business and John Jacob had sent his brother
£3,000. He now recommended that his sister-in-law Elizabeth not try to carry on the business herself. She did not
heed his advice and lost the business. J. J. gave her £200
yearly for life.

The hostilities that had broken out in June 1812 as
a result of political bluster, diplomatic incompetence, and
an element of bad luck ended in January 1815. Peace was
negotiated without third-party mediation in the Belgian city

of Ghent. The British insisted on an Indian buffer territory north of the Ohio River and revision of the boundary line between British Canada and the United States that would give Canada access to the upper Mississippi. John Quincy Adams and Gallatin feared the negotiations would break off as Admiral Lord Gambier, the head of the British team, sent every counterproposal to London for review. The defeat of Napoleon also played into British hands as peace on the Continent freed up crack troops to be sent to fight in North America. With the upcoming Congress of Vienna to decide the future of Europe, the negotiations in Ghent became a sideshow for Lord Castlereagh and the government in London. Tracings on maps of North American wilderness were a distraction, and the British dropped a proposal to carve out a neutral Native American buffer between British and American possessions in the Great Lakes region. British military failures at Baltimore and at Fort Erie stiffened the attitude of Gallatin and his fellow commissioners. Peace terms were signed on Christmas Eve 1814 with Gallatin lending a diplomatic hand, and John Jacob's son-in-law Bentzon hovering over the proceedings. On Christmas Day, the delegates were entertained to roast beef and plum pudding at the British embassy. James Gallatin, Albert's son and secretary, recorded the mood of the occasion: "The band played first 'God Save the King,' to the toast of the King, and 'Yankie [*sic*] Doodle,' to the toast of the President. Congratulations on all sides and a general atmosphere of serenity; it was a scene to be remarked. God grant there may be always peace between the two nations."

The Yule cheer had its measure of ironies. The pact allowed British warships to continue boarding American vessels to search for British nationals, but that point, over which Madison had declared war, meant little for Britain since it and its Russian, Austrian, and Prussian allies defeated Napoleon at Waterloo a few months later. On the principle of *status ante bellum,* the Treaty of Ghent, which the Senate ratified on February 16, 1815, restored to the United States the vast northwest hinterland now called the Oregon Territory. On paper, Astoria belonged once more to John Jacob.

16

—⚂—

"So Long as I Have a Dollar"

Duncan McDougal was in charge of Astoria for the Northwest Company's new owners. John McTavish was hunting in the environs while John Clarke, the latest Pacific Fur Company partner who had come out on the *Beaver,* was at the Okanogan outpost. Wilson Price Hunt was heading toward the Columbia River aboard the *Albatross* and, now that the war was over, Captain Sowle had summoned up enough courage to sail back from Canton. Robert Stuart and Ramsay Crooks were in Michilimackinac, Montreal, and points in-between rustling pelts across the border. In New York, John Jacob thought more about the injury inflicted on his reputation and self-respect than about financial losses. To McKenzie, whose complicity in the sellout J. J. did not yet suspect, he wrote: "While I breath & so long as I have a dollar to spend I'll pursue a course to have our injuries repair'd & when I am no more I hope you'll act in my place. We have been sold, but I do not despond."

The scratching of diplomatic goose quills in Ghent meant little west of the Rockies. In accidental or willful ignorance of political agreements in distant capitals, the Northwesters remained in control of the Columbia and its chief tributaries, holding the posts at Okanogan, Snake River, and the Spokane and trading throughout the region. David Thompson, the Northwest Company's formidable surveyor-trader, had found a northern route around the ever-hostile Piegans that allowed the Northwesters to come through the Suwapta Pass in the Rockies, float down the Wood River to the big hairpin bend of the Columbia, and make their way southwest through today's southern British Columbia and Washington State into what everybody knew was the last virgin frontier of the fur trade. To even out the ironies, it should be added that Northwest's long and bloody contest with Hudson's Bay was about to end in the defeat of the Northwest Company and the ruin of its partners. In 1821, the British government put a stop to the two companies' trade war on the Saskatchewan and Red Rivers by imposing a takeover of Northwest by the Hudson's Bay monopoly. What was not understood yet was that after a century of ruthless hunting the beaver population was shrinking.

In hindsight it was naive for the Montreal fur traders to believe they could hold on to an outpost 3,500 miles from Montreal and, via Cape Horn and Hawaii, almost 20,000 miles from London. The future of the West and of the Oregon Territory was not to belong to fur traders, but to the settlers and homesteaders, cowboys and gold diggers of the expansionist United States. Even British Columbia only stayed Canadian because Canadian and U.S. financiers bought an insolvent railway and, with government help, eventually built the transcontinental Canadian Pacific Railway.

Some contemporaries said the collapse of Astor's grand venture left him unsociable and taciturn. Others saw anger, bitterness, and frustration in him. Out of public view, he was scheming to get Astoria back. In early 1815, he optimistically wrote to his nephew George Ehninger in Canton: "By the peace we shall have a right to the Columbia River & I rather think that I shall again engage in that business." He had ships in the Pacific. Even if the outpost could not be wrested from the Northwesters, it was possible the rich stores of pelts could somehow be hijacked and taken to New Archangel. "After their treatment of me," he wrote to Hunt, "I have no idea of remaining quiet and idle." He toyed with the idea of sending a strong force of his own, not to oust the Northwesters but to establish a rival post. To chase the Northwest's skilled and well-armed agents back across the Rockies, he realized, demanded military support.

His most influential friend in government, however, was not in Washington to advise and to plead his cause. Gallatin and his family were still in Europe. They were in Paris when Napoleon made his triumphant but short-lived return from Elba in March 1815, and in London a hundred days later when the city learned the news of the Allies' final triumph at Waterloo. Gallatin was wondering what he should do now that his peace negotiation appointment was over. He was by no means rich after years in public service, and while President Madison offered him the post of ambassador to France, friends in Pennsylvania suggested he run for Congress. His private income was $2,500 a year. He estimated it would cost him $2,000 to take his family to France. His son James was nineteen, his second son Albert Rolaz was in his junior year at Princeton, and thirteen-year-old Frances was in a school for young ladies in Philadelphia. Besides, the annual pay for ambassadors was $9,000 a year, far less than the cost of living in Paris. In turning down the offer to become a congressional candidate, he wrote to Philadelphia party chairman Richard Bache that he owed it to his family to enter "into some active business." As he was weighing his options, Astor came with a third proposal. In a letter dated October 9, 1815, John Jacob suggested a partnership. J. J. would put up all the money, and give Gallatin a 20 percent stake while charging him the legal interest until his one-fifth share was paid off. "Of course you know it is not possible to say what the profits may be," he wrote, "but I presume it will not be extravagant to calculate from $50,000 to $100,000 clear per annum after interest and all expenses are deducted."

The proposition was attractive, but in the end Gallatin declined his old friend's offer. He also said no to running for Congress. He left England for the United States still undecided about his future plans. Now back in Washington, Secretary of State Monroe persuaded him to take the ambassadorial post. Perhaps in gratitude for Astor's partnership offer, Gallatin asked President Madison to appoint Astor as one of the commissioners to receive subscriptions to a new central bank.

The first Bank of the United States, chartered in 1791 by the Federalist majority in Congress, had resulted in a lasting controversy. As depository of the government, it constantly received funds from collectors of revenue notes issued by private banks. As fast as it received these notes, it called for their redemption in gold and silver, thereby effectively restricting the credit market. Political lobbying by a growing number of state banks and powerful individuals like Astor had led to the lapse of its charter in 1811. The war changed his mind. In lending money to the government, Astor, Girard, and Dallas found virtues in a central bank because it could help protect their investment. By 1814, J. J. was campaigning for a new Bank of the United States, organizing petitions, lobbying congressmen, and preparing a detailed funding plan. He went to Washington to help expedite things, but after unproductive meetings in the House of Representatives with foreign affairs committee member (and future vice president) John Caldwell Calhoun, he returned home. "It appears to me that it will take some weeks before Congress get to pass the Bank bill and if they go on Mr. Calhoune's [sic] plans they must fail and ruin the country and themselves."

Besides banking—Congress chartered a second Bank of the United States in 1816—Astoria was on J. J.'s mind in the fall of 1815. In a letter to Madison, he offered to reestablish the outpost on the mouth of the Columbia provided it be made a military post. The mission, he suggested, could be accomplished with a force not exceeding a lieutenant's command.

Madison's leadership as commander in chief had been less than inspired, and although American victories had brightened the last months of the two-year conflict, he was in no mood to provoke another war. Still, the news was not unpromising. In July, Monroe, to whom Astor had loaned $5,000 on easy terms in 1814, informed the British ambassador that the president intended to reoccupy the post at the mouth of the Columbia. This determination was made "partly at the insistence of Mr. Astor, who was anxious, if possible, to recommence operations on his former plan in North-West America."

—⚏—

No British armada had ever arrived at the Columbia. The Northwest Company's own vessel *Isaac Todd* had been lost off Cape Horn, and the HMS *Phoebe* had gone chasing the U.S. Navy's Commodore David Porter, who, on board the frigate *Essex,* was inflicting heavy damage to British ships in the Pacific. This meant that only the twenty-six-gun sloop of war *Raccoon,* under the command of a Captain Black, had been spared to offer backup assistance in the purely commercial endeavor on the Columbia. On board was a Northwest partner, John McDonald, who whetted Captain Black's appetite for action by telling him and his officers of the war booty that would be theirs once they got their hands on the Astoria storehouse.

On November 20, 1813, Chief Comcomly was the first to alert his son-in-law Duncan McDougal that sail was seen off Cape Disappointment. The vessel was a warship. Of what nationality? Fearing it was American, John McTavish, who since the sellout to the Northwest Company had been in charge, quickly loaded two barges with furs and pushed three miles up the river to Tongue Point. There he would await a signal from McDougal. If the ship proved to be American, McTavish could haul his rich cargo farther inland. Alexander Ross made a dramatic entry in his diary:

> The moment Comcomly left Astoria, Laframboise, the interpreter, was called in, decked and painted in full Chinook costume, and dispatched to Cape Disappointment to report whether the vessel was to be seen and if so, whether British or American. Laframboise has scarcely reached the Cape

when the ship hove in sight, and soon afterwards came dashing over the bar in fine style, and anchored in Baker's Bay, within the Cape. Laframboise immediately returned, and on his way back met McDougal, in a boat well manned, going to the ship.

With the king's soldiers bobbing offshore and fearful for his son-in-law, Chief Comcomly arrived at the fort in something of an opéra bouffe act with his men armed and painted, and offered to kill every one of the king's men if they dared come ashore. Comcomly and his warriors would take cover in the woods that reached the water's edge, and kill the enemy as fast as he waded on shore. The chief was puzzled when McDougal told him his solicitude for his and the princess's safety was touching but unnecessary, because although the *Raccoon* belonged to the king of England, her crew would not injure the Americans, nor their Indian allies. McDougal told his father-in-law and his men to go home, lay down their weapons, wash off the war paint, and come back like clean and civilized people to receive the strangers. Comcomly acquiesced to McDougal's singular demand.

On December 12, 1813, Captain Black, attended by his officers, entered the settlement, ran the Union Jack up the flagpole, broke open a bottle of wine, and declared, in a loud voice, that he was taking possession of the establishment and of the country in the name of his Britannic majesty, and changed the name to Fort George. The Indians shook their heads in disbelief when it was explained to them the ceremony was a friendly arrangement and transfer. "As to Comcomly," Washington Irving would narrate, "he no longer prided himself upon his white son-in-law, but, whenever he was asked about him, shook his head, and replied that his daughter had made a mistake, and instead of getting a great warrior for a husband, had married herself to a squaw." Irving makes his readers feel for Captain Black. The commander of the *Raccoon* believed he had been sent to batter down the walls of an important fort, only to find a wooden palisade and furs already sold to British subjects. He wanted to inventory the peltries, apparently to present the Northwest Company with a bill for the cost of engaging the Royal Navy. He sailed away, however, without exacting a down payment in furs or, to Comcomly's surprise, without taking American or Indian prisoners.

Two months later, Hunt had arrived aboard his chartered brig *Albatross*. He was furious when he learned how his erstwhile second in command had not only bargained away the Astoria assets, but how McDougal had become a Northwest Company partner. Hunt's comportment toward McTavish was frosty and veered toward smoldering fury when McTavish hinted that with a 50 percent advance from Astor the whole caboodle might yet again revert to the Pacific Fur Company.

Hunt judged there was nothing he could do, and on April 3, reembarked. When he reached the Marquesas Islands, he found Commodore Porter with a booty of British whaling ships. Hunt tried to persuade the commodore to send an armed ship to the Columbia or to sell him one of the spoils so that he might return himself. Porter refused. Astor's 1920s biographer Arthur Howden Smith would speculate that behind the refusal was the navy's contempt for the fur trader's wealth, for his unwillingness to invest in privateering, and for his "partiality for the Canadians." "Whatever the reason," Smith would write, "Porter was strangely unwilling to assist the outpost on the Pacific, declining also to send a naval detachment in one of the prizes to bring off the American property and nationals in Astoria."

Hunt got to Hawaii, only to learn the fate of the *Lark*. He bought the *Peddler,* a 225-ton brig, manned it with the survivors of the *Lark,* and in February 1814 was again at the mouth of the Columbia. With some difficulty he secured all the Pacific Fur Company's important papers. When he learned that Donald McKenzie and the clerks Alexander Ross and Gabriel Franchère were ready to set out for Montreal, Hunt entrusted the papers to McKenzie with orders to deliver them to Astor in New York. Hunt took several clerks with him when he sailed again, this time to New Archangel.

—m—

Robert Stuart's overland party had been paddling upstream on the Columbia near Walla Walla when they heard what they thought was a child shouting, *"Arretez donc! Arretez donc!"* They put to shore and found the cries came from the Sioux wife of Pierre Dorion. She and her children were the only survivors of a winter of massacre by Nez Percé tribesmen angered over the killing of one of theirs by John Clarke. Everybody had been murdered, including the Kentuckians and the Canadian voyageurs. In *Adventures of the First Settlers on the Oregon or Columbia River,* Alexander Ross let the woman tell her own story:

Late one evening, about the 10th of January, a friendly Indian came running to our house in a great fright and told Mr. Reed that a band of the bad Snakes, called the Dogrib tribe, had burnt the first that we had built and that they were coming on whooping and singing the war song. After communicating this intelligence the Indian went off immediately, and I took up my two children, got upon a horse, and set off to where my husband was, and the other men were hunting, but just as I was approaching the place, I observed a man coming from the opposite side and staggering as if unwell. I stopped where I was till he came to me. Le Clerc, wounded and faint from loss of blood, was the man. He told me that La Chapelle, Resner, and my husband had been robbed and murdered that morning. I did not go into the hut, but putting Le Clerc and one of my children on the horse I had with me, I turned round immediately, took to the woods, and I retraced my steps again to Mr. Reed's. Le Clerc, however, could not bear the jolting of the horse and he fell once or twice, so that we had to remain for nearly a day in one place. But in the night he died, and I covered him over with brushwood and snow, put my children on the horse, I myself walking and leading the animal by the halter. The second day I got back again to the house. But sad was the sight. Mr. Reed and the men were all murdered, scalped, and cut to pieces. Desolation and horror stared me in the face. I turned from the shocking sight in agony and despair, took to the woods with my children and horse, and passed the cold and lonely night without food or fire.

I was now at a loss what to do; the snow was deep, the weather cold, and we had nothing to eat. To undertake a long journey under such circumstances was inevitable. Had I been alone I would have run all risks and proceeded, but the thought of my children perishing with hunger distracted me. At this moment a sad alternative crossed my mind: should I venture to the house among the dead to seek food for the living? I knew there was a good stock of fish, but it might have been destroyed or carried off by the murderers; and, besides, they might still be lurking about and see me; yet I thought of my children. Next morning, after a sleepless night, I wrapped my children in my robe, tied my horse in a thicket, and then went to a rising ground that overlooked the house, to see if I could observe anything stirring about the place.

She decided to wait until night, and returned to find her children nearly frozen. Knowing the smoke from a campfire would betray her position, she nevertheless lit a fire to save the children. Once warmed, she wrapped them in her robe again and at nightfall sneaked back and found fish scattered about in the storeroom. She returned to the children at dawn, built a fire, and for the first time in three days she, the children, and the horse ate. She hoisted the children on the horse and led it by the halter through deep snow for nine days until she and the horse were exhausted. At the foot of a rocky precipice, she killed the horse and hung up the flesh on a tree, built a small hut with pine branches, long grass, and moss, and packed it all around with snow to keep the children and herself warm. With only a knife to cut wood, she spent fifty-three days in her shelter. She kept herself and the children alive through the winter and descended to the banks of the Walla Walla. She had spent two weeks with the friendly Walla Wallas and was on her way down the Columbia when she saw the McKenzie party.

The hardships and sufferings of this woman and the men who straggled across the continent to establish Astoria were terrible. Some deserted, some went mad, some were drowned or murdered. Alexander Ross listed the death toll:

The tragic list stands thus:

Lost on the bar	8
Land expedition	5
Tonquin	27
Astoria	3
Lark	8
Snake country	9
Final departure	1
Total	61

Astor had wanted the Pacific Fur Company to extend its influence from ocean to ocean, destroy any St. Louis rivals, outdo the Northwest Company and the Russians, and conquer the China trade. Ross came away from the experience an embittered man. "How vain are the designs of man!" he wrote. "That undertaking which but yesterday promised such mighty things is today no more." He blamed Astor's ambition, while admitting that no one could have foreseen the outcome.

—⁂—

John Jacob picked up the pieces. He had already found work for Ramsay Crooks and Robert Stuart, and when McKenzie showed up in New York he gave such a good account of himself that he, too, was offered work in Canada. It was only later that J. J. learned how McKenzie had double-crossed him. But who was calling the kettle black here? J. J.'s wartime activities had verged on the treasonable, even if his loans to the Treasury to finance the conflict saved him from popular wrath and judicial pursuit, even after it turned out that he had offered a $50,000 loan to the British in Montreal, ostensibly to get his furs out of Michilimackinac.

Though the United States had gained none of its avowed aims in the war, popular mythology quickly converted stalemate into victory. Americans preferred to remember the series of military successes during the closing months to the humiliations of the first year and the near sedition in New England. The Federalist Party went into decline because its opposition to the war came to be seen as pro-British Tory. With the election of James Monroe, a man in Astor's debt occupied the White House. We do not know whether the new president acted on his own or whether Gallatin nudged him, but Monroe ordered that "Mr. Astor, of New York, be informed of the measure contemplated in relation to the Columbia River." The measure was to send the sloop of war *Ontario,* under the command of James Biddle, to the Columbia. John Jacob filled Captain Biddle in on how conspiracy and deception had lost him Astoria, yet did little to actively promote the recapture. The gamble had been too big for him. This was not a time for expansion, but for consolidation.

While the *Ontario* rounded Cape Horn and made a stopover in Valparaíso, Chile, British and American diplomats negotiated the details of a treaty to settle the *status ante bellum* questions left unresolved in Ghent. One of the details they stumbled on was Captain Black's taking possession of Astoria. The question was whether Astoria had merely changed ownership through McDougal's sale to the Northwest Company or had been taken by Captain Black in an "act of war." The negotiators decided Astoria had been sold *before* Black had occupied the post.

The *Ontario* arrived at the bar on October 6, 1818. Captain Biddle raised the American flag over the fort, taking "temporary" possession of the Columbia River country in the name of the United States, then sailed away to the South Pacific. There was not much else he could do. As Arthur Howden Smith would write in 1929:

> Captain Biddle, a dozen Captain Biddles, might fire a salute to the flag of the United States, and brandish his sword and recite whatever legalistic formula his superiors had devised for him, but unless he and his blue jackets were prepared to disembark and devote themselves to the unfamiliar warfare of mountain and forests they could not expect to displace the alert Canadians. And the Administration in Washington, mighty glad to have gotten out of the recent war so easily, was in no mood to bring about a resumption of hostilities, especially when the stake was so remote as the fur trade of

a country separated by two thousand miles from the nearest permanent settlement.

McDougal stayed at the renamed Fort George until 1817 when he left for the Northwest Company's Lake Superior depot at Grand Portage. He died a miserable death, date not ascertained. Alexander Ross married an Indian woman, became the first sheriff of Red River, Manitoba, and established the Presbyterian Church of Red River Valley.

Exactly two weeks after Captain Biddle's flag raising, the treaty of October 20, 1818, between the United States and Great Britain proclaimed "all territories and waters claimed by either power, west of the Rocky Mountains, should be free and open to the vessels, citizens, and subjects of both for the space of ten years." The United States owned the Oregon Territory; the Northwest Company owned the fur trade conducted at Astoria/Fort George. Astor could send his ships, but so could any other American citizen and British subject. In 1828, the treaty would be extended for another ten years. John Jacob didn't complain, but he didn't forget. He had attended the theater the night of May 12, 1812, when the *New York Gazette and General Advertiser* had printed the news of the *Tonquin* disaster. A friend had expressed surprise at seeing him in his seat. "What would you have me do?" John Jacob had responded. "Would you have me stay at home and weep for what I cannot help?"

When it came to write the postscript, Washington Irving would blame an irresolute government in Washington for missed opportunities. If the Madison administration had grasped Astor's gambit, the United States could have taken full possession of the region as a matter of course. "Our statesmen have become sensible, when too late, of the importance of this measure." Irving was too kind. Although the treaty of October 20, 1818, restored the territory to the United States, its government made no effort to occupy it for another thirty years.

After 1821, the Hudson's Bay monopoly took over the Columbia fur trade, and for all practical purposes provided

Fort Vancouver

the only white occupancy of the territory. John McLoughlin, the head of the Columbia operations, moved the headquarters upriver and on the northern shore built Fort Vancouver in today's Washington State, across from Portland, Oregon.

Astor's ships sailed around the world, but as his friend Albert Gallatin was one of the first to realize, the fall of Napoleon put an end to unparalleled expansion of American commerce and prosperity. Gallatin was in Paris and understood that a peaceful, stable, and productive Europe would not demand the volume of American imports it had absorbed during the thirty years of nearly continuous war. In retirement, Madison also recognized that glutted foreign markets meant falling prices, that only war or natural disasters could sustain the economy. If peace continued, he wrote, "nothing but seasons extensively unfavorable [in Europe] can give us an adequate market for our grain crop."

John Jacob would soon sense the economic change, but peace brought opportunities that were too tempting. One lucrative novelty was opium.

Until 1816, no Astor ship had carried opium. On July 15, 1816, the *Macedonean* arrived in Canton with, among other things, $110,000 in specie, 27 metric tons of ebony, 8 tons of mercury, and nearly 2.4 tons of opium. It was the first time an Astor vessel had gone to China without furs. The quicksilver had been picked up in Gibraltar, the *papaver somniferum* taken aboard in Smyrna, Turkey. In February 1817, the Astor ship *Seneca* reached Canton with a cargo that included 5.7 metric tons of opium, also picked up in Smyrna. During the next two years the Astor vessels *Boxer, Alexander, William and John,* and *Peddler* carried opium cargos to Canton.

The upper end of the opium trade, however, belonged to a British monopoly. The East India Company devoted thousands of hectares of fertile land in Bengal to the cultivation of opium. The harvest was auctioned at Calcutta, while the yields of individual growers were sold in Bombay. Chinese dealers preferred chests that bore the stamp of the East India Company because the crops of independent growers were often adulterated with molasses or cow dung. Turkish opium was inferior to Bengal imports. Still, one picul—a Malay unit of weight used throughout Southeast Asia and equal to 60 kilograms—of unrefined Turkish opium fetched $500 in Canton. Here, dealers used it to adulterate the high-grade opium from India. Horrified at the harm done to China's health, Emperor Daoguang, a reformer who came to the throne in 1821, ordered that all those convicted of opium smoking be given one hundred strokes. A sentence also stipulated that for two months an addict should wear a heavy wooden collar through which the hands were locked. A number of dealers were executed. These measures, however, proved futile.

Astor dabbled in the opium trade because nearly everybody else did. Olyphant & Company, one American firm that refused to carry opium in its vessels, was nicknamed "Zion's Corner." J. J. didn't hide behind the pieties of those who claimed they sent narcotics to China to accelerate the conversion of the heathen Chinese to Christianity. He was in it because it increased profits.

17

—⚌—

John Jacob Astor & Son

With John Jacob II sinking into dementia, Astor put his hopes in his second son. The bookish William Backhouse was given a European education, first at Heidelberg University and later at Göttingen, Germany's most prestigious center of learning, where Arthur Schopenhauer was also a student.

William was a rather shy and silent young man. An acquaintance described him as "the richest and least attractive young man of his time." By upbringing, temperament, and inclination, he was a dutiful administrator of the businesses his father told him to attend to. He kept track of every parcel of Astor real estate. He knew how and where to buy more of Manhattan with the profits existing holdings generated, but besides his own residence he never built anything. The extraordinary growth of the city during his lifetime assured ever-rising returns on the family investment.

William loved Göttingen and the study of philosophy, history, and languages. He made a lifelong friend in Christian Bunsen, a year his senior and a future ambassador.

Bunsen was happy to write to his fiancée that "I am now in a very convenient position, residing with the son of an American merchant named Astor, boarded and lodged in the best manner, and am to receive between this time and Easter 30 louis d'or for which I give him instructions in German and other things." The two young men set out on a European grand tour in the fall of 1913, but only got as far as Frankfurt. The joint armies of Russia, Austria, and Prussia defeated Napoleon at the battle of Leipzig. After the victory the Allies pushed their offensive and for the first time took the war into France. For William and Christian it meant the borders were closed.

News of what looked like the beginning of the end of nearly twenty years of war on the Continent had John Jacob and Sarah worried. At length a letter arrived. William and his friend were all right and planning to resume their journey to Vienna and northern Italy. J. J. ordered Adrian Bentzon to bring William home with him. Son-in-law and prodigal son arrived aboard the "Prussian" *Hannibal*. The Astor business interests were becoming so multifaceted that J. J. needed someone he could trust. Willliam, however, made his father agree to another stay in Europe, and the young man was back in Paris during the summer of 1815. Napoleon's flight to Elba Island was followed by the restoration of the Bourbon monarchy, and the capital was full of Russian and Prussian troops. Returning royalists, out to extract revenge on Bonapartists, claimed Napoleon's left-behind wife Joséphine and his sister Pauline were turning the head of Czar Alexander. By fleecing tourists like himself, William noted how the French blamed the British and, by extension, the Americans for the restoration of the ancien régime. William was to rendezvous with Christian Bunsen in Florence, but instead of going to Italy, William was on his way to the United States, apparently summoned by his father. Bunsen married a young Englishwoman only known as Miss Waddington, who besides her gifts of mind and heart brought with her a rich dowry.

John Jacob was both proud of the cultured, cosmopolitan young man and worried that William would turn into a

dabbler in intellectual fads—his letters home enthusiasti-
cally quoted Schopenhauer. William was twenty-four. In his
father's mind, it was high time for the boy to study how to
manage the fortune that in due time would be his. William
should be in New York, learn to speak to fur traders, study
the tea market, and pore over rent rolls and bills of lading.
J. J. sensed William was not cut out to make money, but at
least he could be taught how to keep it.

A year after his return, William pleased his papa by
wanting to marry Margaret Rebecca Armstrong. The young
lady was no hard-eyed socialite but the plain Jane daughter
of General John Armstrong, a member of Madison's inner
circle who had been ambassador to France shortly after
Napoleon offered Louisiana for sale and secretary of war
during the War of 1812 until his handling of the conflict
forced him from office. On her mother's side, Margaret was
related to the illustrious Livingston and Beekman families.

Margaret was eighteen, a girl of deep Christian con-
victions, when William met her during a business visit to
Albany. She had spent much of her girlhood at Livingston
Acres, her parents' country home on the Hudson. The estate
was also known as La Bergerie, in memory of Napoleon's gift
of a flock of merino sheep to General Armstrong at the end
of his diplomatic service in Paris. The Hudson Valley was
changing as wealthy city folk built homes on farmland with
river views. Washington Irving captured much of the change
in his short story "Rip Van Winkle." When the bedraggled
Rip staggers down from the Catskills after his twenty-year
sleep, "the very character of the people seemed changed,"
Irving wrote. "There was a busy, disputatious tone about it,
instead of the accustomed phlegm and drowsy tranquility."

The young people were a match in reserve and piety.
Unlike his father, William was a regular churchgoer. John
Jacob approved of the match. Yet, while sensitive to the
young couple's feelings, he was fearful of spoliation. He insisted on a prenuptial agreement for his son, and suggested
to General Armstrong that Margaret renounce her entitle-
ment to a share of William's patrimony in return for a cash
settlement on marriage. The general might have branded

Astor and Albert Gallatin as traitors for their criticism of his handling of the war, but his finances were not such that he could object. He signed away his daughter's legal dower right to one-third of the many millions William would eventually inherit. The arrangement set a precedent that several future Astor wives were to regret.

William and Margaret were married in an Episcopalian ceremony as befitted the bride's lineage. William loosened up enough to call his wife Peachy, a compliment on her fine complexion. She delighted in Gothic novels and mystical poetry. Their first child was a girl they named Emily after the heroine of Ann Radcliffe's popular Gothic novel *The Mysteries of Udolpho.* William, too, was an avid reader. He built himself a large octagonal library and in the evening liked nothing better than to sit by its fire reading lexicons and reference works. Margaret had her garden and eventually a greenhouse. Emily grew up to be pretty and lively, with a quick sense of humor. Six children followed Emily. A girl named Sarah died in infancy, but John Jacob Astor III and his sisters Laura and Mary lived to ripe old age. Emily remained her parents' favorite.

John Jacob gave them a house at Broadway and White Street, eleven blocks north of his and Sarah's home, took William into a partnership, and set up John Jacob Astor & Son to control overseas trading. The firm shared the Pine Street headquarters with the American Fur Company.

William's part in the operation of J. J. Astor & Son, and its chief subsidiary, was always subordinate. J. J. and Ramsay Crooks, in St. Louis, continued to dictate policies and methods. Christian pieties were not what characterized American Fur. If John Jacob made no move to take back Astoria, he spearheaded a ruthless and predatory expansion that spread misery and despair among the continent's original inhabitants.

Manuel Lisa was again extending his trading on the upper Missouri, and thinking of expeditions to the Yellowstone and the great mountains. The war years had not been kind to him. After suffering disastrous losses, the Missouri Fur Company had shrunk from an association of 150 veteran traders to an outfit of 20 men. Gros Ventre Indians had robbed and murdered one Lisa party, and trading posts on the upper river were abandoned. The company's 1812 and 1813 expeditions had been small and brought little profits. Partners pulled out. Once more, Lisa lacked capital. But he was still St. Louis's premier trader because his competitors, including the Chouteau clan, were smaller and weaker than he.

The St. Louis merchant who kept Astor informed of all this was Charles Gratiot, who back in 1808 had offered J. J. his services and still owed him £1,000. During the war, when importing from Canada was costly and against the law, J. J. had written Gratiot, asking if deerskins might be purchased in St. Louis. Gratiot had obtained 120 packs and sent them by keelboat to Astor representatives in Pittsburgh who forwarded them overland to New York. It was slow haulage, but in 1816 Gratiot sent Astor twice as many deerskin packs plus bearskins. J. J. paid Gratiot a 5 percent commission, but instead of forwarding money deducted the sum from Gratiot's debt. No doubt aiming to get out of the debt, Gratiot now suggested Astor move in on the St. Louis market.

Astor wrote back: "I have thought a good Deal on the propositions made me Some time Asince by your frinds to make Some genral arrangement for the Indian Trade & if our Government Do exclude Canada traders from aur Cauntry as I believe they will the trade will become an object & I would Licke to cam to the arrangement of which I will thank you to Inform tham."

Voices in Congress did want to forbid Canadians from trading out West. However, Astor's lobbying to exclude Canadians from fur trading on American soil nearly backfired on him shortly after Congress enacted in 1816 the law he wanted. Major William H. Puthuff, the government's Indian agent at Mackinac, reasoned that since the new law forbade Canadians from operating fur companies in the United States, it followed that they should also be barred from working for American fur traders. John Jacob disagreed. He was anxious to keep hiring Canadians. Major Puthuff's logic made Ramsay Crooks realize how much the St. Louis traders' hostility toward Astor had been communicated to government officials.

Astor wrote to newly elected President Monroe to say he was satisfied with the new law, but added that for the first year an exception must be made so that "some few Canadian traders" could supply Indians. If Monroe would grant him six to nine blank licenses, to be filled out at Michilimackinac, the Indians would not face any "great distress." Monroe, the beneficiary of easy loans from J. J., decided he was not the best-placed person to make a judgment on the public interest, and passed the decision down to Michigan Territory governor Lewis Cass with the comment that American Fur be helped in every possible way.

If American Fur was the most hated outfit on the frontier, Lewis Cass was the man who pocketed Astor's bribes and sold the government down the drain. This former U.S. army officer and future ambassador and presidential candidate was a native of Exeter, New Hampshire, who had come west at the end of the War of 1812. His appointment as governor of the territory of Michigan, which covered an area much larger than the present state, gave him control of Indian affairs. With less than six thousand white settlers, the territory was almost entirely inhabited by Native Americans. To make sure Cass saw the situation Astor's way, American Fur Company paid the governor $35,000 in 1817 for unspecified services.*

Cass instructed Indian Agent Puthuff to grant licenses to Astor while taking care not to give too many to his competitors. The major was incensed and fired back a letter to Cass:

> I wish to God the President knew this man Astor as well as he is known here. Licenses would not be placed at his discretion to be distributed among British subjects, agents or

---

*The amount was considerable enough to be inserted in the American Fur ledgers. However, the page on which the transaction was entered on May 3 or 13, 1817, was torn from the ledger owned by the Detroit Public Library a hundred years later.

pensioners. I hope in God no such licence will be granted. His British friends here calculate confident on his success in this matter, that they may be disappointed is my most sincere wish. Should they succeed incalculable evil will assuredly grow out of the measure.

Puthuff was fired and Astor got his licenses for the workers he wanted.

Colonel Talbot Chambers was another civil servant who learned the hard way that the American Fur Company was not to be trifled with. Crooks and Stuart recruited mainly Canadians and when Chambers interpreted the act of 1816 as excluding British subjects to mean American Fur could not have Canadians accompany American traders on the Mississippi, Crooks brought suit against the colonel. After four years of litigation, the case was decided against Colonel Chambers. The court victory inspired Crooks to write to Governor Cass that the verdict was especially gratifying because it showed how the company had been the victim of unreasonable persecution.

Ironically, the act of 1816 did not apply on the western slopes of the Rockies where Pierre Chouteau Jr. and other St. Louis traders discovered bountiful new beaver streams on the Snake River, because on October 20, 1818, Britain and the United States signed a treaty that declared "all territories and waters claimed by either power, west of the Rocky Mountains," open to the ships, citizens, and subjects of both countries for ten years.

The American Fur Company was divided into two geographical units—the Great Lakes-Missouri division, run from Michilimackinac by Robert Stuart, and the increasingly more important western, or trans-Missouri, division, headquartered in St. Louis and headed by Ramsay Crooks. Stuart had only passed through St. Louis on his way back from Astoria, but Crooks was a former Missouri River trader with friends in town. With discreet help from Gratiot, Crooks fashioned agreements with a pair of midsized trading companies. In return for Astor not sending his own outfits to trade on the Missouri, Cabanne & Company and Berthold

& Chouteau agreed to sell exclusively to Astor. Chouteau Jr. was the nephew of René Auguste Chouteau, born in St. Louis, who at the age of twenty-four had formed a partnership with Bernard Berthold. Like Astor, he adapted his methods to conditions as he found them and made no attempt at introducing a higher standard of business ethics than the trade was accustomed to.

Then something momentous happened that upset even Astor's applecart. On July 27, 1817, the first steamboat to reach St. Louis tied up among the keelboats, canoes, and barges. The *Pike*'s paddle wheels had pushed the little vessel up the strong currents of the Mississippi all the way from New Orleans. Astor was not there to see it, but everybody else was. Steamboats would change everything. Trade with New Orleans and the sea would be accomplished in a fraction of the time it took barges to float downriver. And what about upriver? The next spring, when the Great Lakes' first steamboat was built in Buffalo, the *Independence* thrashed its way into the Missouri, defying the spring flood, and chugged clear to Franklin, halfway to the Mandan villages. Next, the *Western Engineer,* belching smoke over the endless Great Plains, battered its way past the campsite where the Hunt expedition had spent the winter of 1808–1809 all the way to Council Bluffs, on today's Iowa-Nebraska border. "In 1817, less than two years ago, the first steamboat arrived at St. Louis," the *Missouri Gazette* noted. "Who could, or would have dared to, conjecture that in 1819 we should have the arrival of a steamboat from Philadelphia or New York. Yet such is the fact!"

Before anyone could grasp the full impact of paddle wheelers, the St. Louis fur trade degenerated into a free-for-all. The sudden death of Lisa in 1820 brought ambitious new men to the forefront of the Missouri Fur Company. One was Joshua Pilcher, who within a short time sent three hundred men up the Missouri and established a strong post at the confluence of the Yellowstone and Bighorn Rivers, at today's Custer, Montana. Another was Joseph Renville, a Northwest Company trader thrown out of work by the company's forced merger with Hudson's Bay. With a number of other

Canadians he formed the Columbia Fur Company and took two Americans into the partnership. Renville and his partners threatened Astor's American Fur Company presence by setting up posts in the upper Mississippi and Wisconsin region. Crooks warned J. J. that buying off competitors like Cabanne, Berthold, and Chouteau was no longer an option. When Columbia Fur became too successful to crush, Astor ordered Crooks to investigate the possibility of a merger.

—◊◊—

Astor was by now a millionaire—and a man in his late fifties. A charcoal drawing shows him as a figure of severe manner. His features are filling out with a double chin, his hair is sparse, his eyes deep set, and his lips thin and stern. People who met him thought he projected a virile force. His name ensured respect. Yet although he and Sarah belonged to New York's important families, they did not escape life's vicissitudes. Adrian and Magdalen had given them two grandchildren, a boy, and a girl who died young. J. J. loved to play with his first grandson. In February 1818, he took the seven-year-old John Jacob Bentzon and his eighteen-year-old daughter Eliza on a trip to Philadelphia and Washington. J. J. explained what happened next in a letter to his old friend Gallatin:

> I was changing my clothes for to dine and while Bentzon [the grandson] was sitting by the street door at or near 5 in the afternoon a boy of 17 years of age came by with his skates and persuaded Bentzon to go with him to the Tiber [Creek]. Bentzon was not 5 minutes absent before I missed him but before we could hear where he had gone, both he and the boy with him were drowned. No one had seen them on the ice and we met while looking about only a little boy who had seen them walking towards it. Bentzon had never been on ice before. I cannot describe to you the distress the misfortune has occasioned.

John Jacob feared he would never live down the tragedy. Magdalen, never very stable emotionally, became unhinged and started brooding after the death of her second child.

The White House and Tiber Creek

She began to drink. When the Congress of Vienna restored St. Croix to Denmark and Adrian was once more asked to take up residence in the governor's mansion, she refused to follow her husband to the Caribbean. There were rumors that Adrian, happy to put distance between himself and his wife, had fallen in love with an island girl. John Jacob sent Benjamin Clapp, one of the Astorians, to the West Indies to spy on Bentzon. The spying job was an easy one. Bentzon lived openly with a Creole girl called Susanna, or Sukey. A year after the death of her son, Magdalen sued for divorce. Her husband admitted his adultery in a sworn affidavit.

Whether in anger over Adrian's nonchalant attitude toward decorum or because he saw big money was to be made, J. J. agreed to level Richmond Hill, where Magdalen and Adrian had lived, and with it the knoll it stood on. By ingenious methods, the old house was lowered as the land was cut away under it. For a while it languished as a road tavern on the north side of Charlton Street, east of Varick Street, only to disappear when Astor leased the now flat land and others built rows of brick houses.

Sarah and he were now enjoying success beyond their wildest dreams. The demands of business had prevented John Jacob from fulfilling a wish to show Magdalen the Old World. William had been to Europe as had their nephew Henry Brevoort, the son of Sarah's sister, who had spent the war years in London and Paris and was a friend of that other expatriate, Washington Irving. Henry had recently returned and married.

In 1818, John Jacob decided to go to Europe. Sarah had never been overseas and this time again stayed home. As a good Calvinist, one can speculate that she might have denied herself the opportunities to sample the frivolities of foreign courts. As we have noted, wives did not travel with their husbands on business (although Magdalen had accompanied Adrian to St. Petersburg). Perhaps John Jacob had no desire to share with his wife the pleasures a wealthy American could find in Europe. Once abroad, however, his letters to other members of the family made affectionate references to Sarah, suggesting the couple viewed long separations with equanimity.

In his absence, William and Crooks out West in St. Louis would be in charge. J. J. would make course corrections from afar. Transatlantic mail was getting faster all the time.

18

—ɷ—

Paris

J ohn Jacob did not spell out his motives for going to Europe. Concern for his eldest son's mental health might have been a deeper reason than the pleasures that foreign capitals offered. Travel, a doctor ventured, might stimulate John Jacob II's mind and help him recover his wits. To try this remedy and to seek second opinions from European physicians, John Jacob decided to take his now twenty-six-year-old son, a trained nurse, and his favorite daughter, Eliza, with him to Europe. Before sailing he spent long hours with William going over the business. He made William Roberts his bookkeeper during his absence, and took pains to dictate a lengthy memorandum in case he should meet with an untimely end. "Supposing it may be useful to those of my family which will survive me, I propose to make some notes of some transactions which are not entered in my books and to explain some which are entered more fully than appear on my books." Letters went out to Ramsay Crooks in St. Louis and Robert Stuart at Michilimackinac warning them not to purchase more merchandise than the market could absorb.

Father, son, and daughter left New York on June 2, 1819, aboard a new ship, the *Stephania,* landed in Le Havre, and

made straight for Paris. There, they met up with the Gallatins. Albert Gallatin was the U.S. ambassador to the court
of King Louis XVIII, who, with the backstage guidance of the
crafty Talleyrand, was perspicacious enough not to reject the
entire legacy of the Revolution. Paris was unconscionably
expensive, Ambassador Gallatin said. With the restoration,
many well-to-do English families had settled in Paris, sending up all costs, especially the cost of servants. Hannah
helped stretch Albert's $9,000 emolument so that they could
offer respectable and tasteful hospitality. Lafayette enjoyed
evenings at the Gallatins' Rue du Bac residence, and so
did the formidable Madame de Staël. Her opposition to
Napoleon had forced her into exile, but the emperor was
now a prisoner of the English on faraway St. Helena Island,
and her salon was again attended by the leading lights of
literature and politics.

Also hobnobbing with the Gallatins was Washington
Irving. He had spent three years in London and his *Sketch
Book,* a collection of short stories that included his best-
loved tales "The Legend of Sleepy Hollow" and "Rip van
Winkle," was about to make him famous in the United States
and in England. He was now writing a drama with John
Howard Payne, the American playwright who had written
Therese, Orphan of Geneva in debtor's prison and earned
enough in royalties to gain his freedom. Irving met the
Astors and found young John Jacob to be "in very bad health
and seems in a state of mental stupor. His situation causes
great anxiety to his father and sister, and there appears
little prospect of his recovery." John Jacob left his son in the
hands of leading experts, and spent a small fortune in efforts
to discover treatments for him.

Eliza was by all accounts the pleasantest of the Astor
children, although she was on the plump side (Irving described her as "a clever agreeable girl"). Her sister Dolly had
defied her parents and married Colonel Langdon, and one
reason J. J. had invited Eliza to come to Europe was to get
her away from Eleazar Parmly and find a suitable, perhaps
titled, husband. Parmly was a Vermonter, an outstanding
dentist who had established a successful practice on Broad-

way not far from the Astors' home. He possessed culture and charm and, like so many young men of his time, wrote poetry. Several biographers of the Astor dynasty suggest John Jacob and Sarah were in total disagreement over Eliza's suitor, that J. J. refused to see his youngest daughter married to a dentist and that his wife was on the suitor's side, giving Parmly ideas on how to win the girl. "Knowing full well that it was useless to argue with her husband, [Sarah] let John Jacob take Eliza away and then wrote to Parmly urging him to follow his beloved to Paris and, since he was already unofficially engaged to her, carry her off and marry her," wrote Astor biographer David Sinclair.

Paris was a busy, fun-loving city. Its population was almost seven hundred thousand, of which at least fifty thousand were visitors or foreigners who had settled down there for good. With its polish, manners, and fine parks, the city excited visitors. "Americans," historian Stephen Longstreet wrote, "noted the frenzy of physical sensation, glory, and high fashion." There were balloon ascents, military ceremonies on the Champ de Mars, fine foods, and, for men of Astor's wealth, high-class gambling, where, he noted disapprovingly, young blades and desperate widows cashed in letters of credit issued by New York, Philadelphia, and Boston bankers. Most American and British women protested the Parisian female style of breasts pushed up by short corsets, nipples often showing, but obeyed the fashion in the matter of the baroque fantasy of hair, jewels, scents, and hats. Felt, straw, and satin bonnets included dizzying constructs called Minerva helmets and *toques à la sphinx.* Men wore waistcoats, narrow shoes or slim boots, box coats with triple collars so that the neck was often hidden up to the jawline. As one Anglo-Saxon recorded; "Powdered queues were cut off, barbers produced a look of the young orangutans—reeking of pomades and perfumes—for eighteen francs."

Through the Gallatins, father and daughter were introduced to prominent figures. One couple who made an impression on them were the duc and duchesse de Broglie.

Victor de Broglie was a moderate member of parliament. His young wife, Albertine, was the daughter of Madame de Staël. The de Broglies entertained John Jacob and Eliza at their Swiss château at Coppet, on Lake Geneva. To John Jacob's delight, Albertine and Eliza, both unaffected young women, became friends. He became alarmed, however, when Eliza and her new friends wanted to go to Italy.

In reorganizing post-Napoleonic Europe, the Congress of Vienna had respected dynastic claims and ignored nationalist urges, thereby making the greater part of Italy fall under direct or indirect Austrian rule. Since Italian patriots were holding protests, committing minor terrorist acts, and plotting revolt, John Jacob decided he'd better come along. The Astor–de Broglie party moved from court to court with letters of introduction from one aristocratic family to the next, but, wrote John Jacob to President Monroe, "All Europe is threatened with revolution. The example of Spain will, I have no doubt, be followed and I am persuaded that those in power are trembling, but none can or dare act." He learned enough Italian to talk with the outrageous Pauline Bonaparte, the most indulged of Napoleon's sisters, married to Prince Camillo Borghese, but living apart from him. During her brother's reign, she had spent half a million francs a year, mostly on clothes,* and, it was said, treated men as she treated frocks. She spent a great deal of money on them, and unless she liked them, she wore them only once. If she did like them, she wore them out. With her in Rome was Maria Letizia Ramolino Bonaparte, the seventy-year-old Madame Mère of the Bonaparte brood. After Waterloo, Napoleon had tried to escape to America, only to be captured by the British blockade and carried off to the desolate South Atlantic island of St. Helena. His imprisonment made Pauline and Madame Mère the center of intrigues by the surviving Bonapartes.

After Italy, John Jacob took his daughter to Baden-Baden to introduce her to the German cousins. Uncle Melchior and Aunt Verona had two daughters a little older than Eliza. Eliza was particularly interested in the Moravian

*In 1820 money, $1 equaled 5 francs.

faith that Uncle Melchior and Aunt Verona practiced. Members of this Protestant community believed in simple Christian teachings, exemplary moral life, and industry. They were the first to treat foreign missions as a church responsibility instead of leaving it to societies of interested persons. From Baden-Baden father and daughter went to Antwerp, The Hague, Amsterdam, and Frankfurt. From there John Jacob planned another visit with relatives in Heidelberg, but Eliza was taken ill. Doctors prescribed mountain air and in December 1823 John Jacob took her to Geneva. The town was a summer capital for a large contingent of nobility. Profiting from the off-season slump in real estate prices, he bought a charming Swiss villa at Genthod on the north shore of Lake Geneva for $50,000. He was in the process of placing John Jacob II in a special school in Geneva when he met the most fascinating American woman in Europe.

Elizabeth Patterson Bonaparte was the daughter of a Baltimore shipbuilder, trader, businessman, and owner of real estate. In 1803, she had fallen in love and married Napoleon's youngest brother, Jérôme Bonaparte. Nicknamed Fifi since his childhood, Jérôme was a wayward, impulsive, undisciplined, and handsome nineteen-year-old when he met William Patterson's daughter in Baltimore. Napoleon had wanted his youngest brother to be the naval member of the family and had sent him on a cruise. Fifi, however, did not find naval uniforms flattering and at diplomatic receptions in Baltimore sported a hussar's sky-blue jacket and scarlet waistcoat. The French ambassador lent Fifi money so he could court the "bewitching Betsy," and by so doing ruined his own diplomatic career. Since neither William Patterson nor his daughter was a fool, the marriage contract stipulated, "If the marriage is annulled, no matter by whom, Elizabeth Patterson is to have the right to a third of her future husband's fortune." Jérôme, having no fortune, signed and the wedding took place on Christmas Eve, 1803, with the archbishop of Baltimore officiating. Fifi wrote to his mother. The ambassador wrote to Napoleon. However, the news did

Betsy Bonaparte

not reach Napoleon by any of these letters, but through a notice in the British press, which heightened his rage. He had dynastic designs for his brothers and sisters and would make Jérôme a king of Westphalia. After the pope refused to annul the marriage, Napoleon had it declared null and void by civic decree. He crowned himself emperor in 1804 and three years later forgave Jérôme, made him rear admiral, paid his 3-million-franc debts, gave him a million francs a year, and married him off to Princess Catherine of Württemberg.

Since the emperor's downfall, Betsy Bonaparte, now in her mid-thirties, had devoted her time and energies to achieving for herself and her teenage son, Jerome Napoleon Bonaparte—she called him Bo or Cricket—the recognition and fortune she considered their due. She limited her own expenses to a comfortable $3,000 a year, but her poverty existed chiefly for her own convenience. As Bo wrote to his grandfather in Baltimore: "Mama goes out nearly every night to a party or ball. She says she looks full ten years younger than she is, and if she had not so large a son she could pass for five and twenty years old."

As a child Betsy had enjoyed staying with her father during his working hours and as a result possessed an unusual knowledge of investment banking, real estate, trade, contracts, and business law (she would die a millionaire in her nineties). She had brains and determination and liked to say she would have married the devil himself to get out of Baltimore. "The men are all merchants, and commerce, although it may fill the purse, clogs the mind," she said. "Beyond their counting-houses they possess not a single idea; they never visit except when they wish to marry. The women are all occupied in *les details de ménage* and nursing children; these are useful occupations, but they do not render people agreeable to their neighbors." She was charming in person and dress, witty and bright, and a great talker. If she could not afford a salon of her own, she knew how to hold forth in the mansions of others, where the subjects ranged from the carnal to the spiritual, the scientific to the occult, to contribute, as the historian Edward Gibbon said, "to the perfection of that inestimable art which softens and refines and embellishes the intercourse of life." According to Albert Gallatin's son, James, she put an Englishman in his place at a dinner party by agreeing that all Americans were vulgarians. "Quite true," she told the English guest seated next to her. "If the Americans had been the descendants of the Indians or the Esquimaux there might have been some reason to be astonished, but as they are the direct descendants of the English it is perfectly natural that they should be vulgarians."

She had tried London for a while with the help of Lady Morgan, an ex-governess who had risen by her pen and wits to the top of Upper Bohemia. Politicians received Betsy once as an interesting incongruity. Great families did not open their houses to her.

She crossed to Paris in 1815. Talleyrand praised her wits, Madame de Staël admired her beauty, and Louis XVIII offered to see her at court, an offer she refused. As a Bonaparte, she did not wish to stoop to the restored Bourbons. "I form no plans," she wrote to her father. "I try to hope that some unexpected happiness may continue me where alone I attach value to existence. The ex-king of Westphalia [Jérôme] is now living at the Court of Würtemberg. He has a large fortune, and is too mean to support his own son."

Pauline Bonaparte, or Princess Borghese as she now styled herself, used John Jacob as a go-between to ask Betsy to come to Rome. After Napoleon's death on St. Helena in 1821, the surviving Bonapartes were regrouping and Betsy was flattered to be solicited. Not that she expected any help from her now poor relations. "They are less wealthy than supposed," she wrote to her father. "I believe some of them are amiable but when there is a question of parting with money, good will is generally exposed to a great trial."

What did Madame Bonaparte think of the plainspoken millionaire fur dealer and shipowner who spoke with a German accent and who had manners no one would call polished and who never mastered the intricacies of court etiquette? Astutely sizing up her man and her prospects, she insinuated herself not by seducing him, but by taking Eliza under her wing. She accepted an invitation to sojourn with the Astors in their new villa. Here is her tart portrait, worthy of a Jane Austen, of her host and his daughter:

> Mr. A and daughter are here. He seems, poor man, afflicted by the possession of a fortune, which he had greater pleasure in amassing than he can ever find in spending. He is ambitious, too, I fancy, for his daughter, to whom nature has been as penurious as fortune has been the reverse. She may marry by the weight of her person, but any idea of disposing of

her except to some painstaking man of business, or ruined French or Italian nobleman, would be absurd. She is not handsome, and sense cannot be bought; therefore they will wander from place to place a long time before their object is accomplished. The father has no small portion of natural sense, and, could he have commanded the advantages of instruction, which he gives his children, he might have made that figure which he desires, but will never attain for his family. Education improves but can never give capacity—a truth some people never discover.

More than a trace of envy colors Elizabeth Patterson Bonaparte's derision. Sooner than she thought, Count

Eliza Astor von Rumpff

Vincent von Rumpff, a Swiss-born diplomat who represented the Hanseatic free cities of northern Germany at the court of Louis XVIII, would demand Eliza's hand. Madame Bonaparte wrote that von Rumpff "is a handsome man of thirty-five and we all think she has been very fortunate in getting him, as she is no beauty. He is well connected, and has it in his power to introduce her into the best company."

Madame Bonaparte was not the only one to write scornful observations. Confided young James Gallatin to his diary: "Really Mr. Astor is dreadful. Father has to be civil to him, as in 1812–1813 he rendered a great service to the Treasury. He came to *déjeuner* today; we were simply *en famille,* he sitting next to Frances [James's teenage sister]. He actually wiped his fingers on her fresh white spencer. Mamma in discreet tones said, 'Oh, Mr. Astor, I must apologize. They have forgotten to give you a *serviette.*' I think he felt foolish."

More than one biographer would wonder about the accuracy of James Gallatin's observation. "Either Astor had suffered a relapse to the days when he sat about campfires in the wilderness on his fur-trading trips," John Upton Terrell wrote in *Furs by Astor,* "or the snobbish young Gallatin was lying." What aggravated James Gallatin's ill will was that his father was far from rich.

Albert Gallatin's distinguished career as a public servant was coming to an end—the ambassadorship was meant as a last sinecure—and John Jacob once more offered his old friend a chance to make some real money and hinted at a dynastic alliance if James and Eliza would marry. John Jacob would finance their joint undertaking to the tune of $800,000, not merely as a charity or a thank-you for years of support and assistance, but because he admired Albert's knowledge of money. Surely, they could make money together. The $800,000 should bring in earnings of between $150,000 and $200,000 a year. Albert could have one-fifth of the profits. As for the young people, should James accept Eliza's hand, J. J. would not only make Albert a partner, but would also find a position for young James. We do not know whether the young people were consulted, but James held no attraction for Eliza and she seemed to have made no impression on him. Hannah Gallatin was against her son marrying Eliza as she considered all the Astor women to be "shrews." Albert refused the "most generous offer" of a partnership, saying that after holding so many government posts it would be unbecoming of him to die rich.

Gallatin was offered the chairmanship of the second U.S. Bank. Back in 1815, Astor had lobbied for the bank's creation, and when Congress had finally chartered the bank a year later, he had been eager to be a commissioner of the New York branch. It hadn't happened, and since then his enthusiasm for central banking had cooled. Americans were deep in debt, he would write to Gallatin in October 1822, and the country was no longer what it had been in their youth:

> For the interest of the United States Bank I am sorry that you will not take it. For your own sake I am glad. It is, as you say, a troublesome situation, and I doubt if much credit is to be got by it. I have been to-day spoken to about your taking the situation, but I stated that you decline it, and I think you are right. Matters here go on irregular enough. It's all the while up and down. So soon as people have a little money they run into extravagancy, get in debt, and down it goes. Exchange is again $12\frac{1}{2}$ to 13 [percent], and people will again ship specie, the banks again curtail discounts, bankruptcy ensues, exchange will fall for a short time, and then we have the same scene over again. You know so well this country and character of the people that I need say no more.

—◆—

When no one in Geneva could jolt the mind of John Jacob II into a resemblance of normalcy, his father quietly sent him back to America. With Eliza, J. J. wintered in Paris, meeting most of the current celebrities of court and capital. In the summer it was back to the villa at Genthod where he enjoyed his role as host. Betsy Bonaparte came down while her nineteen-year-old son continued his education in Geneva. So did Washington Irving and Count Vincent von Rumpff. Vincent had no fortune and the $300,000 Astor was prepared to settle on his daughter might have added to von Rumpff's ardor. Washington Irving made a note in his diary of "Mrs. Patterson," as he called Betsy, sitting for a portrait in the Genthod garden.

Why would the sophisticated Madame Bonaparte sojourn with the coarse nouveau riche fur trader and his overweight daughter? Because she could use him in her dynastic designs for her son. She had failed in securing the hand of Joseph Bonaparte's daughter for Bo. Napoleon had crowned his elder brother king of Spain. Her second unsuccessful try was the wealthy daughter of Napoleon's eldest sister Maria-Anna (Elisa), whom the emperor had crowned grand duchess of Tuscany. Astor was important for Betsy. He had met Pauline in Rome, and Betsy now wrote her former sister-in-law to thank her for having asked J. J. about herself and her son, and to announce her plans to come to Rome to lobby for her son's interests.

Astor played along. A month later when he was in Florence, he wrote Betsy to tell her he had met Pauline again and presented her case: "I told her what I thought was the case; that your father is very wealthy, but that his property consisted chiefly in houses and lands, which at present did not produce much; that he has a large family, say seven besides yourself; and that I believed you had to economize to educate your son." Pauline was not well and the mission ended inconclusively. With a down-to-earth earnestness that perhaps only a self-made man would express, he added: "Your son will have sense enough not be flattered with prospects which may prove vain."

Sound advice. Pauline never received her former sister-in-law. As Betsy wrote to her father, "The Bonapartes are all alike, very affectionate in words, but without the least intention of parting with a farthing. Their fortune is less than is supposed, their expenses very great, and the chance is that they will spend more than they possess."

John Jacob prolonged his stay in Europe. William's unimaginative but competent management—and Ramsay Crooks's sharper grip on affairs in St. Louis—allowed him to fine-tune the American Fur Company operations by mail, and to accept the invitations Vincent von Rumpff secured at the courts in Paris, Vienna, and Naples. Speculation about Eliza's marriage to Vincent was the subject of letters to and from New York. Dorothy asked her father for a portrait of her sister and fiancé. By return letter, he told her he was having his own "likeness" painted: "Eliza is very well & very happy I never knew her So much So. Some time ago She was very Cross with me but I belive it arose from Indisposition which [she] feels ocatinally."

We don't know whether Ramsay Crooks was summoned or he decided he could combine business with leisure, but during the winter of 1820–1821, he was in Paris. Competition was heating up on the Missouri and the question John Jacob and he had to decide was whether to accept an offer by the St. Louis outfit of Berthold & Chouteau to buy part of American Fur Company. There was something surreal in this tail-wagging-the-dog proposal, but Bernard Berthold had indeed made overtures to buy the western department, that is, the most aggressive division of American Fur. Old rivals with new money were moving in on Berthold & Chouteau. One was an outfit headed by David Stone, a Detroit trader who had challenged Astor on the Great Lakes. Now, Stone's success in the West sowed alarms among St. Louis merchants, including Berthold & Chouteau. William was cut in on these events, but on July 27, 1820, Crooks had written Astor in Paris:

> To address Messrs Berthold and Chouteau on a subject so often canvassed, appears to me more than useless, as their conduct has hitherto betrayed an undecision [*sic*] that small hopes ought to be entertained of their determination now. Perhaps the appearance of David Stone & Company at St. Louis may rouse them from their fancied security and turn their attention seriously this way. Lest that should be the case, and to clear myself from all blame, I shall in a few days write them and request an immediate and specific reply at New York.

There were days when Astor allowed despondency to take hold. His conversation with Crooks about Berthold & Chouteau turned into a larger question of the future of American Fur.

John Jacob's flair for business was undiminished. Better than most men in business he understood the impermanence of success. He understood the volatility of markets and how to anticipate change. By incessant instructions to William, he had seen to it that John Jacob Astor & Son deliberately withdrew from the China trade. Little by little, they sold off the fleet of clippers and dockside warehouses. Now the family business was at a crossroads and only John Jacob could divine the future. Sometime in 1822, he made his decision. Instead of folding the tent, he would redouble the effort to squash any and all competitors in the western fur trade.

Albert and Hannah wanted to return to the United States and John Jacob decided he and Eliza would travel with them the following spring. The Gallatins' spoiled son James, they decided, was "wasting time to no purpose" in Europe. But the young man found Paris more to his liking than the backwoods of western Pennsylvania. His sister Frances also resisted. Turning twenty, Frances was a beauty much admired in Paris society, but, as Betsy Bonaparte remarked, "the beauty of Venus would never marry any one in France without money," and Ambassador Gallatin had no fortune with which to endow his daughter. It must have grated on the Gallatins when Vincent von Rumpff married Eliza Astor in 1825. We do not know how much John Jacob settled on Eliza, but he was always generous to his favorite daughter. When she died, he bequeathed to Vincent $50,000 and the "lands and estate in the Canton of Geneva."

—⚏—

The marriage would not put an end to the story of the besotted dentist. By the time Parmly got to Paris, Eliza and Vincent were married. Eleazar himself found another love and, a year and a half later, married. Unrequited love, of course, was the stuff of poetry, and Countess Eliza Astor von Rumpff's money and name apparently caused Parmly to persist in writing verses about aching hearts and broken flowers. The story was widely believed and given credence by Eliza's embrace of deep religious faith shortly after her marriage. She founded Sunday schools for children and presided over prayer meetings. Although she and Vincent enjoyed a happy marriage, her death at the age of thirty-seven prompted Parmly to say she died of grief for him. Twice, the New York poet-dentist traveled to Rolle, Switzerland, to bow his head in contemplation at her grave.

The story of the smitten dentist gave rise to a biographers' tiff. In his 1929 biography *John Jacob Astor: Landlord of New York,* Arthur D. Howden Smith maintained that J. J. broke up a love affair between Eliza and Eleazar, and hauled his daughter to Paris to show what she would miss if she married the dentist. Two years later, Kenneth W. Porter's exhaustive *John Jacob Astor, Business Man* said Smith's story was riddled with contradictions, that Smith had the lovers meet and fall in love in 1823 or 1824 when Eliza had sailed to Europe with her father in 1819. Even if Sarah had been in Parmly's corner, he was extraordinarily slow in trying to capture his beloved Eliza:

> He is said in July 1825 to have referred in a poem "to his imminent departure for 'far distant countries'"—and yet he could not manage to get to Paris in the four or five months between the date of this poem and Eliza's wedding! Certainly he did not long mourn his bereavement, since he himself married within a year and a half of Eliza's wedding. Moreover it is not true that Eliza "only lived eight years after her marriage"; she did not die until 1838, or more than thirteen years after the event which is supposed to have been responsible for her early decease. But this point need not be stressed; if a heart is to be eight years in breaking, it may as well take an additional five.

The Gallatins postponed their return to America and so did John Jacob. News from home during J. J.'s sojourn abroad was not always pleasant. At thirty-two, Magdalen had become pregnant and on March 9, 1820, hurriedly married John Bristed. He was an Englishman working in New York as a writer, lecturer, and magazine editor. The marriage was a failure. Bristed, however, stayed long enough to see the child born then returned to London, finding it "impossible," as Sarah's nephew, Henry Brevoort, wrote, "to bear the matrimonial yoke any longer."

There was speculation that Magdalen suffered some of the mental instability that afflicted her elder brother. Why else would two men renounce a portion of the Astor fortune rather than continue under the same roof with her? To escape the marriage, Bentzon had pleaded guilty to adultery. Bristed ran away, although he later returned to the United States and for thirteen years served as rector to the church of St. Michael in Bristol, Rhode Island. After his death in 1855, the grateful parishioners raised a monument to his memory. Magdalen and John's son, Charles Bristed, would become John Jacob's favorite grandson.

19

—ɯ—

This Land Is My Land

Ramsay Crooks returned to St. Louis in 1822 shortly after his thirty-fourth birthday and set in motion the expansion that would turn the American Fur Company into the most hated entity on the frontier. "Many are the stories, largely exaggerated, no doubt, that have come down to us of its hard and cruel ways," Hiram M. Chittenden would write in *The American Fur Trade of the Far West*. "Small traders stood no show whatever and the most desperate measures were resorted to without scruple to get them out of the way. Many an employee, it is said, who had finished his term of service and had started for St. Louis with a letter of credit for his pay fell by the way and was reported as killed by the Indians." President Zachary Taylor, whose early soldiering in the War of 1812 and billeting at Prairie du Chien during the Black Hawk War twenty years later brought him into contact with Astor's agents on the Mississippi, considered American Fur's employees to be "the greatest scoundrels the world ever knew."

John Jacob and Eliza sailed for New York in May. Crooks went to St. Louis via London. Leading fur houses expressed

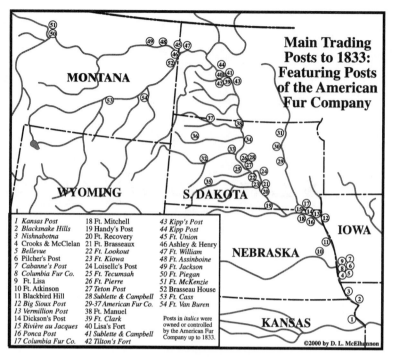

Main Trading Posts to 1833: Featuring Posts of the American Fur Company

MONTANA

WYOMING

S. DAKOTA

NEBRASKA

IOWA

KANSAS

1 Kansas Post	18 Ft. Mitchell	*43 Kipp's Post*
2 Blacksnake Hills	19 Handy's Post	*44 Kipp Post*
3 Nishnabotna	20 Ft. Recovery	*45 Ft. Union*
4 Crooks & McClelan	21 Ft. Brasseaux	46 Ashley & Henry
5 Bellevue	*22 Ft. Lookout*	*47 Ft. William*
6 Pilcher's Post	23 Ft. Kiowa	48 Ft. Assinboine
7 Cabanne's Post	24 Loisellc's Post	*49 Ft. Jackson*
8 Columbia Fur Co.	25 Ft. Tecumsah	50 Ft. Piegan
9 Ft. Lisa	26 Ft. Pierre	*51 Ft. McKenzie*
10 Ft. Atkinson	27 Teton Post	52 Brasseau House
11 Blackbird Hill	*28 Sublette & Campbell*	*53 Ft. Cass*
12 Big Sioux Post	*29-37 American Fur Co.*	*54 Ft. Van Buren*
13 Vermillion Post	38 Ft. Manuel	
14 Dickson's Post	*39 Ft. Clark*	Posts in *italics* were
15 Rivière au Jacques	40 Lisa's Fort	owned or controlled
16 Ponca Post	*41 Sublette & Campbell*	by the American Fur
17 Columbia Fur Co.	42 Tilton's Fort	Company up to 1833.

©2000 by D. L. McElhannon

Western department of the American Fur Company

alarm at rumors that Astor planned to bring all his continental buyers to London and auction all his furs there. London furriers didn't need competition from Astor. From Montreal, Crooks hurried on to Michilimackinac, where, under Robert Stuart's management, American Fur was now in control of the trade. John Jacob and Eliza sailed shortly after Crooks.

The year Astor had given up the opium trade, along with much of the China commerce, 1821, was also the year liquor became the American Fur Company's chief medium of exchange. The ravages of alcohol on Native Americans were well known, and successive administrations in Washington earnestly tried to forbid the sale of liquor in Indian territories. Government action, however, was wholly ineffectual, as alcohol was the most powerful weapon one trader could use to get an advantage over another. "So violent is the attachment of the Indian for it that he who gives most is sure to obtain the furs, while should any one attempt to trade without it he is sure of losing ground with his antagonist,"

Thomas Biddle wrote General Henry Atkinson in October 1819. "No bargain is ever made without it." A shrewd trader first got his victim so intoxicated that the Indian could no longer drive a good bargain.

Chittenden would write:

> The Indian, becoming more and more greedy for liquor, would yield all he possessed for an additional cup or two. The voracious trader, not satisfied with selling his alcohol at a profit of many thousand percent, would now begin to cheat in quantity. As he filled the little cup, which was the standard of measure, he would thrust in his big thumb and diminish its capacity by one-third. Sometimes he would substitute another cup with the bottom thickened up by running tallow until it was a third full. He would also dilute the liquor until, as the Indian's senses become more and more befogged, he would treat him to water pure and simple. In all this outrageous imposition, by which the Indian was robbed of his goods, it must be confessed that the tricks of the trader had at least this in their favor that they spared the unhappy and deluded savage from a portion of the liquor which he supposed he was getting. The duplicity and crime for which this unallowable traffic is responsible in our relations with the Indians have been equaled but seldom in even the most corrupt nations.

Black Hawk, the chief of the Sac (Sauk) Indians, had repudiated an 1804 agreement to cede Sac and Fox lands in Illinois to the United States, declaring the whites had persuaded the Native Americans to sign after getting them drunk. The cession of the disputed territory was again arranged by new treaties and by the time Congress considered a bill for the absolute prohibition of importing liquor into Indian country, most of the Sac and Fox were suffering from hunger on new, less fertile lands west of the Mississippi. When Black Hawk learned that whites were occupying the Sac and Fox homelands, he once more refused to recognize the agreement and plotted a return.

Because liquor was not sold to Indians at government posts, the first thing Astor did was to lobby Washington to get the government out of the fur trade. He had railed against the government posts at the time of their creation in 1796. His agents were now told to do everything to lure Indians away from trade with government agents. Reports that a manager at American Fur's Michilimackinac station had taken delivery of 3,300 gallons of whiskey and 2,500 gallons of fortified wines during 1825 provoked the military commander of the Detroit region to write to his superiors in Washington that "the neighborhood of the trading houses where whiskey is sold presents a disgusting scene of drunkenness, debauchery and misery; it is the fruitful source of all our difficulties, and of nearly all the murders committed in the Indian country."

The commander was not alone. The ravages of alcohol revolted David Thompson, the Northwest partner and surveyor who had come down the Columbia to see for himself that Astoria existed. He saw so many Indian men and women debased or made murderous by spirits that he vigorously opposed the Northwest Company's liquor policy. Like outfits in Mackinac and St. Louis, however, the partners in Montreal could not imagine staying in business without using alcohol as a sweetener.

—⁊⁊—

Michigan Territory governor Lewis Cass was not the only public servant who helped choke off trade at the "dry" government posts. When the Indian Trade Department asked Congress for extra money to make its posts more effective, newly elected Senator Thomas Hart Benton from Missouri was the eloquent defender of free trade with the Indians. Benton, who just happened to be American Fur's attorney, helped win the day for abolishing government trading posts. Ramsay Crooks wrote to the senator, saying he deserved the unqualified thanks of the community for destroying a pious monster.

Army officers asked Washington for instructions on how to stop the flow of whiskey. What, for example, was Indian territory? Astor's Green Bay post was not, Governor Cass ruled. Could white men be deprived of liquor rations? Obviously not. And while liquor could not be sold to Indians, there was no provision against giving it away. Smaller traders in small craft evaded government inspectors at Leavenworth on the Missouri and Bellevue on the upper Mississippi by either going overland or taking a chance running the inspection stations at night. In overland journeys the alcohol was generally carried in short, flat kegs, which would rest conveniently on the sides of a pack mule. When carried by water it was hidden in flour barrels or bales of merchandise.

Historians have searched in vain the Astor and Crooks correspondence for evidence of criminal collusion. A scrutiny of the St. Louis office archives, however, show the western department conducted its business one way in transactions with New York and differently when dealing with the men in the far-flung field. "It may indeed be said that the history of the company upon the Upper Missouri was uniformly on the side of the advancement of knowledge and its assistance to enterprises of this character was of permanent value," Chittenden wrote in *The American Fur Trade of the Far West* in 1903. "But to the average individual the American Fur Company was the personification of monopoly, determined to rule or ruin, and hence it was thoroughly hated even by those who respected its power." When the head of the Fort Union depot had a still smuggled in, his superior in St. Louis, Pierre Chouteau Jr., obligingly sent him a ton of corn for making whiskey. When a rival trader informed government agents, Chouteau wrote the Indian Affairs Department that he was looking into the outrageous and no doubt scurrilous allegation of whiskey distilling at an American Fur Company post.

The company shipped its goods in great cargoes that had to stop at Leavenworth, in today's Kansas, and Bellevue, now in Iowa. As we have seen, Indian Affairs inspectors could not deprive white men of alcohol. In fact, the government permitted one gill (0.14 liter) per day per boatman during their absence, which was calculated to be twelve months. For fifty men, that amounted to three hundred gallons of liquor going upriver. The pure article never found its way to the Indians. The alcohol was cut again and again with everything from molasses to sugar water.

Curbing the sale of alcohol could have worked to Astor's advantage. Public opinion was appalled by the whole sorry mess and demanded energetic government action. In the spring of 1822, Congress considered a bill for the absolute prohibition of importing liquor into Indian country. Had John Jacob boldly proposed outlawing alcohol from Indian territories, he might have obtained in exchange what he had always wanted—a monopoly of the western fur trade. But he was still in Paris and did not see or seize the opportunity. Instead, he relied on the argument that the other guys were doing it.

In a letter-perfect submission to General William H. Ashley, first lieutenant governor of the new state of Missouri, he wrote:

> Wherever the trade is exclusively in the hands of our own citizens, there can be no doubt that the uniform and complete enforcement of such a law will be beneficial both to the Indians and the traders, but at those points where we come in contact with the Hudson's Bay Company we must either abandon the trade or be permitted to use it, to a limited extent at least, in order to counteract, in some measure, the influence of our rivals, who can introduce any quantity they please.
>
> Our new posts on the Missouri River above the Mandans must yield to the superior attractions of our opponents, unless the government will permit us like them to use spirituous liquors; and the friendly relations we have at last succeeded in establishing with the Blackfeet (those inveterate enemies of the Americans) at so much expense and personal hazard, must inevitably be destroyed, and the British be restored to the unlimited control they have heretofore exercised over these Indians.
>
> If the Hudson's Bay Company did not employ ardent spirits against us, we would not ask for a single drop. But without it, competition is hopeless; for the attraction is irresistible; and if the British traders alone possess the temptation, they will unquestionably not only maintain, but rivet their influence over all the Indians within their reach, to the detriment of the United States, in alienating their affections from us, and in the loss of trade to which we have an undoubted claim.

Ashley was a Virginian who had settled in St. Louis in 1808. After turning lead mining into a flourishing industry, he had gone into politics and taken an active part in developing the Missouri militia. It was understood that if he had opposed the prohibition bill, it would not have become law in July 1822. American Fur never ceased to lobby for its repeal. Ten years later, Crooks wrote to Pierre Chouteau:

> I regret truly the blindness of the government in refusing liquor for the trade of the country in the vicinity of Hudson's Bay posts, because the prohibition will not prevent the Indians getting it from our rivals, to our most serious injury. It *might* have been possible last winter at Washington to accomplish some modification had we been there together. I have very strong doubts on the subject, however, because Governor Cass is a temperance society man in every sense of the word, and it was with his full consent and approbation that the law for its exclusion from the Indian country was passed by the last Congress, and though I did not go to the Great City, the Chairmen of the Indian Committees were made as fully acquainted with the subject in all its bearing as if I had detailed all the facts to them, in person.

An explanation for Ashley's endorsement of the bill came in the form of an advertisement in the March 20, 1822, edition of the *Missouri Republic* that jolted Astor enough to make him return to New York:

> To enterprising young men. The subscriber wishes to engage one hundred young men to ascend the Missouri river to its source, there to be employed for one, two, or three years. For particulars enquire of Major Andrew Henry, near the lead mines in the county of Washington, who will ascend with, and command, the party; or the subscriber near St. Louis.
> [signed] William H. Ashley

Major Henry was a tall, slender, blue-eyed Pennsylvanian fond of reading and playing the violin. He married a beautiful woman of French birth much younger than himself, whom he had once carried as a child in his arms, and playfully predicted she would be his wife. In 1809, he had joined Manuel Lisa's Missouri Fur Company, and suffered an attack by the Blackfeet the following year. Fleeing west instead of east, he had built a post on a tributary of the Snake River. It was at this deserted Fort Henry that the Astorians had found refuge during their trek over the Rockies.

Henry's plan was innovative and ingenious. Best of all, it conformed to the new law. Instead of relying on Indian trappers to come to company posts to barter their pelts, Henry would take white men into the upper river country and the western mountains and train them to hunt and trap. No costly and vulnerable posts were to be established. Instead, the white trappers—and any Indian ready to trade without booze—would bring their furs to trade at rendezvous that could be changed according to the season and afforded the most advantageous place. Who needed liquor if the main workforce was not Indian?

Just as Crooks was recruiting for American Fur, Ashley's ad brought enthusiastic responses. Among the mostly young men who signed up were Jedediah Smith, a fearless New Yorker who went to the Mexican provinces and pronounced California the most beautiful country he had ever seen, and Etienne Provôt, a seasoned trader who was to rediscover the invaluable South Pass, which the returning Stuart party had missed in 1814. Along with the Sublette brothers— Andrew, Solomon, Milton, and William—Jim Beckwourth, a French mulatto who discovered Beckwourth's Pass, the 5,212-foot passage in California's High Sierra, also joined. So did James Bridger, a former blacksmith who was considered the ablest hunter, mountaineer, and guide in the West, and Thomas Fitzpatrick, an Irishman who had lost a finger and crippled his left hand by a rifle burst and was known among Indians as Bad Hand, Broken Hand, and Withered Hand. The Ashley outfit called itself the Rocky Mountain Fur Company. Under Henry's command, a first contingent left St. Louis in April 1823. Ashley recruited another hundred men and in March 1824 headed this second, follow-up expedition himself.

The field was getting crowded. Besides the would-be trailblazers of the Ashley outfits, the most formidable competitor was David Stone, the head of Stone, Bostwick & Company after Stone's Mackinac agent O. N. Bostwick joined the partnership and got the better of the hesitant Berthold & Chouteau. There was also Joseph Renville's Columbia Fur Company, which traded from the Great Lakes to the Rockies. Its capital was not large, but its partners were skilled and enterprising men who, in what is today's central South Dakota, established at the mouth of the Cheyenne River a post they named Fort Tecumseh. And there were the laid-off Northwest men, victims of the Hudson's Bay takeover, freelancing or ready to sign up with old or new outfits.

Astor and Crooks agreed there was no reason to provoke a clash with Ashley. Why not let Ashley, Stone, Renville, and Joshua Pilcher, who after Manuel Lisa's death had taken over the Missouri Fur Company, do the hard work of opening the country? Why not let them suffer the losses of men, merchandise, and furs that were unavoidable in overcoming and perhaps pacifying the Blackfeet and the other Bighorn, Yellowstone, and Snake River tribes? After that, American Fur could step in and, by its sheer financial heft, buy them out or absorb or destroy them. In writing *The American Fur Trade of the Far West,* Chittenden would attribute the company's power to Astor himself: "The chief elements of strength which gave the American Fur Company such a power in the Indian country was the great wealth and business sagacity of its founder. Its formidable financial backing gave to its operations a degree of force and stability which none of the other American fur companies possessed."

Crooks made several trips to New York and held long meetings with Astor. Maps had improved, and the Missouri had been charted. J. J and Crooks pored over reports and maps. They were in a business that stretched over a million square miles, and for someone who had never been farther west than Fort William, on Lake Superior, Astor's knowledge and understanding of the country and the trade were astute. No detail, it was said, was too small. His mind retained every fragment of information gathered through the years. Besides, Crooks and Robert Stuart at Michilimackinac were not his only source of information. However observant and accurate their reports, John Jacob supplemented them with intelligence from Senator Benton and the obliging President Monroe, who during his last years in office worked to improve relations with Britain, France, Spain, and Canada. With agents in London, Montreal, St. Petersburg, and Canton, John Jacob was both the market and its benchmark. Prices moved according to what he bid, offered, and paid.

—m—

In June 1823, John Jacob and Eliza set sail for Europe. They were on the high seas on July 17 when he celebrated his sixtieth birthday. America, he had written to Gallatin before leaving, no longer agreed with him: "Here I cannot pass my time but by being constantly engaged in business, which is a trouble to me and causes anxieties which I wish to avoid . . . I can do better in Europe or more pleasantly." Between William and Crooks the business was in solid hands, and he had every intention of staying on top of it. His privileged position gave him a perspective that others didn't have. He saw clearly that too many competitors were diminishing the returns for everybody, that trade would inevitably fall off. Worse, it would degenerate into a brutish, lawless free-for-all as the mountains filled with rivals, each using every means to undermine the rest. The Indians would be demoralized by the conduct of whites toward each other and lose all confidence and incentives to set traps and prepare skins. From Washington, he heard of fears that the fur trade was undermining the government's policy of keeping Indians peaceful. Before he could decide the next move, however, the dominoes began to drop into his lap.

Two days after his birthday, Stone, Bostwick & Company agreed to be absorbed by American Fur. The deal was temporary, running for three and a half years, not that anybody envisaged a breakup come January 1827. From Michilimackinac, Stuart wrote David Stone: "Permit me to welcome you as a member of the American Fur Company & I think you have all acted wisely, but if the junction had been formed five years ago there would have been cause of mutual congratulation."

Of the many, William Ashley's Rocky Mountain Fur Company was now the new formidable competitor. The success of its young recruits was measured in the massive cargoes of pelts they brought back from beyond the Rockies. The hauls made a deep impression in St. Louis, as did the tales of Jedediah Smith's scrapes with Indians, grizzly bears, and starvation. The other piece of gossip that animated St. Louis parlors was Ramsay Crooks's courtship of Emelie Pratte. The Pratte family was associated with the Chouteaus by blood ties and the fur trade. The prospect of marriage made Crooks—and after him, Stuart—ask for more money. John Jacob was smart enough to see the value of his two deputies. Stuart's contract was the easiest to settle. He would get a salary of $2,500 a year and 15 percent of the northern department's net profits. Neither Astor nor Crooks divulged the remuneration they settled on for the head of the western department. Crooks was satisfied enough to sign a new contract and, in March 1825, to marry Ms. Pratte. From then on, however, a certain coolness entered his relationship with his distant boss for whom he had worked for nearly fourteen years. The reserve was mutual. From Astor's point of view, Crooks, a man half his age, was too timid. What grated on J. J. was not what Crooks did, but what he didn't do. American Fur should control the West before the trade disintegrated or sell out.

As he had done many times before, Astor pored over the structure, strength, and personnel of the various St. Louis houses. To buy out Ashley's Rocky Mountain Fur Company would be costly. J. J. decided to wait, and in the meantime consolidate his own assets by shaking up the recent acquisition of Stone, Bostwick & Company. David Stone was an able trader, but the others, J. J. felt, were liabilities. Unfortunately, William Astor had just agreed to a year's extension of the agreement with Stone, Bostwick. John Jacob decided not to wait a year and sent instructions to Crooks to arrange a termination of the agreement. Also, Crooks should try to make a deal with his new in-laws' firm, Bernard Pratte & Company.

"Old Astor," as the St. Louis agents called the boss, was way ahead of Crooks. Acquiring Bernard Pratte &

Company would of course add profits, but the company's bigger asset was its partner, Pierre Chouteau Jr. Behind the shuffle, Astor was headhunting for a replacement for Crooks. Now thirty-five, Chouteau was smart enough to see Astor's moves. "He had no illusions about Astor's power, no foolish hopes that the spreading tentacles of the American Fur Company could be avoided," John Upton Terrell wrote in *Furs by Astor.* "Astor had more resources, money, brains, affiliations, political power than all the other St. Louis traders combined. He had agents in Europe who purchased manufactured goods for him at the lowest possible cost, directly from the factories. He was the largest fur dealer in the world."

In discussions with Pratte, Chouteau said he had wanted to buy shares in American Fur, that it would be folly to defy Astor. Astor wanted him, meaning Astor would make concessions. The alternative would be a bitter and costly fight they would ultimately lose. Bernard Pratte & Company signed a four-year deal with Astor. The agreement, running until the end of 1833, gave American Fur posts at the forks of the Cheyenne and at the confluence of the Cheyenne and the Missouri in today's South Dakota.

Anticipating overcrowding and anarchy, Astor ordered cutbacks in the northern department. Stuart was to retrench Detroit, the easternmost company post. The completion of the Erie Canal sent homesteaders to the Great Lakes, and settlement meant the destruction of wild animals. Stuart did not share Astor's view. John Jacob compromised, authorizing Stuart to continue the Detroit operations but to try to liquidate.

In the West, American Fur gave every indication of vigorous profits, but J. J. told Crooks the prices of buffalo robes, muskrats, beaver, raccoons, martens, and deerskins were depressed, that only otters fetched good profits. "On the whole Prospects for furrs is Bade." In the spring of 1827, prices rose in New York but remained low in London. Astor sensed a bull market in the making and bought over $1 million worth of furs, thereby cornering the market on beaver, buffalo, muskrat, bear, and otter.

On July 6, 1827, the last big competitor besides General Ashley's outfit fell into Astor's hands. The prize was Joseph Renville's underfinanced but asset-rich Columbia Fur. The valuation of its various posts on the Missouri was $17 million. In buying out Renville and his partners, John Jacob eliminated competition from the Great Lakes and the upper Mississippi. The northern department was now without major opposition. With Renville and his partners came seven major posts in Council Bluffs, Teton River, and the Mandan villages, more than fifteen hundred miles above the mouth of the Missouri, and many clerks, trappers, and voyageurs. One was Lucien Fontenelle, a dashing native of New Orleans, who at the age of fifteen had run away from his aristocratic family and disappeared into the fur trade. Years later when he went back to New Orleans, he found that his sister Amelie had married wealth and position. She refused to recognize the still handsome but gnarled Lucien, even though a nursemaid identified him by a birthmark on his foot. Once more Fontenelle returned to the Missouri, where he married an Oto woman and raised a family, never to see New Orleans again.

Columbia Fur was renamed the Upper Missouri Outfit, or UMO. Astor was shrewd enough to offer jobs to Fontenelle and the most experienced men in the new acquisition. The same year, General Ashley sold out, and later ran for Congress and won. The buyers of the Rocky Mountain Fur Company were his ablest lieutenants: William Sublette, Smith, and David E. Jackson.

American Fur was now the most powerful trading company. The mergers had cost money, but they also brought Astor new wealth. The northern department, headed by Stuart, was all Astor's as were 90 percent of its profits. Crooks's western department was different, insofar as some partners furnished some capital. Nevertheless, Astor received interest on the capital he invested in both departments. At one time the interest reached $1 million. He also paid himself a salary, the size of which he kept secret.

An old mountain coot who wore tattered buckskins, spoke the Blackfoot tongue, and had a knack for diplomacy gave Astor a one-shot windfall. His name was Jacob Berger, and his appearance at Fort Union, a trading post on the Missouri at the confluence of the Yellowstone, surprised the fort's Scottish commander. Kenneth McKenzie affected a military uniform, polished belt and holster, a tunic with shiny metal buttons, and a plumed hat. He was the lord and master of Fort Union, which had become an American Fur outpost with the acquisition of the Upper Missouri Outfit. He was no kin of Donald McKenzie of the Astoria venture, but was a relative of the explorer of Canada, Alexander Mackenzie.

Kenneth McKenzie had been another victim of Hudson's Bay's takeover of the Northwest Company. With no seniority, the twenty-two-year-old trader had thrown in his lot with Joseph Renville, and with him sold out to American Fur in 1827. Now a thirty-year-old energetic trader, he was the head of Fort Union. The new post represented the partial realization of John Jacob's dream of a continent-spanning string of trading posts. Because it was on the edge of Blackfoot country, Fort Union was indeed a fort guarded by palisades, and partially built of stone. McKenzie's residence faced the heavy cross-beamed main gate and featured windows, a stone fireplace, and the rare convenience, an inside commode. Everybody at Fort Union dreaded his authority. "Imagine my surprise," wrote Charles Larpenteur, an American Fur clerk, in his diary, "to find myself in the presence of Mr. McKenzie, who was at that time considered the king of the Missouri; and, from the style in which he was dressed, I really thought he was a king." McKenzie was lavishly hospitable toward visitors. His guests included John James Audubon and the Pennsylvania artist George Catlin, whose portraits and watercolors of western life were admired in Paris and London but who would die ignored in his own country.

If McKenzie had one fear it was that William Sublette, Jedediah Smith, and David E. Jackson would beat him to establishing trade with the Blackfeet. General Ashley's successors were aggressive, fearless, and coordinated, and roamed all over the West. Smith had been to California twice. When Indians in Oregon had killed several of his men and stolen their pelts, Jedediah had made his way alone to the Hudson's Bay station at Fort Vancouver and borrowed a force to punish the Indians and recover most of his furs. Although the head of Fort Vancouver considered Smith a poacher, he bought Smith's furs and gave him a draft on a London bank for $20,000. Lately, Sublette, Smith, and Jackson were operating on the Snake River, in the Tetons, and—in the valley named after the latter—Jackson Hole.

In the spring of 1830, McKenzie went down to St. Louis to talk countermeasures. While he strategized with Crooks and Chouteau, Jedediah Smith did exactly what McKenzie feared. With young James Bridger, the former blacksmith, Jedediah entered the edges of Blackfoot country. Although he met no Blackfeet, he had a successful hunt, and returned on the Wind River in today's Bridger-Teton National Park.

A few months after McKenzie returned to Fort Union, Jacob Berger walked into the post. He had wandered these mountains longer than he could remember and lived long enough among Indians to speak the Blackfoot tongue. He told McKenzie of rivers deep in the Blackfoot country, where no white trapper had ever taken beaver. McKenzie was both eager and suspicious. When he asked why Berger was showing up at Fort Union, the old man shrugged. He had just come to have a look. He knew Hudson's Bay traders, but he knew the Blackfeet better, and had no loyalty to anybody.

McKenzie had to overcome his own men's reservations. Only an army could enter the Blackfoot country and come back alive, they said. After much talk, however, five men volunteered to accompany Berger on the diplomatic mission to the Blackfoot chiefs. McKenzie watched the six men and their packhorses leave and immediately wrote to Chouteau. Besides stressing the magnificent prospects if trade could be established, his letter suggested they set up steamboat service to Fort Union, or at least try to run a steamboat up the Missouri. A small, powerful side-wheeler could be built at a cost of no more than $7,000. It could leave St. Louis after the last ice broke and by June be back with the previous winter's furs.

It took Astor's approval to go forward. By return mail to Chouteau, John Jacob gave the go-ahead, and in October

1830, a contract was signed with a St. Louis firm to build the steamboat. McKenzie knew nothing of the contract. His worry was the fate of Berger and the five men.

Berger and the volunteers rode west for four weeks without seeing an Indian. As a precaution, they carried an unfurled flag so Indians would know at a distance that they were white men. They were at the Marias River in today's Chouteau County in north-central Montana when the volunteers froze in horror at the sight of mounted warriors coming toward them. Berger halted his little party, rode forward alone with the flag, and stopped. To his men's astonishment, he was recognized and soon welcomed to the Blackfoot village. The chiefs trusted him, but the negotiations were difficult. Their long hatred and distrust of all Americans were difficult to overcome, and the chiefs moved slowly. Winter turned into spring before they agreed to send a delegation of forty warriors and headmen to talk to McKenzie. The party set off, but when Fort Union came into view, the warriors and headmen hesitated. Only Jacob's gentle prodding made them move forward.

McKenzie handed the warriors expensive gifts, set bottles of good wine before them, and swore eternal friendship, honest trade, and generous prices. Negotiations resumed several days later after the warriors had recovered from their hangovers. In a letter to Chouteau, McKenzie took all the credit: "On my arrival at Fort Union last fall I fortunately found a Blackfoot interpreter, Berger, and by this means have been enabled to make those Indians acquainted with my views regarding them." He also claimed he had prepared the treaty that brought a temporary peace to the Blackfoot country, telling Chouteau, "I have lately negotiated a treaty of peace between the Assiniboine and the Blackfoot Indians, which I expect will be ratified." Historians would see old Berger's understanding of both Blackfoot and Assiniboine mores in the text:

> We send greeting to all mankind! Be it known unto all nations
> that the most ancient, most illustrious, and most numerous
> tribes of the redskins, lords of the soil from the banks of
> the great waters unto the top of the mountains upon which

the heavens rest, have entered into a solemn league and covenant to make, preserve and cherish a firm and lasting peace, that so long as the water runs, or the grass grows, they may hail each other as brethren, and smoke the calumet in friendship and security.

It was agreed that McKenzie could erect a trading post at a Blackfoot village at the confluence of the Missouri and the Marias. In October 1831, a Fort Union crew of thirty men arrived and began constructing a trading post they named Fort Piegan to flatter the nearby Piegans who traded with Hudson's Bay agents. During the first ten days after the post was built, twenty-four hundred beaver skins were traded, and before the end of the winter another four thousand beaver pelts were brought in. Unfortunately, a keelboat under the command of Lucien Fontenelle coming up the Missouri with $30,000 worth of goods for the 1832 trading was swept from its moorings one stormy night and sank. Two men drowned. Also lost were presents McKenzie was sending to the Blackfeet. A number of Indians accompanying the party suspected the boat had been scuttled deliberately. In their anger they burned down Fort Piegan.

Native American anger and desperation led to warfare between Indians and whites that year. Black Hawk and a thousand hungry Sac and Fox warriors, old men, women, and children began a trek east to their old homeland. Alarmed by their "invasion," Governor John Reynolds of Illinois called out the militia, and the federal government dispatched troops. Black Hawk's band caught the militia unaware and inflicted a stinging defeat. Reinforcements from other tribes did not arrive, however, and food supplies were exhausted. As the Indians tried to cross the Mississippi River, most of them were slaughtered. Black Hawk was captured and the survivors settled in Iowa. At the same time, the Cherokee were removed from Georgia, and in Mississippi and Alabama the remaining Cree were also expelled.

At Fort Union, the thirty men arrived safely with the sixty-four-hundred-pelt haul. They found McKenzie and the fort's residents impatiently awaiting the arrival of a steamboat.

Named the *Yellowstone,* the side-wheeler had set out from St. Louis on April 16, 1831. On board, sharing the quarterdeck with Captain B. Young, was Pierre Chouteau. The artist Catlin was Chouteau's guest. For six weeks the sturdy little side-wheeler had chugged upriver. On March 31, it passed the mouth of the Niobrara, where back in 1811 Manuel Lisa had sent a messenger asking Hunt to wait for him before entering Sioux country. The next stretch stopped all progress. The water level sank and the *Yellowstone* was stuck in mud. Days passed as Chouteau paced the riverbank watching the Nebraska sky for signs of rain. When no rain came, he sent two men upriver to Fort Tecumseh with orders to bring barges down to the stranded steamship. After a large part of the cargo was transferred to keelboats, the *Yellowstone* reached Fort Tecumseh on June 19. From here Chouteau wrote an enthusiastic letter to Astor in Paris. Six days were given over to making repairs and cleaning the machinery. In the amazingly short time of twelve days, the *Yellowstone* came within sight of Fort Union, her lofty twin chimneys pouring clouds of wood smoke into the pristine prairie air and the blasts from her whistle sending wild game fleeing. A thousand miles of the Missouri had been conquered by steam. Furs would come down to St. Louis in a matter of days. From France, John Jacob wrote Chouteau: "Your voyage in the *Yellowstone* attracted much attention in Europe, and has been noted in all the papers here."

Chouteau scrutinized the Upper Missouri Outfit's bottom line and found it far from profitable. The extraordinary haul of 6,400 beaver skins—which, if sold at St. Louis and not shipped to New York and London, would have fetched $50,000—was a onetime windfall. The Blackfeet and Assiniboine were difficult to deal with. They had burned down Fort Piegan over the keelboat whose loss was the UMO's, not theirs, even if it was carrying goods destined for them. If it wasn't for fear of losing face with Indians, trappers, and Sublette, Smith, and Jackson, Chouteau was ready to abandon the UMO outposts altogether. In a May 4, 1833, letter to Astor, he stated his concerns:

I am convinced that these expeditions have been an annual loss. But we have hopes for improvements from year to year. Generally the loss falls upon the traders. If the expeditions to the Upper Missouri had confined themselves entirely to the trade [at regular posts] its returns would have been greater and its expenses much less. Nevertheless, in spite of the unfavorable prospect, I do not think it politic to abandon this trade for the present. Just at the time when Sublette and Company are opposing us on the Missouri it is not for us to leave the mountains exclusively to them.

The Sublette brothers and Jedediah Smith had opened new territories where no Americans had ever traded—the upper reaches of the Colorado and the valley of the Great Salt Lake—and returned to St. Louis with beaver skins valued at $76,000. Like Ashley had done, the trio sold out to James Bridger and the other younger men in their company. The new Rocky Mountain Fur Company team set out with two hundred men and penetrated the Blackfoot country at Great Falls, Montana. The Blackfeet found the force too big to attack, and after a successful hunt, the Rocky Mountain men repaired to the northeast shore of Great Salt Lake. Here, they found a cache of Hudson's Bay furs, which they looted. They came back to St. Louis with pelts valued at $200,000.

John Jacob curbed his own urges to match the Rocky Mountain Company in men and resources. With the various acquisitions, American Fur had acquired forty-three strategic and permanent posts on the waters of the Missouri River system. The first one was Fort Leavenworth and the last one Fort McKenzie on the Marias, in the shadow of the Rockies in northwestern Montana.

In 1822, when Astor had decided to redouble the effort to squash any and all competitors in the western fur trade, he had been the largest fur trader in the world. Five years later, he was the most powerful. Better informed than most and with an undiminished knack for reading tea leaves, he approached his seventieth birthday with thoughts of withdrawing from the fur trade.

20

—⚉—

Estimable Grand-Papa

He was the richest man in America and was fond of saying, "The only hard step in building up my fortune was the first thousand dollars. After that it was easy." By 1830, he was also New York's only millionaire. Contemporaries described him as stout and square, with a high forehead and heavy features. Sketches and caricatures show him with a sharp, somewhat haughty stare under a thinning head of hair brushed forward to cover his pate. The nose is sharp, the jowls prominent with a hint of a double chin. As for his character, Horace Greeley, the journalist and reform politician, thought him a man in command of his passions, but selfish, grasping, and ruthless. There were numerous stories about his stinginess, exacting acquisitiveness, and merciless aggression. Fitz-Greene Halleck, who served as J. J.'s confidential secretary for sixteen years, teased his employer into making him a small legacy. "Mr. Astor, of what use is all this money to you?" Halleck asked once. "I would be content to live upon a couple of hundreds a year for the rest of my life, if I was only sure of it." Astor's will included a provision for paying an annuity to Halleck of just that— $200. He upbraided Charles Bristed, his favorite grandson, for taking butter and leaving it on his plate. Joseph Green Cogswell, a man of letters who met Astor through Washington Irving, would remember how the millionaire and he had visited a hotel dining room where J. J. said the owner would never make a success of the establishment. When Cogswell asked why, Astor said: "Don't you see what large lumps of sugar he puts in the bowl?" Another time when Cogswell and Astor were walking toward the pier for one of the harbor cruises that J. J. loved, Cogswell said he figured it cost them twenty-five cents every minute the boat was waiting. Astor tried to break into a run.

His effigy appeared on coins. The idea originated with Kenneth McKenzie. As a former Northwest trader, McKenzie had appreciated the way the now defunct Montreal company attached importance to giving gifts to Indians. American Fur should adopt the Northwest tradition and have medals struck, he told Pierre Chouteau Jr. Such a gesture would be especially appropriate for the planned post in Blackfoot country. Chouteau forwarded the idea to Ramsay Crooks. Could the government be persuaded to place at the disposal of American Fur Company medals, which would be delivered to the Indians in the name of the president of the United States? "A little indulgence of this nature on the part of the government will secure the confidence and friendship of these savages toward us," he wrote. Ramsay Crooks took the idea to Washington, where Lewis Cass, former governor of Michigan Territory and now secretary of war, agreed so long as the proposed gifts were not called medals but ornaments. In November, Crooks wrote back to Chouteau that the medals were "in the hands of the die-maker, who, I hope, will give us a good likeness *de notre estimable grand-papa.*"

Astor's profile was ample, virile, and severe in the manner of Roman emperors. Like coins struck during the reign of Louis XIV, the president of the American Fur Company is ennobled with a swirl of neck-long tresses. The strong, square face is softened by a double chin. The privilege of using the Astor coins was revoked by order of the secretary of war in 1844. By 1900, only three of the medals were known

Astor medal

to be in existence. No other entrepreneur ever had the U. S. government's permission to strike coins in his likeness.

For Astor, the business was indeed imperial.

—⚒—

A ten-pound keg of gunpowder cost him $2 in London. It reached New Orleans on one of his vessels and by steamboat was transported up the Mississippi to St. Louis. From here the keg traveled by keelboat to the post at Yellowstone, where it was transferred to packhorse or canoe to Bighorn country. Here it was parceled out, pound for pound. The price to Indians was $4 a pound or $40 for the keg. Indians paid in beaver skins. It took ten prime two-pound pelts to pay for the keg. The skins traveled to London the way the gunpowder had come and fetched $7 a pound, bringing Astor $140.

For buying the gunpowder, Astor deducted a 2 percent commission and 5 percent for handling the fur sale, leaving a gross of $132.96. Transportation, wages, and other expenses amounted to 25 percent. The remaining $97.96 was considered net profit. On his original investment of $2.00 in gunpowder, Astor's commissions and 50 percent of the net gave him $56.02. There was more. He charged interest on the $2 working capital he advanced, and in using his own ships made money on freight charges.

At the request of Secretary of War Cass, Thomas Forsyth, an agent who had been on the frontier for forty years, undertook a study of Astor's profits: His report listed American Fur by its chief traders:

> Mr. [J. P.] Cabanne, a member of the American Fur Company, has in his division all the Indians on the Missouri as high as a point above Council Bluffs, including the Pawnee Indians of the interior, in about a southwest direction from his establishment. Mr. Auguste O. Chouteau (Pierre's brother) has within his department all the Indians of the Osage Country, and others who may visit his establishment, such as Cherokees, Chickasaw, and other Indians. Messrs McKenzie, Laidlaw & Lamont have in their limits the Sioux Indians of the Missouri, and as high up the river as they choose to send or go.

James Parton, who knew the octogenarian Astor, called him "one of the ablest boldest and most successful operators that ever lived" in an 1863 *Harper's Magazine* piece. *Harper's* was less generous and editorialized that Astor's goal was "to get all that he could and to keep nearly all that he got." But John Jacob was reaching the age where the verdict of posterity began to preoccupy him. He might have wanted to be portrayed as a broad-minded humanitarian, but civic duties had never been his forte. He had given $5,000 of the $20,000 required to build a home for old women and made donations to New York City's fire department, but that was all. He was lumped together with Stephen Girard, the Philadelphia banker with whom he had propped up the Madison administration with war loans. Horace Mann, the leader of the Whig Party in Massachusetts and known as the "father" of the public school system, called the two men insane for not giving back more to the society that had enriched them. We do not know whether the criticism hit home or if Washington Irving whispered the idea of endowing the city of New York with a library. In any case it was to Cogswell that Astor confided his desire to devote a part of his fortune to a worthy cause. A public library, Cogswell told him, would enhance the Astor name and give New Yorkers access to the cultural heritage of the world.

—⁓—

Astor had first hinted at his retirement to Crooks in a letter from Geneva dated August 20, 1825.

> With regard as to whether I continue in the trade I really cannot now tell. Much will depend on situation of matters when I get home, but whether I do or not I never had any other thought than that I did retire, I would like you and Mr. Stuart to be fully satisfied. I must say that I never intended to make any arrangements contrary to your interest. Quite otherwise, nor did I contemplate that you or Mr. Stuart would ever separate from the concern while I continued. I hope that both of you on reflection have come in the late agreement. You tell me indeed that you will at all events go on.

The millions gave John Jacob and his family notoriety— people pointed to them in the streets—if not respect. New York's rich were their neighbors in town and in the country. The best addresses for wellborn New Yorkers were on Broadway below Cortlandt Street, with the Battery the favorite place for Sunday strolls. At Hellgate, John Jacob and Sarah's neighbors were old Dutch and English families— the Rhinelanders, the Crugers, the Schermerhorns, and the Gracies. Sarah was a relation of the Brevoorts, her son William had married Margaret Armstrong, and two of their sons in turn would wed patrician daughters, but Sarah never attained, nor perhaps aspired to, the rank of hostess. The Astors experienced the joys and sorrows common to most households, but their celebrity made it difficult for them to keep disputes, jealousies, and tragedies to themselves.

As if being the heir to his father's millions wasn't enough, William inherited $1 million from childless Uncle Henry and Aunt Dorothea in 1832. In Lafayette Place, a leafy street running between Broadway and the Bowery, William built a magnificent brick mansion, which, in English fashion, Margaret staffed with servants dressed in livery. For her husband she hired a valet, who supposedly became so disgusted with what he considered his master's untidiness that he quit and went to work for President Martin Van Buren. There was enough money left for Margaret to renovate her late father's country home. She added a wing and a tower with a superb view of the Hudson and the Catskills. Inspired by Sir Walter Scott's poem, she renamed the estate Rokeby.

Margaret was a trendsetter both in town and country. Lafayette Place became a fashionable address after the Schermerhorns took the plot next to William and Margaret's. Other first-rank families moved in. Like his father, William remained a man of routine, rising early to deal with correspondence before breakfast at nine, and a walk to his office on Prince Street. Whereas J. J. allowed himself to leave the office at two in the afternoon, William stayed until five-thirty, when he closed up and walked home again. Margaret and he often entertained at home. Guests included in-laws, the Livingstons, and the Brevoorts—Henry had married Laura Carson of South Carolina. Also present at the William B. Astors' soirees were young, rich, and more or less idle foundations of the social register, the Stuyvesants, the Jays, the Crugers, and the Schermerhorns.

His father's typical day was more unassuming. John Jacob had dinner at three in the afternoon, followed by a glass of beer and three games of checkers. If the weather was fine, he might have a horse saddled up for a sunset ride to look for land to buy. At night, it was either the theater or entertaining at home. He enjoyed having his granddaughter Emily Ward sing to him. He was credited with organizing the first orchestra in the city of more than twelve musicians. With John K. Beekman, a distant relative of Sarah's, he bought the Park Theater in 1806 for $50,000. The playhouse was destroyed by fire fourteen years later and rebuilt as New York's best. He read a lot of history, perhaps books William lent him. Parton, the first Astor biographer, maintained John Jacob did not collect books, but William Waldorf claimed his great-grandfather had several thousand volumes.

—◊◊◊—

Tragedy and scandal touched the principled Mr. and Mrs. William Backhouse Astor when their pretty and vivacious daughter Emily married. Her husband was Sam Ward Jr., heir to a banking fortune, and famous for his wit, charm, and love of good food and wine. The newlyweds moved into a large house on Bond Street just a few blocks south of Lafayette Place. A daughter, Margaret Astor Ward, to be known as "Maddie," was born. Emily was soon pregnant again. Sadly, she died during the birth and the son she bore was dead within a few days.

The family was devastated. The death brought William closer to his eldest son, John Jacob III, but Margaret never quite recovered from the shock of her daughter's death. When doctors insisted the grief-stricken woman take a walk every day, she had seventeen-year-old Laura and fifteen-year-old Mary accompany her. Mother and daughters, veiled and dressed in black, were a sight on Broadway.

The bereavement of son-in-law Sam, however, was brief. He married a beautiful Creole girl named Marie Angeline Grymes, known as "Medora" and described as showy and fascinating. Sam's sister Louisa was visiting at Rokeby when William first heard the news. For once, he lost his habitual self-possession and ordered Louisa out of the house. John Jacob's wrath matched his son's when Sam turned over the Bond Street house to his new wife. Henry Brevoort recorded J. J.'s feelings and noted how salutary anger was in stirring the "estimable grand-papa" into action:

> An untoward event has just happened in his family, which has stirred his ire; a thing which always does him good. Master Sam W—— has married Miss Medora Grymes and settled upon her his house in Bond Street, which house had been purchased & previously given or settled upon his first

wife, but by our laws, became his, after her decease. This affair sticks deep into the old gentleman's gizzard. He views it as a sort of impeachment of his accustomed sagacity; a sort of outwitting & overreaching in the part of bargaining.

Historians would wonder whether John Jacob was right. Sam's father, some records show, gave the Bond Street house to his son and Emily. Sam Ward Sr. lived in Bond Street himself. If the Astors had given Sam and Emily a house, the young couple might have been expected to settle in Lafayette Place. Young Sam backed down, however, not by handing the Bond Street house to the Astors, but by agreeing to J. J.'s demand that one-year-old Maddie be brought up by William and Margaret.

John Jacob's energies had been concentrated too much on amassing wealth for him to learn to give away money to strangers. Toward his extended family, however, he was more than generous. His sister Catherine and her husband, George Ehninger, had settled in New Jersey, where George became a distiller. John Jacob and Catherine had their fights. She thought her brother's wealth was going to his head, and needled him by reminding him of his humble beginnings as a baker's peddler. Yet when George Ehninger was imprisoned for insolvency, his brother-in-law allowed him to make a fresh start in New York. When George died in an accident while burning spirits, John Jacob sent the couple's son, also named George, on voyages to Canton. Young George married the daughter of one of the Astor captains. Besides his sisters Catherine and Elisabeth, John Jacob had brought his half sister Ann Eve to New York. Elisabeth married one of her brother's employees, and J. J. set the couple up in business.

William and Margaret had given John Jacob and Sarah seven grandchildren. A girl named Sarah, after her grandmother, died young and Emily of fever after childbirth. Dorothea brought her total of Langdon children to four boys and four girls. In 1827, Eliza and Vincent arrived from Paris, taking the opportunity of a diplomatic mission that von Rumpff was making to Washington. Three years later, Eliza was back alone. Vincent wanted his wife out of harm's way when pent-up opposition to King Charles X resulted in barricades in Paris. By the time Eliza reached New York, however, the monarchy was restored with "Citizen King" Louis-Philippe on the throne. Although anxious to get back to Paris, she stayed to help nurse Dorothea, ill after the birth of her last child, Eugene. When doctors recommended a change of air, it was agreed that Dorothea and her children should go to Europe with Eliza. The sisters took young Charles Bristed with them. John Jacob's munificence toward this grandson was special. He brought up Magdalen's son, sent him to Yale and later to Trinity College, Cambridge, and bequeathed to him both the Broadway residence and Hellgate and enough money to allow him to live a gentleman's life. He became an author of twenty-one books. His most famous was *The Upper Ten Thousand: Sketches of American Society.* He told his readers the title, coined by a fashion magazine, was an exaggeration. Society should be counted in the hundreds, not the thousands. His nephew's wife, Caroline (née Schermerhorn), would put the number at four hundred, the number of guests her ballroom could accommodate.

Dorothea Langdon spent four years in Paris. We know little of her religious sentiments, but a woman in her entourage reinforced her sister Eliza's faith. Under the influence of Phoebe Maybee, Eliza reaffirmed the religious fervor she had first expressed when J. J. had taken her to meet Uncle Melchior and Aunt Verona and their Moravian brethren. Although the von Rumpffs were welcome at the court of the liberal Louis-Philippe and Queen Marie-Amélie, Eliza gave up court appearances, balls, theatergoing, and other worldly leisure, and with her friend Albertine de Broglie became active in charities. Nature had denied Eliza children of her own, but her husband's position and her father's wealth allowed her to import inspirational books and establish a library for the children of English-speaking residents of Paris. The library proved so popular that similar amenities were opened in two provincial towns and in Brussels, Naples,

Florence, and St. Petersburg. John Jacob gave her the villa at Genthod, where she opened a school.

In 1832, as the *Yellowstone* was chugging up the Missouri, John Jacob followed Eliza, Vincent, Dorothea, and the children to Paris. Daughters, son-in-law, and grandchildren welcomed him. He renewed old friendships and secured an introduction to Louis-Philippe. He also met Marie-Joseph Motier, and the marquis de Lafayette, the last great link with the French and American Revolutions. Lafayette was out of favor with the Citizen King and told Astor the monarchy was losing touch.

The news from home was not all as cheerful as Chouteau's report on the *Yellowstone*'s triumph. Magdalen's death in 1832 was followed by the death of William's infant daughter and John Jacob's sister, Catherine Ehninger. In 1833, Henry, his last surviving brother, passed away, four years after Melchior had died.

J. J.'s stay in Paris was less enjoyable than earlier sojourns. Poor health and "bad nerves" led him to consult a succession of physicians, and to contemplate retirement. A nasty fall was followed by a painful ulcer operation. The surgery prompted him to write to Chouteau: "I think now to Remain in Europe till Spring in Deed I am not able to go back & in winter I Do not wish to." He was under the care of Baron Guillaume Dupuytren, surgeon to Louis XVIII, and famous for his research in surgical pathology and treatment of aneurysms. Dr. Dupuytren believed in exercise and on some days went riding in the Bois de Boulogne with Astor. On one such outing, his patient remained obstinately silent for so long that Dupuytren began to fear Astor was suffering from some secret pain or trouble. When Astor finally talked, it was to say that the 2.5 percent interest rate Parisian banks were willing to pay on the 2 million francs he had on deposit would make any man's blood boil.

Instead of sailing to New York in the spring of 1833, he went for a lengthy convalescence at Genthod. He had worked since he was fifteen and was the richest man in America. Still, the idea of sitting wrapped in a shawl on the veranda at Hellgate and watching the ships on the East

River didn't appeal to him. In New York, William thought his father needed the jolt of activity, the bustle of the office. In January 1834, William wrote to his brother-in-law Vincent von Rumpff: "I was much disappointed by my father's not returning to this Country in October. I hope he will however certainly return in the Spring. Occupation of mind which he will get here is, I believe, the only cure for his nervous affliction."

Astor had begun to dispose of his ships, and his executives wondered what to believe. When Green Bay trader John Lawe wrote to David Stuart that he had heard rumors that Astor was about to withdraw from the fur trade, Stuart had written back: "Pray, give yourself no concern about Mr. Astor's retiring . . . my opinion is that he will never retire until he is called." Crooks was of the same opinion, writing to Chouteau: "The business seems to him like an only child and he cannot muster the courage to part with it." As usual, John Jacob was ahead of his lieutenants. He wrote to William to let him know if Crooks forwarded any proposals for the future of American Fur. In Geneva, he dictated a letter in March 1833 to Crooks's in-laws and Pierre Chouteau's former partners:

> Messrs. Bernard Pratte and Company, St. Louis
> Gentlemen,
> Wishing to retire from the concern in which I am engaged with your house, you will please take this as notice thereof, and that the engagement entered into on the 7th of May 1829, between your house and me, on the part of the American Fur Company, will expire with the [end] of the present year on the terms expressed in said agreement.
> I am Gentlemen your humble Servt.

21

—◊—

The Bigger Picture

John Jacob's return to New York in the spring of 1834
was precipitous. He wanted to attend the wedding of
Sarah Langdon, who as a six-year-old had told him she
was his granddaughter. By the time he applied for passage
aboard the *Utica,* the first available packet, all staterooms
were booked. The captain, however, sacrificed his cabin for
the wealthy passenger.

John Jacob had crossed the Atlantic in all kinds of
weather, but when the *Utica* hit storms in the English
Channel, he panicked and demanded to be put ashore in
England. The captain of the *Utica* was none other than
Frederick de Peyster, who some thirty years earlier had
extricated nearly three-quarters of a million dollars' worth
of Astor merchandise from a legal snarl in Canton. Now
John Jacob offered de Peyster $1,000 to place him aboard
a pilot boat. So persistent was the aging millionaire that
the onetime China skipper agreed to alter course if the ship
failed to reach the open sea in the next few hours. A change
of wind took the *Utica* into the Atlantic, but gales forced
the ship toward the Irish coast. This time, Astor upped his
offer to $10,000 if de Peyster would deliver him from the

bucking vessel. The captain said that if he tried to put into an unfamiliar harbor he would lose his insurance coverage. "But I'll insure you," the frantic Astor shouted.

There are at least two versions of what happened next. In one retelling, John Jacob rushed below deck and came back up with a piece of paper filled with illegible scrawl. "No one can read it," de Peyster objected. "Let one of the other gentlemen draw up a proper draft. You sign it. Then I'll get you to land." In another version, de Peyster suggested *he* write out the promissory note for Astor to sign. One way or another, Astor came to his senses.

Within hours the wind abated and the *Utica* resumed her course. The paranoia repeated itself, however, when the ship was off Newfoundland. This time, Astor wanted the captain to hail an outbound vessel and tell its master he'd pay $1,000 to be taken *back* to Europe. The nightmare crossing ended April 4 when the *Utica* berthed in New York. As he came down the gangplank, William and Mayor Philip Hone were there to tell him his wife had died. Sarah had expired eight days earlier.

He returned to a home peopled only by servants. William and Margaret did their best to comfort him. When Dorothea heard of her mother's death, she hurried back with the children. In his diary, Hone noted how J. J. appeared feeble and ill, adding that he doubted the ailing millionaire would survive by much his wife of nearly fifty years. On May 4, 1834, John Jacob described his feelings to Wilson Price Hunt: "While absent, I lost wife, brother, daughter, sister, grandchildren and many friends and I expect to follow very soon."

Premonitions of his own demise led to introspection. He had set things in motion with his letter from Switzerland to Bernard Pratte & Company, but that was just one contract. We do not know whether Sarah's death or a reassessment of his remaining days was responsible, but within weeks he decided to sell the American Fur Company. The last fifteen years had been fruitful. How fruitful? The government agent John Dougherty made the following estimate on the 1815–1830 fur trade:

26,000 buffalo skins a year for 15 years @ $3 each	$1,170,000
25,000 beaver skins a year for 15 years @ $4 each	1,500,000
4,000 otter skins a year for 15 years @ $3 each	180,000
12,000 coon skins a year for 15 years @25¢ each	45,000
150,000 lbs deer skins a year for 15 years @ 33¢ per lb	742,500
37,500 muskrat skins a year for 15 years @ 15¢ each	112,500
Total	$3,750,000

Minus expenses		
20 clerks, 15 years @ $500 a year	150,000	
200 men, 15 years @ $150 a year	450,000	
Merchandise	1,500,000	
Total profits		$1,650,000
Average annual profit		$110,000

For comparison, one Northwest Company outfit that set out for the McKenzie River in 1804 returned in 1806 with the following:

	Large skins	Small skins	
Fine beavers	23,438	11,402	
Common beavers	25,319	13,438	
	48,757	24,840	Total 73,597

Muskrats	51,003
Martens	40,440
Fine otters	4,001
Common otters	2,132
Minks	4,338
Fishers	2,268
Cervier wolves	1,131
Large black bears	1,591
Cubs	529
Large brown and grizzlies	272

Cubs	53
Bears, damaged and staged	290
Cubs	65
Deer skins	4,065
Dressed original skins	3,497
Kitts	2,508
Wolves	4,502
Wolves, bad	582
Raccoons	745
Wolverines	798
Red and cross foxes	1,746
Silver foxes	26
Dressed cariboux skins	173
Deer skins, damaged	906
Parchment and shaved original	323
Buffalo robes	1,135

What stuns the modern reader is the mass slaughter of animals. The American Fur Company figures—390,000 buffalo and 375,000 beavers over fifteen years—represent only the admittedly busy years between 1815 and 1830, and do not include Canadian and Russian culls. At the February 15, 1847, anniversary celebration of the founding of St. Louis, the value of the the city's fur trade had been between $200,000 and $300,000 a year, or between $8 and $12 million over the previous forty years. The arrival of the steamboat in the heart of buffalo country caused hide hunting by the Kiowa, Blackfeet, Sioux, and other Plains tribes to soar. For the first time, there was a way to haul the bulky robes east, where they were becoming popular as a covering during cold weather travel and for leather goods. Modern scholars estimate that before 1840, sixty thousand Plains Indians killed half a million bison a year.*

—∞—

John Jacob had his finger on the American Fur Company's ledger. He was conscious of the diminishing returns and

*Dr. Drew Isenberg, *The Destruction of the Bison: An Environmental History, 1750–1920,* Cambridge, U.K.: Cambridge University Press, 2000.

saw a bigger picture than William and Ramsay Crooks
and Pierre Chouteau out West. Not that he was secretive
about his insights. Before illness made him a patient of Dr.
Dupuytren, he had visited London and from there written:
"I very much fear beaver will not sell very soon unless
very fine. It appears that they make hats of silk in place
of beaver." Crooks and Chouteau could also read *Silliman's
Journal,* the fur industry trade paper. One hundred fifty
years before the acceptance of environmental and ecological
parameters, *Silliman's Journal* informed its readers in its
June 1834 issue:

> It appears that the fur trade must henceforth decline. The
> advanced state of geographical science shows that no new
> countries remain to be explored. In North America the ani-
> mals are slowly decreasing from the persevering efforts and
> indiscriminate slaughter practiced by the hunters and by
> the appropriation of the uses of man of those forests and
> rivers, which have afforded protection. They recede with the
> aborigines before the tide of civilization, but a diminished
> supply will remain in the mountains and uncultivated tracts
> of this and other countries, if the avidity of the hunter can
> be restrained within proper limitations.

Astor also saw the other end of the picture. He might
not be the trendiest of dandies, but his money allowed
him to travel among aristocrats in Europe and to move in
influential circles in New York and Washington. Besides his
fashion-plate granddaughters, he was the mature friend of
trendsetters such as Henry Brevoort and his former tenant
Aaron Burr. Chinese silk was losing its cachet as European
textile mills produced more varied materials. Even the taste
in tea was changing as leaves from Japan and Java and,
within a few years, India, reached the West. In London, he
had noticed that smart gentlemen were wearing silk hats.
"Beavers" were disappearing because it was now cheaper
to make the felt from the skins of rabbits. In addition
to changes in fashion, the growing suspicion that pelts
were responsible for the spread of cholera accelerated his
exit from the fur trade. The second of the great cholera
pandemics had reached Europe while he was sick in Paris. It

began in India in 1817, reached Russia in 1830, spread from Moscow to St. Petersburg, and went into Germany in 1832. Cholera was carried to North America, entering Canada and spreading south along the Mississippi Valley before heading east to New York and Boston. The infection was present in most of the United States and did not disappear until 1838. It was only in 1883 that the German physician Robert Koch discovered that the *Vibrio cholerae* bacterium was the cause of the disease.

—⁓—

Loneliness made Astor ask his personal secretary to move in with him. Fitz-Greene Halleck was a man of letters twenty-seven years Astor's junior. Halleck's business skills were no doubt a requisite for his position, but his social polish and literary standing were decisive qualifications as well.

Edgar Allan Poe would rate Halleck a close second to William Cullen Bryant among American poets. Fourteen years before Halleck entered Astor's employ, he and his friend Joseph Rodman Drake had written the lively *Croaker Papers* for New York newspapers. When Drake died in 1820, Halleck had composed his most famous elegy, beginning "Green be the turf above thee." His long poem "Fanny" was in the vein of social satire and his "Red Jacket" eulogized the Indian chief of the Tuscarora. Working for Astor made him neglect his poetry. "In literary circles the blame for his silence was, of course, ascribed to the pressure of official duties, together with a desire not to expose himself to the prejudice which business men of the day felt toward the literati," Kenneth Porter wrote. A literary journal blamed Astor for the poet's silence with the battle cry: Discharge Halleck, oh Astor! Halleck himself lamented in "Alnwick Castle" that

> The power that bore my spirit up
> Above this bank-note world—is gone.

Once Astor made the decision to sell out, deals fell quickly into place. On June 1, 1834, the first business monopoly in American history was split into two. J. J. had great respect for Ramsay Crooks's abilities and sold the northern department to a company of which Crooks was the principal partner. The new owners retained the name American Fur Company. The same day, the western department was sold to Pratte, Chouteau & Company. William had no objections. At forty-two, he was happy to be free of responsibilities for an empire that, he told Secretary of War Lewis Cass, was worth $1 million.

The sale and partition inevitably reshuffled the fur trade. They also provoked clashes of personalities, quarrels, and conflicts. Chouteau wanted to drop the underperforming Upper Missouri Outfit, and when an alarmed Kenneth McKenzie rushed to St. Louis, the new boss only offered a four-year extension of the current contract. McKenzie swallowed and signed, only to see James Bridger, his nemesis from the Blackfoot trade war, take trapping parties through the mountains for Chouteau. Lucien Fontenelle also switched sides. Crooks suggested Chouteau abandon the mountain trade altogether.

New, inexperienced men moved in, thinking they could become the next John Jacob Astor. The most famous was Benjamin Louis de Bonneville, a Frenchman who had come to America with Thomas Paine and, at Lafayette's recommendation, entered West Point in 1819. Captain Bonneville met Astor in New York several times, resigned his commission, and with one of the old Astorians funded and led an expedition that set out for the Rockies in 1832. In the Absaroka Range in western Wyoming, he erected a post that became known as Fort Nonsense, or Bonneville's Folly, because it was so high up it was snowbound over half the year and no use was ever made of it. Five years later Bonneville wrote his story and sought to have it published. When the manuscript found no publisher, Washington Irving bought it, added to the text, and issued it as *The Rocky Mountains: Or Scenes, Incidents and Adventures in the Far West.* His brother Peter Irving wrote after reading it: "It is a picture of a singular class of people midway between the savage state and civilization, who will soon cease to exist."

In 1843, organized fur trade in the Rockies came to an end.

—⚹—

The Oregon Territory—and its boundaries—remained the subject of tortuous, decade-long negotiations. Britain wanted a boundary westward along the forty-ninth parallel only to the Columbia. From there the U.S.-Canadian border should follow the river to the sea, which would have made today's Seattle and three-quarters of the state of Washington Canadian. After all, hadn't Astor's people sold the Columbia River foothold in 1813? A bill was brought before Congress in 1840 that assumed Oregon to be American, recommended a series of fortifications, and offered land to pioneers. Louis McLane, a friend of Astor, was a former senator from Delaware who, as U.S. ambassador to England had negotiated a resumption of trade between the British West Indies and the United States. He believed he could soothe British irritation and nudge London to agree to a border along the forty-ninth parallel all the way to the Pacific. Presidential hopeful Daniel Webster, who had spent 1839 in London, wanted the United States to have a deepwater port on the West Coast: not at the mouth of the Columbia with its sandbar, but San Francisco or, failing that, a harbor on Puget Sound. In negotiations with his British counterpart, Foreign Secretary Lord Ashburton, Webster suggested Britain help persuade Mexico to sell San Francisco to the United States. In return, perhaps Puget Sound and the Strait of Juan de Fuca could be finessed so that the United States would get the Olympic Peninsula and Canada maybe a chunk of the mainland. The Webster-Ashburton Treaty of 1842 was not entirely satisfactory to either party and a war loomed when Democratic presidential candidate James Polk barnstormed with demands that Oregon be "reoccupied" right up to the 54° 40' parallel—that is, to the southern tip of Alaska. Once elected, President Polk moderated his stance and, in 1846, agreed to the boundary with Canada at the forty-ninth parallel.*

---

*The Oregon Territory was organized in 1848 and the state of Washington carved out of the territory in 1853.

The Oregon Trail, the 2,170-mile road from Independence, Missouri, to Fort Vancouver on the Columbia River (across from the future Portland, Oregon) that was used by nearly four hundred thousand people, began with the Astorians. David Stuart and Ramsay Crooks had discovered the South Pass, in Wyoming, only seven thousand feet above sea level and with easy gradients. They published an account of their journey in which they pronounced the route entirely practicable for wagons. From South Pass the main trail went south to Fort Bridger, in the southwestern corner of today's Wyoming, before turning into the Bear River Valley and heading north to Fort Hall in present-day Idaho. From here, the trail followed the Boise River to the Snake, where it entered what is now Oregon and continued north across the Blue Mountains to reach the Columbia River at The Dalles. Shorter and more direct routes were found along some parts of the trail, but they were often more difficult. In 1826, Jedediah Smith connected the route with southern California by an extension from Great Salt Lake to the Colorado River and across the Mojave to the Spanish settlements. The following year he opened the route between San Francisco and the Great Salt Lake across the Sierra Nevada.*
As travel increased with the inflow of emigrants, various shortcuts were found; but as late as the 1840s, there were no settlements between Independence and Fort Vancouver. The only evidence of white men's presence travelers saw on the trek were two dozen or so fur traders' posts.

Steamboats came to the Columbia and quickly took over communications with the interior. Railways followed—the first wood-burning locomotives were shipped out via Cape Horn—and the Oregon Railway & Navigation Company was born. Astor was an investor and a director of the Mohawk & Hudson Railroad, the first railway in New York State. The Baltimore & Ohio Railroad began carrying revenue traffic

---

*Jedediah Smith withdrew from the fur trade in 1830. The following year he entered the Santa Fe Trail trade, but on the first expedition, he was killed by Comanche Indians at a water hole on the Cimarron River.

in 1827 and over the next eighteen years lengthened its tracks to Chicago, St. Louis, and the Great Lakes. The Civil War slowed the expansion and it would be 1869 before the Union Pacific, laying track west from Omaha, Nebraska, met the Central Pacific, building east from Sacramento, California, created the first transcontinental link. Settlements, commerce, industry, agriculture, and other railroads followed. To the north, the tracks were laid along the Astorians' trail from Independence to Casper, Wyoming, and again from the Bear River on the Utah-Wyoming line to Willamette, Oregon. The names of fur traders survived as railway depots—Laramie, Wyoming, from the trapper Jacques La Ramie; Bridger and Chouteau in Montana; Smith's Fork (for Jedediah) and Boise (for a Hudson's Bay post) in Idaho. Fontenelle got a reservoir named after him just south of Sublette County in western Wyoming, while John Day gave his name to a river in Oregon.

22

—◊—

Writing about It

Self-made rich men want to be remembered for their triumphs. Astor had a book written about a failure. To make sure the story got told right, he commissioned the best-selling author of the day. Washington Irving was shrewd enough not to accept compensation from J. J., preferring instead to own 100 percent of the publishing rights. "He was too proverbially rich a man for me to permit the shadow of a pecuniary favor to rest on our intercourse," Irving wrote some years later.

Irving felt he had known Astor most of his life. He had traveled to Montreal as a twenty-year-old law graduate and there met Henry Brevoort. At a loss as to what to do in life, young Henry had listened to his aunt Sarah's advice and agreed to learn to become an Astor fur agent. The two young men had agreed to meet again after they returned to New York. Irving had entered the law offices of Henry Masterton and for a summer fell in love with Brevoort's sister Margaret. Since then, Henry Brevoort had done well working for Astor and was among the wealthiest men in New York.

In 1832, when the author dined with the widowed John Jacob and the subject of Astoria came up, he was New

York's prodigal son back from seventeen years overseas. At forty-nine, he was the most popular short-story writer, an essayist, a historian, and a diplomat, and the first American author to gain recognition in European literary circles. Born in New York City, the youngest of eleven children of a petty officer and the granddaughter of an Anglican curate, he grew up indulged by parents and siblings. He was schooled at home. Two of his brothers were newspaper and magazine editors, and Washington made his writing debut at twenty-five with light verse, satiric pieces, and the energetic parody *Diedrich Knickerbocker's A History of New York from the Beginning of the World to the End of the Dutch Dynasty.* The story, told by the fictional Diedrich Knickerbocker, mocks the pretensions of early historians, and the tone becomes increasingly pointed. The writing was interrupted by the death of Washington's fiancée Mathilde Hoffman and only finished in 1809. Mathilde's death was the great tragedy of his life. He never married, but was said to have been enamored of Mary Wollstonecraft Shelley. He and the Astors had met in Paris the year after *The Sketch Book of Geoffrey Crayon, Gent.* made him famous in London and New York. The thirty-two whimsical and sentimental pieces of *The Sketch Book* include his two famous tales, "Rip Van Winkle" and "The Legend of Sleepy Hollow."

After years of wanderings in Spain and writings on Christopher Columbus, Irving's attentive and ever-protective brothers got him a post as embassy secretary in London. According to Ambassador Louis McLane and Martin Van Buren, who as secretary of state in the Jackson administration was in London negotiating a U.S.-British West Indies trade treaty, Irving's devotion to secretarial work was less than inspiring. His return to the United States, however, was triumphant. The May 31, 1832, edition of the *New York Evening Post* described in detail the toasts and eulogies of a grandiose dinner headed by Mayor Philip Hone and attended by three hundred eminent citizens. In a tactful speech Irving assured his countrymen of his unchanging love for them and America, although he found them "all pervadingly commonplace." He was restless in New York, and joined an expedition to the land of the Osages and the Pawnee. In St. Louis he met Pierre Chouteau, who told him tales of a frontiersman returning to an Indian village in search of his betrothed and of the burial and returning spirit of the Great Manitou. Via steamboat, Irving reached Independence, Missouri. He scribbled quick impressions for the book he was planning:

> Steam boat aground with two flats each side of her. We take part of cargo on board—moonlight—light of fires—chant & chorus of Negro boat men—men strolling about docks with cigars negros dancing before furnaces glassy surface of River. Undulations made by boat wavering light of moon & stars. Silent, primeval forest sleeping in sunshine on each side still; forest—forest—forest. . . . Beautiful moon rise on Illinois— fire of woodman at front of island red-yellow moon—silver star—calm, cobalt-green sky reflected in river—here & there at far distance a solitary light twinkles.

Catering to public taste, Irving wrote *A Tour on the Prairies* (1835), with prettified portraits of buffalo, wild horses, and the customs of the Osages instead of what was in fact a rough experience for the author. The rancorous James Fenimore Cooper, who since the Leatherstocking novels thought the frontier history and folklore was his territory, hated the book.

Irving was in search of financial security when, over dinner, Astor told him he had boxes and trunks full of documents that in the hands of someone like Irving would add up to a grand story of men who, for the most part, were still alive. The widower saw the book as a chapter of history and wanted the biographer of Christopher Columbus to write it. He added that he himself felt "the want of occupation and amusement." Perhaps Irving might "find something of both in the progress of the work."

Irving nodded. The story was colorful enough, but did it add up to special pleading? Astor said he still hoped Congress would agree to put the now abandoned outpost, as well as its upriver Fort Vancouver rival, under the American flag. Irving asked himself if he could put his name to such a corporate hagiography. Or was it one for the record, the story of a thrilling roll of the dice that had come up snake eyes? He believed part of his task might be to add to the literature on the Indians. After the book was published, he would write to S. G. Drake, the author of several books on Native Americans, that he wished "a complete depository of facts concerning these singular and heroic races that are gradually disappearing from the face of the earth." We do not know whether it was out of the question for him to spend time and money to travel to the coast of Oregon himself. Perhaps he considered it unnecessary, as Astor promised him masses of documentation.

Irving would need a researcher, someone to go through the papers, classify them, and put them in chronological order, and suggested his nephew Pierre Munro Irving for the job. Pierre was William Irving's eldest son, a twenty-four-year-old would-be writer who three years earlier had arrived unexpectedly at his uncle's residence in Madrid. Pierre admired Washington Irving, who in turn had developed a fondness for the young man. He had suggested Pierre might finish his grand tour of Europe in London and help with the publication of the Columbus manuscript. The offer had proved premature. Perhaps for a fee, Washington now suggested, Pierre would be willing to undertake the preliminary work of examining the records and preparing a rough outline of the Astoria chronicle. A deal was struck. Astor agreed to pay Pierre Munro Irving $3,000 as a researcher. In addition, he suggested that author and researcher move in with him and Fitz-Greene Halleck at Hellgate, the country residence overlooking the East River.

Pierre had recently gone to Jacksonville, Illinois, on a business venture, where Irving wrote him:

> John Jacob Astor is extremely desirous of having a work written on the subject of his settlement of Astoria . . . something that might secure to him the reputation of having originated the enterprise and founded the colony that are likely to have such important results in the history of commerce and colonization.

The old gentleman has applied to me repeatedly in the matter, offering to furnish abundance of materials in letters, journals, and verbal narratives, and to pay liberally for time and trouble. Mr. Astor is a strong-minded man, and one from whose conversation much curious information is to be derived. He feels the want of occupation and amusement, and thinks he may find something of both in the progress of this work. You would find him very kindly disposed, for he was an early friend of your father, for whose memory he entertains great regard; and he has always been on terms of intimacy with your uncle Peter and myself, besides knowing more or less of others of our family. Halleck, the poet, resides a great deal with him at present, having a handsome salary for conducting his affairs.

Pierre found the proposition attractive and was soon in New York. In August 1835, uncle and nephew moved in at Hellgate. While Pierre was busy sorting the Astoria papers, which included letters from the ill-fated Captain Thorn and complete accounts of the Pacific Fur Company, Washington polished various manuscripts and wrote the memories of his 1817 visit to Walter Scott at Abbotsford, and, a year after Lord Byron's death in 1824, to Byron's ancestral seat at Newstead Abbey.

John Jacob loved the literary activity. Friends who visited and stayed for bachelor dinners included former secretary of state McLane and Mayor Hone. Uninvited, Fenimore Cooper snorted, "Columbus and John Jacob Astor! I dare say Irving will make the last the greatest."

During the day, "Astor was hovering in the next room," Irving wrote to a friend, "emanating anecdotes, ready to send, if necessary, for every survivor of the expedition," and doing everything possible "to render our residence with him agreeable, and to detain us with him." Comfortably installed, Irving filled notebooks with queries for Pierre to research, and wrote letters to Albert Gallatin requesting details. In queries to Pierre he wanted to know if Crooks and McClellan's business with the Sioux Tetons was "one or two years previous to the expedition of Mr. Hunt and what were the particulars." He also read the memoirs of John Bradbury and Thomas Nuttall, the two British naturalists Wilson Price Hunt had allowed to tag along to the Mandan villages. Bradbury had enriched the story of the West with his *Travels in the Interior of America* (1817), while Nuttall's *Journal of Travels into the Arkansas Territory* (1821) contributed to *Genera of American Plants.* To understand the surrender of Astoria, Irving read Gabriel Franchère's French eyewitness account of the events, published in 1820. Franchère had returned to Montreal in 1814 to the surprise of his family, who after four years' silence assumed he had perished with the *Tonquin.* He married his patient sweetheart, Sophie Routhier, the following year, and sired ten children between 1817 and 1838, when his wife died. As with Crooks, Stuart, and McKenzie, Astor kept Franchère in his employ as his Montreal agent.

The first eyewitness account written in English to reach print was the memoirs of Ross Cox, who had started his journal on the deck of the *Tonquin.* His *Adventures on the Columbia River* was published in London in 1832 and a year later in New York. It was an entertaining book full of details Irving didn't find in Franchère. Among the unpublished sources Irving read were the rough notes of Robert Stuart on his return trip from Astoria to Saint Louis, which included Squaw Dorion's own story of the harrowing winter she and her children spent in the Snake River region after the Nez Percé killed her husband and Jacob Rezner.

Irving had visited Montreal and several Northwest Company establishments in his youth and was just back from the prairies. Fur traders, he once wrote, "have always been themes of charmed interest to me, and I have felt anxious to get at the details of their adventurous expeditions." In *Relation d'un voyage à la cote du nord-ouest de l'Amérique septentrionale, dans les années 1810, 11, 12, 13, et 14,* Franchère made no mention of Astorians spoiling for a fight with John McTavish and the Northwesters. The absence of plans to fight McTavish would make later historians wonder if Washington Irving invented the standoff for dramatic effect. When an English edition of Franchère's narrative was published in New York in 1854, however, the now sixty-eight-year-old Astoria survivor, or his editor, added an Irvingesque description of Astorians raring to fight the Brits.

Out of Astor's documents, the accounts of Franchère and Cox, out of Hunt and Crooks's letters, Stuart's eyewitness account, and other authentic writings of the frontier, Irving spun an epic retelling of the *Tonquin* story and the Astorians' overland trek.* A first draft was finished in the fall of 1835 and Irving spent the winter revising it. Carey and Lea paid him $4,000 for the American publication rights and he got $500 from the London firm of Bentley for the British rights.

Astoria, or, Anecdotes of an Enterprize [sic] *Beyond the Rocky Mountains* was an instant best-seller when it came out in October 1836. Irving knew he had written the book in a hurry and was suspicious of the acclaim it brought him. Henry Wadsworth Longfellow said the appeal of the book was that the author made "John Jacob stand out like a statute of granite. A sublime enterprise." The *New York Mirror* called the book romantic, but found it superior to *A Tour on the Prairies.* The London *Spectator* called the book "a masterpiece. It has all the minute fullness and enough of the polished and elaborate elegance of other works, with more of closeness, pith and substance, " and said it "is the history of as grand and comprehensive a commercial enterprise as ever was planned with any well-grounded prospect of success, and which was prosecuted among scenes as vast and nations as wild, gave rise to incidents as ludicrous, as interesting, as appalling, and developed characters and manners as marked and striking as anything on record respecting the adventurous explorers of the Middle Ages, or the hardy discoveries of the modern days."

In the United States, the *Quarterly Review* chimed in: "From being an obscure stranger [Astor] has made himself one of the celebrities of the country . . . Nations have taken

---

*Alexander Ross, the third Astorian clerk to write an eyewitness account, did not publish his *Adventures of the First Settlers on the Oregon or Columbia River* until 1849.

cognizance of his individual enterprises, statesmen have studied them and labored to favor or thwart them. A masterpiece." The *Southern Literary Messenger* found Irving to be a brilliant rewrite man: "The modesty of the title [affords] no indication of the fullness, comprehensiveness, and beauty, with which a long and entangled series of detail, collection, necessarily from a mass of vague and imperfect data, has been wrought into completeness and unity."

The book presented Irving's patron in the best light, giving him all the credit for dreaming up and financing the enterprise while placing the blame for its failure on others, including the government leaders of the day:

> He [Astor] was already wealthy beyond the ordinary desires of man, but he now aspired to that honorable fame which is awarded to men of similar scope of mind, who by their great commercial enterprises have enriched nations, peopled wildernesses, and extended the bounds of empire. He considered his projected settlement at the mouth of the Columbia as the emporium to an immense commerce; as a colony that would form the germ of a wide civilization; that would, in fact, carry the American population across the Rocky Mountains and spread it along the shores of the Pacific, as it already animated the shores of the Atlantic.

Astoria's severest critic was Hubert Howe Bancroft. The California historian and chronicler of social reforms considered the book propaganda, and pronounced himself "deeply pained to see Mr. Irving lend his brilliant faculties to so base purposes." Others talked of the vast sum Irving must have received from Astor for the perfunctory and flattering book. Later historians were of several minds about *Astoria*. Some charged Irving with embellishments at the expense of accuracy, of allowing his friendship for Astor to bias his judgment. *Astoria,* they said, is both history and propaganda, full of biased political intent. Still others, however, found Irving's book remarkably sturdy. In 1903, Hiram Chittenden wrote: "It has been a matter of growing astonishment throughout these studies to find with what detail the illustrious author had worked out his theme. In the essential respects of accuracy and comprehensive treatment, Irving's work stands immeasurably above all others upon the subject." What especially struck Chittenden was the accuracy of Irving's geographical descriptions considering the lack of detailed maps at the time the author wrote the book: "Pen pictures which would probably pass for the effusions of a versatile pen are found to be true to the localities even to the present day." Others, however, said they had a hard time following the Astorians' return trek in the Irving book. In the *Literary History of the United States,* Irving is praised for drawing his own conclusions from the half dozen different accounts: "*Astoria* is neither profound scholarship nor brilliant writing, but it is at least that somewhat rare combination of good scholarship and good writing."

While working on *Astoria,* Irving met Bonneville at Astor's, rewrote the captain's book, and added recollections from another American Fur Company trader. Irving's English publisher gave the book its enduring title: *The Adventures of Captain Bonneville.**

Astoria, meanwhile, was quickly translated into French, German, and Russian. The Russian edition was censored, no doubt because of its unflattering portrait of Alaska Governor Alexander Baranov and Adrian Bentzon's cunning negotiations in St. Petersburg.

"Old Mr. Astor," Irving noted, "seems greatly gratified."

---

*How much Irving used of Bonneville's book is unknown, as both Bonneville's and Irving's manuscripts have disappeared.

23

—〰—

A Third Fortune

Astor had been annoyed at the low interest Paris banks paid when he was a patient of Dr. Dupuytren. He was equally displeased by the rates New York banks offered on the money rolling in from the American Fur sale. In exasperation, he plowed the money into New York real estate. Luck and playing the market contrarian gave him his third, and biggest, fortune.

New York was surpassing Paris in population and catching up with London, the world's most populous city. More than forty thousand jostling immigrants landed at Whitehall and the Battery every year, only a few streets from Prince Street where William still functioned in an old-fashioned cubbyhole office. Among the newcomers were a number of young Germans who knocked on Astor's door, claiming they were from Walldorf. To one such John Jacob gave a $5 bill. When the fellow said, "Your son gave me ten dollars," John Jacob replied: "Well he may, the dog has a rich father."

Brokerage and commission houses were rising along Broadway, but hogs still rooted in its gutters. The stock exchange occupied a space between Broad and New Streets and also had an entrance on Wall Street. The yellow fever epidemic of 1822 had accelerated the growth of the city northward as many of the people fleeing the lower part of the island kept their suburban homes after the fever passed. Rows of brick fronts ran north of Canal Street to house the city's two hundred thousand inhabitants, but in the gaps in between were fetid back alleys where clapboard tenements were erected. Since 1825—a year when sixteen hundred houses were built, as a contemporary chronicler noted— city blocks had reached Greenwich Village. Newly rich grain brokers, shipping operators, canal promoters, and contract-labor importers swarmed noisily over Park Place.

Even disasters played into Astor's hands. During the night of December 16 and 17, 1835, the most devastating fire in New York's history swept the tinderbox city of wooden buildings. It was one of the coldest winters in memory. The East River had frozen so hard that it was possible to walk between Manhattan and Brooklyn. Firemen poured liquor in their boots to prevent their feet from freezing, but the seven degrees below zero Fahrenheit temperature froze the water in their hoses. Ships trapped by ice at their docks went up in flames, as did blocks of tenements built on the Astor lots. The inferno continued for two days. When it was all over, the losses were put at $25 million. Insurance companies went bankrupt and Henry Brevoort lost $40,000. J. J. didn't lose anything since, apart from his own home, he didn't own any structures in the city. Owners of gutted buildings standing on leased Astor land had two choices. They could rebuild at their own expense. Or they could walk away and watch Astor repossess his land and lease it out to a new entrepreneur.

Lending money to a whiskey distiller who got into debt gave him a good chunk of today's midtown Manhattan. Medeef Eden had inherited Eden Farm with its gambrel-roofed Dutch homestead in 1797. The twenty-two-acre rectangle of fields extended from the old Bloomingdale Road (Broadway) between what are now Forty-second and Forty-sixth Streets all the way west to the shore of the Hudson River. When John Jacob heard young Medeef was in financial difficulties and had secured a mortgage on the farm, he rode out to meet him and purchased a third interest in the mortgage. Medeef defaulted on the mortgage, and Astor found himself the owner of Eden Farm for an investment of $25,000. Eden's heirs thought they discovered irregularities in Astor's title and sued. The case dragged on for twenty years. When John Jacob offered the heirs $9,000 for their claim, they happily settled. J. J. sold 141 lots around Times Square for $5.1 million, and still left the greater part of Eden Farm in one piece.

—m—

John Jacob's biggest real estate killing was the result of a protracted legal fight devised and orchestrated by Aaron Burr. It was called the Morris Case. The way Burr first explained it to Astor, Roger Morris and his wife, Mary, had bet on the wrong horse during the Revolution and, after the success of the Patriot cause, had fled the country. Their 51,000-acre estate—nearly one-third of Putnam County—had been Mary's inheritance from her grandfather, Frederick Phillips, who had financed the pirate Captain Samuel Burgess. After Roger and Mary fled, the state of New York sequestrated their property and sold off parcels to seven hundred farmers. In London in 1809, Burr learned that when Mary Morris died the property would become the possession of her heirs. The way he figured it, American law could not punish the three Morris children for their parents' political sins, meaning that when Mary died, the estate would irrevocably belong to them. With Burr acting as his lawyer, Astor had no difficulty persuading the Morris children to sell him their rights to the confiscated farms for $100,000. Burr no doubt encouraged them to think title to the properties in far-off, unfriendly New York State was clouded, that it would take years of uncertain litigation to settle, and there was no guarantee of success. Besides, since J. J. bought the title from the children, not Mary Morris, he was powerless to move until she died. When she did at the age of ninety-four in 1825, he commemorated her demise by sending eviction notices to the seven hundred farmers.

The farmers rose in a chorus of cries of injustice that was so loud the New York State legislature appointed commissioners who, after a title search, asked Astor to name his price. John Jacob offered to take one-half of the value of the land, now estimated at $667,000. The state refused. The case dragged on. Astor resubmitted his offer, with interest added. Again the state declined. Finally pressed by the farmers, who could neither secure mortgages, nor sell the land, nor make wills, the legislature enacted a law providing compensation for Astor if he obtained judgment in his favor from the Supreme Court of the United States.

With Burr advising in the background, Thomas Emmet, counsel to a number of businessmen, represented Astor. Pleading the state's case were Daniel Webster, who ten years earlier had been retained by Astor on a case in Boston, and Martin Van Buren. Webster had no equal as an orator. But his golden tongue failed to persuade the Supreme Court. In June 1830, the court found for Astor. Mary Morris's children, the court ruled, had never been dispossessed. They had been the rightful owners when they sold their rights to the property to Astor. J. J. gracefully relinquished his rights when the state offered him $520,000 in 5 percent stock that gave him a yearly income, ad infinitum, of $26,000.

Burr was going on seventy-five, an aging pariah who in the streets recalled the tiewig Hamiltonian days (he would die in 1836). New men intrigued the city. In the Astor mold were Cornelius Vanderbilt, a semiliterate, onetime steamboat captain on his way to a fortune by owning the ferries that serviced the still bridgeless metropolis, and James Gordon Bennett—an "ill-looking, squinting man," Astor's friend Philip Hone said—a Scottish immigrant who founded the aggressive *New York Herald* and whose son would send Stanley to Africa to find Livingston. Shipowners and railway tycoons were becoming famous. Transatlantic shipping lines established fixed dates for sailing. One was the Black Ball Line with four 500-ton ships. Another was the Red Star with departures for Liverpool on the twenty-fourth of every month. Black Ball added ships that sailed on the sixteenth of every month, and was followed by the

Swallowtail Line, which moved its departures to the eighth. During his lifetime, John Jacob saw transatlantic travel time slashed to a quarter of the nine weeks of his youth. The sixty-six-day crossing had been halved by the 1830s, and cut in half again in 1838 when the steamship *Great Western* sailed from Bristol to New York in fifteen days.

To the west, the railways changed everything. Vacant places in the states east of the Mississippi filled up and the emigrant wagons gave way to the new and better methods of transport. Chicago had been a frontier fort in 1832. Six years later it was a flourishing town with eight steamships connecting it with Buffalo, New York. Two new states, Arkansas and Michigan, were admitted to the Union and the population of the country grew from 12.8 million in 1830 to 17 million ten years later.

—⚅—

Public land out West had been meant as a source of development, not a source of revenue, but government land sales were so robust they wiped out the national debt. When the U.S. Treasury surplus reached almost $37 million, the Jackson administration decided to loan part of it to the states. Money was cheap. Foreign, particularly English, capital was abundant and states which had been accustomed to thinking twice about a $100,000 bond issue began to negotiate loans of millions of dollars to dig canals and build railways. Many projects were badly conceived and managed. Everybody wanted to buy. The assessed value of real estate in New York City in 1832 was $104 million; four years later it reached $253 million.

President Jackson ordered the government's surplus revenues deposited in institutions other than the Bank of the United States and ordered the secretary of the treasury to select various banks. In most states banks were freely organized, with or without tangible assets. Their notes were now sent west for the purchase of government lands, which needed to be held only a couple of months to gain a handsome profit. "Wildcat banks" sprang up all over the country and the "pet banks," as those chosen for the deposit of government revenue were called, went into a speculative frenzy as eagerly as banks that hardly pretended to have any capital.

Congress had always been denied the power to issue anything but gold or silver coins as legal tender. "Hard money" supporters in the Jackson cabinet wanted to keep it that way. In the dying months of the Jackson administration—Vice President Martin Van Buren had already been elected president—the government caved in to the hard money advocates and ordered land agents to accept land payments in gold and silver only. This "specie circular" turned the tide of paper back East and when notes were presented for payment most banks suspended payouts in coin. Prices collapsed faster than they had run up. Failures on a scale unprecedented in U.S. history had some states wash their hands of their debt, a repudiation made easy by the fact that a state could not be sued except by its own consent. Thousands of businesses went bankrupt. Even the federal government felt the strain. The dispersal of its surplus revenues to state institutions meant the government's resources were locked up in suspended banks. A little more than a year after Congress had authorized the distribution of surplus revenues among the states, President Van Buren was forced to call Congress into a special session to provide relief for the government itself.

John Jacob was debt free, and the Panic of 1837 could only make him richer when those who owed him money couldn't pay. Since his brother Henry had sold him lots near the junction of Bowery Lane and Elizabeth Street in 1789 for "£47 current money of the State of New York," J. J. had participated in hundreds, even thousands, of transactions, buying, selling, leasing, renting, and lending money on real estate security. In 1804–1805, he had invested $80,000 each year in Manhattan real estate, then dropped off to $170,000 over the next ten years. The most famous purchase was the Trinity Church leases to Richmond Hill from Aaron Burr and purchasing the half share J. J. didn't own of Greenwich Village from Governor Clinton's heirs.

There were no more Morris Case gold mines, and many of his acquisitions had been short-term distractions to the fur and shipping interests, a means of increasing working capital or providing collateral for raising working capital. In 1815, he had told Gallatin his annual profit from the China trade fluctuated between $50,000 and $100,000. After William joined John Jacob Astor & Son, the emphasis had shifted to long-term appreciation. At $46,000 a year, the real estate returns nearly equaled the China profits by 1830, only to triple ten years later. And the Astor realm was wholly self-financing. In a snowballing effect, income from sales of leases went into acquiring yet more property. William bought one of the most valuable Astor holdings, the Thompson farm, east and west of Fifth Avenue, between Thirty-second and Thirty-sixth Streets.

With one exception, John Jacob didn't believe in building.

The exception was Astor House. He had lived in luxurious hotels in Europe and in 1828 picked up the City Hotel at an auction for $101,000. The establishment was considered New York's best, but not quite the luxury hotel J. J. decided his adopted city deserved. Houses were torn down from Barclay to Vesey Street on Broadway, including his own home. One homeowner on the block refused to sell until John Jacob offered $20,000 more than the value put on the house by a committee of three people, two appointed by the owner, one by Astor. In the end, the wife of the owner persuaded her husband they should accept $60,000. The stone-laying ceremony was held the Fourth of July, 1834, and construction proceeded rapidly under John Jacob's supervision. His enthusiasm for the project, it was said, was an antidote to his grief over Sarah's death. When the new six-story hotel was finished it was described as "the marvel of the age." It boasted three hundred rooms and seventeen bathrooms, and was furnished throughout in black walnut. For $2 a night, well-heeled guests had their own door key, maid service, pitcher and bowl, and free soap. The corridors were carpeted and the walls hung with pictures.

When Davy Crockett stayed at the Astor House he was amazed to hear how much the owner had spent. British visitors were loud in their praise—except Charles Dickens, who was horrified when he walked out the main entrance and saw pigs gobbling up garbage. Celebrity guests included Jenny Lind, Abraham Lincoln, William Makepeace Thackeray, the Prince of Wales (later Edward VII), and Edgar Allan Poe, who got the idea for the armchair detection essay "The Mystery of Marie Roget" at Astor House. A Whig party dinner in 1836 for 220 guests began at 7:30 and lasted all night. After other senators spoke, presidential hopeful Daniel Webster—Van Buren was elected—didn't get to speak until 2 A.M., but he held his audience spellbound until four in the morning. "Not another speaker on the globe," Philip Hone noted, "could thus have fixed their attention at such an unseasonable hour." Webster claimed that if he were ever denied a room at Astor House, he would never again visit New York City. Realizing society news sold newspapers, James Gordon Bennett began to print the Astor House guest list in the *New York Herald*. "Anyone who can pay two dollars a day for a room must be important," he told his staff.

The hotel restaurant was famous for its literary and political dinners (specialties included kidneys in champagne and vanilla custard), while the lounges were thronged with "highly dressed ladies," and the sumptuously decorated corridors were known as "flirtation galleries." John Jacob turned the hotel over to William in return for "one Spanish milled dollar, and love and affection." William immediately leased the hotel at a yearly rent of $20,000.

Erecting Astor House had left John Jacob homeless. He built himself a four-story brownstone at 485 Broadway, on the corner of Prince Street, then filled it with the finest works of art and furniture brought back from Europe and Asia. The new *Harper's Magazine* called it one of the most conspicuous of the New York palaces and lovingly described the picture gallery, dining room, and a staircase accentuated by a piece of sculpture executed by J. J.'s grandson William Waldorf Astor.

The master of the house craved a place among the city's cultural elite, and gave dinners and musical soirees for a wide circle of friends that included merchants, sea captains, politicians, and the glitterati. The dinners were Lucullan feasts, starting with oysters and Moselle wine, followed by boned turkey, filet de boeuf aux champignons, fried oysters, quail, and canvasback duck. Louis McLane was a frequent guest. The former congressman, who would soon be President Martin Van Buren's secretary of state, was an internationalist in J. J.'s mold; as ambassador to the Court of St. James, he had done much to heal old Anglo-American wounds. Besides grandson Charles Bristed and Washington Irving, the fashionable Philip Hone was there to dispense the latest gossip. He was deeply involved in politics and in the theater. His lady friend was the British star and playwright Fanny Kemble, whose slightly condescending verse about the brash new nation echoed a prevailing sentiment when she declaimed: "Some of it is very beautiful, all of it is in good feeling—it made me cry. Oh my home, my land, England, glorious little England! From which this bragging big baby was born."

John Jacob's other pleasures included horseback riding, listening to music with a glass of beer and a pipe, and the theater—he remained the half-owner of the rebuilt Park Theater on Broadway.

John Jacob invested $224,000 in Manhattan real estate at the bottom of the 1837 financial crash. Many people believed the market would never recover and regarded him as mad for throwing his capital into a "bottomless pit." When interest rates climbed to 7 percent and owners with properties mortgaged to the Astors could no longer service their debt, J. J. Astor & Son foreclosed on seventy properties. For $2,000 John Jacob and William got a block in Harlem said to be worth $1 million. An East Side radish patch was theirs for $20,000. At one foreclosure sale alone J. J. bought lots at so low a figure that the Court of Chancery later made him pay an additional sum. So extreme became the plight of people falling behind in mortgage payments that the New York State legislature passed a bill that allowed a year's redemption at 10 percent interest.

Astor was accused of picking up most of his land through foreclosures. However, of one hundred properties transferred to him during a twenty-year period, the master in chancery conveyed eight and the U.S. marshal only one. He appeared as complainant in only five of these conveyances; in the others he was merely the highest bidder at auction sales. He secured grants to reclaim public land lying below high-water marks, and usually succeeded in petitioning the city for better terms, such as a reduction of the rent or its remission for a period of thirty years. He also bought wedge-shaped strips formed by closing old roads bordering his land, and was accused of being tardy in filling the lots granted to him, some of which became public nuisances. "Evidently Astor was by no means so eager to do his part in the improvement of the city as he was to acquire all the public lands which the corporation [city] could give him," Kenneth Porter would write. "But of course he was not unique in this attitude." Horace Greeley spoke out against this feudal notion of land tenure and against "land speculators like Mr. A." Reformers such as Gerrit Smith, the son of John Jacob's long-ago associate in upstate New York, Peter Smith, also objected. Young Gerrit was a candidate for governor of New York in 1840 on an antislavery platform.

We do not know what Astor thought of slavery or whether he had any slaves himself. For years his ships had carried cotton from Charleston, but slave owning remained overwhelmingly rural. As an ex-shipowner he must have been interested in the *Amistad* case. Hone was. His sympathies were with the slaves in an August 31 entry in his diary: "The ringleader in this revolt is a Congo negro, named Joseph Cinques, about twenty-six years of age, a fine, intelligent fellow, who would be exalted into a hero instead of a pirate and murderer if his colour was right, and he had been taken under other circumstances." The former mayor's attitude changed when the two Spanish owners of the *Amistad* were jailed in Connecticut. In an October 22, 1839, entry in his diary, Hone called abolitionists "fanatics" who, "under the cloak of an abstract opposition to slavery, are blowing up a flame which may destroy the Union, and light up a civil war." This view echoed the general sentiment among

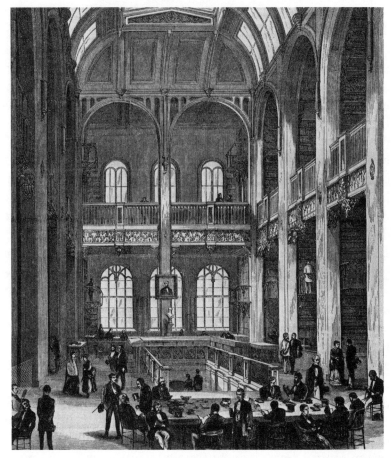

Astor Library

the working and upper classes. Abolitionism was gaining strength, but its estimated 160,000 supporters were mostly educated church people of middle-class New England or Quaker heritage.

In 1835, Astor's investments in Manhattan had totaled $832,000, but his rental income was larger. From 1840 to 1848, his rental income reached more than $1,265,000. In 1890, William Waldorf Astor, the Third Viscount Astor, still possessed an 1840s ledger of his ancestor's properties and transactions. Each right-hand page had a colored drawing showing the boundaries of every plot bought and sold. On the opposite leaf, in tiny handwriting, were details of purchase or lease, buildings and rents.

The 300-odd Astor leases brought in $128,000 annually in 1840. Eight years later, rent from 470 leases topped $200,000. Such power aroused hostility—and obsequiousness. In 1839, Hallet's Cove, the stretch of northwestern Queens across from Hellgate, was renamed Astoria.

—⚹—

Two years earlier, J. J. had agreed to endow the city with a library. In October 1837, when Joseph Green Cogswell returned from a scouting trip of private libraries in Europe, he was summoned to Hellgate. Wrote Cogswell:

> I went out [to Hellgate] the next day and found him very cordial but feeble. I learnt that he had been beset by innumerable applications for money, in all possible amounts from five to five thousand dollars, since his great act of munificence had been made known. This his own penetrating mind had foreseen, and it had induced him to change his intended donations to a legacy.

It would be years before land, architecture, personnel, and the purchase of books were agreed upon. Astor repeatedly changed his mind about where to locate the Astor Library. He finally assigned less valuable lots in Lafayette Place. Cogswell, however, could never persuade "the old gentleman" to actually start construction. In 1839, William asked the scholar to travel to Germany to check up on William's son, John Jacob III, the second generation of Astors to study at Göttingen University. Cogswell thought this was his chance. He would only go, he said, if John Jacob provided him with substantial funds to buy any private European library that might come on the market. J. J. huffed and puffed and gave Cogswell the money.

24

—⁓—

Richest Man in America

John Jacob was famously America's richest man. How rich was the question everybody tried to guess. In 1845, when Moses Y. Beach, publisher of the *New York Sun,* printed a list of the city's wealthiest people, it ran thirty-two pages. It began, in the low end, with A. T. Stewart, the immigrant from Belfast who had turned Irish laces and linens into a department store emporium towering above Broadway and dispensed dry goods of every sort. Stewart, the *Sun* calculated, was worth $400,000. Cornelius Vanderbilt, whose only schooling had been the docks of New York and whose ferries made him the newest millionaire, was estimated to be worth $1.2 million. With $25 million, John Jacob Astor topped the list. The list provoked Horace Greeley to a mocking jibe in the *New York Tribune*: "It is our deliberate estimate, the result of much inquiry, that the average earnings of those who live by simple labor in our city—embracing at least two-thirds of our population— scarcely, if at all, exceed one dollar per week." Conservative Whigs in turn attacked Greeley, as he himself reported, for

John Jacob Astor in middle age

"attempting incessantly to incite the prejudices of the poor against the rich."

How to reconcile the portrait of the war profiteer and slumlord who charged goods to his traders at such high prices they were forced to mortgage their lands to him, who wrecked the government's trading houses, who sold liquor to Indians knowing the devastating consequences with the courtly widower with the long silver hair and silver shoe buckles, never so happy as when surrounded by grandchildren for an evening concert at Hellgate? Always a shrewd judge of character, he was quick to see the best of people, but in his later years the onrushing world left him indifferent. He cared little for clubs, schools, churches, public works, or neglected children, but he was openhanded to his kin, even overindulgent, and not ungenerous in dealings with subordinates he knew personally.

Ramsay Crooks and Robert Stuart were not the only beneficiaries. While he felt no responsibility toward the thousands of men who had contributed to his wealth and those who had died to feed his—and their own—greed, he accorded people with whom he was in close contact a special claim to his consideration. Astorians making it back to New York had been given jobs: Gabriel Franchère, Donald McKenzie, Russell Farnham, and Benjamin Clapp, whom J. J. had sent to the West Indies to spy on his son-in-law. John Ebbets and several other captains stayed with Astor for decades, and many of his clerks became successful merchants. He paid for Ebbets's son's education at Yale, and at his graduation in 1832 offered him a position with American Fur. Employee families could sometimes count on him. Widows were sent checks. When Jacob B. Taylor, described as Astor's "rent collector," died, his son Moses could count on Astor. Moses Taylor was an importer of Cuban sugar, and it was said "old Mr. Astor always backed up Moses when he needed aid." Except when he had roamed the woods of upstate New York to exchange trinkets for beaver skins and canoed with Northwesters to the end of Lake Superior, he never saw the misery among the Indians or the sweat his voyageurs put into their work.

—◊—

Fame made him wonder how posterity would judge him. Washington Irving had painted a handsome portrait of Astor's golden vision, but the writer was not J. J.'s only confidant. Among his younger friends were Gerrit Smith, Fitz-Greene Halleck, and Joseph Cogswell, the latter the person closest to Astor during his declining years.

These friends found him to be an astonishing character, astute and imaginative and with a sense of humor. Once when he refused to subscribe to a charity on the grounds he had no money, Halleck said: "Mr. Astor, if you're out of money, I'll endorse your note for a few hundred dollars." To which the old man burst out laughing and signed a check. Cogswell wrote to a friend the first night he met Astor: "He talks well on many subjects and shows a great interest in the arts and literature." Astor had enjoyed Cogswell's cultured company and urged him to join his household.

Philip Hone discovered that the way to open Astor's fount of memories was to mention Sarah. For all her piety, Astor told his dinner guests, Sarah had been sharp and clever in business. She always kept the house open to ministers from all denominations and read a little in the Bible every day. He, too, had read the Good Book when he had boarded in his brother's house in London. He had been awakened by Bow bells—the bells of St. Mary-le-Bow Church, which since the Middle Ages had begged Londoners to return to the city—and had read a few verses before getting up. Sarah liked books with religious themes. No, he and his wife had never had a serious disagreement. Oh, yes, he remembered once they had quarreled over discipline. She had upbraided one of their granddaughters, one of the Langdons. Maybe it was little Sarah. He had always spoiled the child and when her grandmother scolded her, the girl asked him, "Grandfather, why did you marry Grandmother, anyway?" "Because she was so pretty, my dear," he had answered. What could Sarah do in front of the child except look frustrated and walk away in a huff? There was also the time when he needed her to go to his warehouse and give her opinion on some skins. "I'm very busy," she had told him. "If I go it will cost you five hundred dollars an hour." "Agreed," he had told her and, in remembering, chuckled. Sarah was a great one.

There were few stories about John Jacob II, but unlike Cornelius Vanderbilt, who had thrown his epileptic son out of the family fold, Astor had always taken care of his. No French or Swiss doctor had been able to cure his son and he lived out his days in comfort in an institution in Cambridgeport, Massachusetts, where he was cared for by a Mr. Chaplin and his wife at the cost of $2,000 a year. Back in

1812, John Jacob had fulminated against Dorothea for elop-
ing with Colonel Walter Langdon, but twenty-five years later
he spared neither money nor affection for the Langdons. He
had built a house, apparently for himself, on the northwest
corner of Astor Place and Lafayette Place, which he gave to
his daughter. In his will he left her a life income of $100,000,
and when her husband died in 1847 he added the income
of another $100,000. He had always been generous to his
favorite daughter, Eliza. In his will he bequeathed $50,000
to her and her husband, Vincent von Rumpff, along with the
"lands and estate in the Canton of Geneva."

Old resentments faded. Great-granddaughter Maddie,
who had been brought up by her grandparents, William

John Jacob II

and Margaret, made a good match and J. J. grudgingly tolerated her father, Sam Ward. The Wards were no longer rich. After the Ward family bank collapsed in the 1837 panic, Sam went off to California with the forty-niners. Sarah Langdon married Baron Frans Robert Boreel, the first secretary of the Dutch embassy in Paris. The couple settled in The Hague, but as a wedding present Astor gave them a house on Broadway between Prince and Spring Streets. He also smothered her teenage sister Louisa with gifts. In his will, he left Louisa a life interest of one-seventh of one hundred lots in New York City, and in one-fourth of four lots on Broadway, a lot on Lafayette Place, and legacies of $25,000 and a one-sixth share of $100,000. In 1841, when Louisa followed her parents' example and eloped with Oliver DeLancey Kane, descendant of the "treacherous" Tory family whose lands had been seized by a bill of attainder during the Revolution, John Jacob rescinded everything. Grandpa mellowed enough, however, to give her mother the right to restore the legacy. Eliza and Cecilia, Dorothea's two other daughters, received the same bequest. Eliza married Matthew Wilks, and at least one of her children was born at Hellgate. Their brothers—John Jacob Langdon, Walter Langdon Jr., Woodbury Langdon, and Eugene Langdon— received similar legacies.

The grandson who was the glint in Astor's eye and received special consideration in his will was John Jacob III. William and Margaret's eldest son, born in 1822, was an energetic graduate of Columbia, studying at Göttingen like his father. In Astor's testament, the namesake grandson was granted a life interest in half the Astor lands "lying between Bloomingdale Road, Hudson River, Forty-second Street, and Fifty-first Street," the other half to be divided between his two brothers. To William and Margaret's two daughters, Alida and Laura, John Jacob bequeathed $200,000, to "be settled on them on their respectively attaining the age of twenty-one years, or their marriage, with the consent of their father or his wife." Only Laura married during Astor's lifetime. She caused a good deal of envy by capturing Franklin Hughes Delano, heir to a Massachusetts whale oil fortune, and said to be one of the handsomest men of his day. A story, never verified, has it that when Laura became his wife, her grandfather gave her a check for $250,000.

Still, how to transmit the greater part of the fortune to John Jacob III? He could trust William, but could he trust lawmakers? The fortunes of the great merchant princes of Europe—the Medicis of Florence, the Rothchilds of Frankfurt, the Fuggers of Augsburg—had been passed from fathers to firstborn sons in patrilineal lines since the Renaissance, but American legislatures enacted laws limiting trusts. There was a tendency in the United States, Alexis de Tocqueville approvingly noted in *Democracy in America,* to disperse and distribute wealth. Yet the notion of keeping riches and tradition in families by transmitting everything to the eldest son had roots in the American Revolution. Washington, Lafayette, and Hamilton were among the founders of the Society of the Cincinnati, named after the Roman general Lucius Quinctius Cincinnatus, who reputedly left his plow to defeat the enemy and then returned without reward or complaint to his farm. The society was formed in 1783 to perpetuate the friendship of a group of Continental army officers, to preserve the liberty they had fought for, and to assist, by acts of beneficence, members and their families who were in need. Membership in the society was transmitted within a family to the eldest male or, lacking this direct descent, to collateral branches that were judged worthy.

We do not know whether John Jacob himself or his attorneys came up with an ingenious will. The simplicity of the idea has the marks of John Jacob; its ability to dodge trust laws suggest lawyerly talent. Instead of leaving the bulk of the estate to William, John Jacob stipulated that William get half outright, with the other half held in trust for John Jacob III. William had always done what his father told him and he in turn drew up a will that left one-half to John Jacob III and the other half to his eldest son, as yet unborn. If successive generations of Astor heirs copied this leapfrogging will, it would be difficult for any one of them to squander everything. It was no doubt John Jacob's wish to have the rollover go on forever. It lasted three generations. Great-grandson William Waldorf, who was the last to benefit from the leapfrog, looked into the Society of the Cincinnati and found that "not one ten-thousandth part" of the possessions of the Revolutionary War families remained in the hands of their male descendants.

—∿—

When Astor was in his eighties, people gathered outside 485 Broadway to catch a glimpse of him. On a crisp January day, the young Walt Whitman saw a

> bent feeble but stoutly-built very old man, bearded, swathed in rich furs, with a great ermine cap on his head, led and assisted, almost carried, down the steps of his high front stoop (a dozen friends and servant, emulous, carefully holding and guiding him) and then lifted and tuck'd in a gorgeous sleigh, envelop'd in other furs, for a ride. The sleigh was drawn by as fine a team of horses as I ever saw.... I remember the spirited champing horses, the driver with his whip, and a fellow driver by his side, for extra prudence. The old man, the subject of so much attention, I can almost see now. It was John Jacob Astor.

In the summer the patriarch liked a boat ride around Manhattan. Another favorite pastime was to sit at water's edge at Hellgate and watch ships sail up and down the East River.

Legends of his stinginess grew with his wealth, beginning with the story of John James Audubon. Astor had promised a thousand dollars toward the publishing costs of the naturalist's classic *Birds of America,* published between 1827 and 1838. When Audubon arrived to collect the pledged sum, Astor told him, "You come at a bad time. Money is vary scarce. I have nothing in the bank. I have invested all my funds." Five visits later, John Jacob still had the same excuse. "William," he called to the next room, "have we any money in the bank?" Either the younger Astor wasn't in on his father's game or he felt sorry for the naturalist, because he replied: "Yes, Father. We have $220,000 in the Bank of New York, $70,000 in the City Bank, $90,000 in the Merchants'—" John Jacob cut him short, and Audubon got his thousand dollars.

Paralysis, digestive disorders, and insomnia plagued him in old age. He would summon Cogswell and other members of the household to his bedside and keep them awake with endless talk. United States Superintendent of Indian Affairs Thomas L. McKenney wrote to Dolley Madison in 1846: "Your old friend Mr. Astor is very feeble and can have no pleasure in life. I am told by those who best know him that his relish for wealth is as keen as ever; that gone, he is gone."

Philip Hone wrote that his old friend "presented a painful example of the insufficiency of wealth" to prolong a life:

> This old gentleman, with his $15 million, would give it all to have my strength and physical ability. He would pay all my debts if I could insure him one year of my health and strength, but nothing else would extort so much from him. His life has been spent in amassing money and he loves it as much as ever. He sat at the dinner table with his head down upon his breast, saying very little, and in a voice almost unintelligible, the saliva dropping down from his mouth, and a servant behind him to guide the victuals, which he was eating, and to watch him as an infant is watched. His mind is good, his observations acute, and he seems to know everything that is going on. But the machinery is all broken up, and there are some people, no doubt, who think he has lived long enough.

On he lived. He was seventy-five when the news reached him that his beloved daughter Eliza had died in Switzerland after a painful illness. After her death at age thirty-seven, William and Dorothea were, besides John Jacob II, the only surviving children. Between them they had thirteen children who in turn married and had children. He enjoyed the company of the children, but many of them found him an embarrassment. Wealth and education had distanced them from the man who had given them both. He was a relic from another age, another world. All he could do was to shower them with riches.

He turned eighty in 1843, clinging to life with tenacity despite his illnesses. Bedridden much of the time, his ser-

William Backhouse Astor

vants tossed him in a blanket to stir up his metabolism. When he could no longer eat, he suckled at the breast of a wet nurse. To New Yorkers of 1848, he was a misty figure, the landlord whose agents trudged the foul streets and back alleys collecting rents. Impassive, William awaited his father's death. Himself a heavyset man with thick jowls and a listless expression, the fifty-five-year-old heir apparent seemed tired of the rent-roll monotony and the surfeit of luxury.

In the morning of March 29, 1848, old John Jacob died, four months short of his eighty-fifth birthday.

25

—⚏—

Heirs and Graces

Under the date March 29, 1848, Philip Hone wrote in his diary: "John Jacob Astor died this morning, at 9 o'clock, in the eighty-fifth year of his age; sensible to the last, but the material of life exhausted, the machinery worn out, the lamp extinguished for want of oil. Bowed down with bodily infirmity for a long time, he has gone at last, and left reluctantly his unbounded wealth."

The telegraph, novelty of the 1840s, clicked the news to Boston, Washington, and Montreal. Obituaries, set in type in advance, told the world that the wealthiest American had died. The conservative press preached the moral of the butcher boy who died, as the editor of the *Recorder* put it, with such wealth as to be "quite out of our small comprehension." "There are few men whose biography would prove more instructive or more acceptable for the present age than the life of John Jacob Astor," declared *Hunt's Merchant Magazine.* "For nearly forty years he has been characterized as perhaps the greatest merchant of this if not of any age— the Napoleon of commerce." *Harper's Magazine* wrote: "In the art of prospering in business, he has had no equal. To

get all that he could and to keep nearly all that he got—
those were the laws of his being." For Horace Greeley, the
moral of Astor's life was to be found in Scriptures: "Lay
not up for yourselves treasures on earth." James Gordon
Bennett wrote in the *Herald* that of Astor's fortune "ten
millions at least belong to the people of the city of New York,"
because it had accrued to the late immigrant not by his own
exertion but "by the industry of the community." Sharpness,
rough humor, and tightfistedness were the characteristics
that stood out in the stories of the day. Although he was
born a Lutheran, his faith had been vague at best. William,
however, thought it fitting that his father should be buried
in the church of the wealthy. Four Episcopalian rectors conducted the final rites in St. Thomas Episcopal Church, a
church John Jacob never attended. Washington Irving was
one of the pallbearers and appointed an executor of the will,
which prompted the ever-jealous James Fenimore Cooper to
circulate the rumor that Irving was to receive $50,000 and
become Astor's biographer.

Everybody wanted to know how much money Astor left
behind. John Jacob's banker friend Stephen Girard had died

John Jacob in later life—a cartoon published by the
London *Spectator* to accompany Astor's obituary in 1848

in 1831 and left an estate of $7 million. Peter Chardon Brooks, a grandfather of Henry Adams and reputed the richest man in Boston, died the same year Astor did and left an estate of $2 million. Speculation on Astor's worth reached $150 million. The *New York Sun* estimated the fortune to be $25 million; the *Illustrated London News* suggested between $30 and $50 million. His executors put the figure at $8 million, but since nearly all the money was tied up in property most biographers accept the total estate to have been between $20 and $30 million.

It would take forty-three years to tie up all the loose ends and settle the estate—Irving was given $10,592.66—but few outside the family benefited. Without neglecting a single member of John Jacob's family, from daughters to granddaughters, cousins and nephews, half sisters and in-laws, his will left half of the greater part of the fortune to William Backhouse Astor, and the other half in trust for John Jacob Astor III. Besides leaving $460,000 for the Astor Library, he remembered his birthplace and left $50,000 to the town of Walldorf, earmarked for the care of the frail and elderly and to provide education for poor and orphaned children. He also left $30,000 to the German Society of New York to be used in helping immigrants and another $30,000 to the Home for Aged Ladies, and minor gifts to the Blind Asylum, Half-orphan Asylum, and German Reformed Church.

The social reformer Horace Mann denounced Astor for not giving more for the benefit of the country that had allowed him to make a fortune in the first place. Mann calculated that Astor had given 6.25 percent of his money to the public. It was far less than Girard, who had died childless and without immediate heirs.

New York got its library. When the library was finally built, Cogswell stocked it with 100,000 books. By contrast, Harvard claimed 72,000 volumes, Philadelphia 60,000, and the Library of Congress 50,000. In the presence of William, grandson Charles Bristed, and Washington Irving, it opened its doors a year after Astor's death in a building that 140 years later would house the New York Shakespeare Festival's Joseph Papp Public Theater. Although books were not loaned out and the hours were limited, the Astor Library was a major source of reference and research. William supplemented his father's endowment of $10,000 a year. In 1895, the library was consolidated with other private trusts to form the New York Public Library. The site chosen was the Croton Reservoir, a popular strolling ground that occupied a two-block section of Fifth Avenue between Fortieth and Forty-second Streets.

—⟰—

Effortlessly, the Astors kept their money longer than any other of America's great families. Other sons of butchers, fur dealers, and farmers rode the steamships and railroads to unparalleled wealth during the post–Civil War years. The foulmouthed Cornelius Vanderbilt, as forceful and fiery as the steam boilers on his ships, died wealthier than John Jacob, and the son of a snake oil salesman, John D. Rockefeller, became the country's first billionaire, only to be brought down by government trustbusters.

John Jacob's descendants constituted an upper class in an avowedly classless society. Not all were slumlords. One tried politics before being drawn to England, where the concept of elitism and wealth disparity was tolerated. One of the granddaughters-in-law gave to the poor, while another gave balls that cost $200,000 and refused to invite the Vanderbilts because she thought manipulating railway stocks was ungentlemanly.

William Backhouse Astor remained the obedient heir who spent no money himself. Rich men delighted in carriages and fine horses, but William walked everywhere, never wasted money on wine, scanned and revised the smallest expenditure, and viewed the transformation of the city with deep satisfaction. Like his father, he paid attention to politics and made friends with the debonair Democratic mayor Fernando Wood. The mayor rewarded William's support by selling him for a pittance the waterlocked block between Twelfth and Thirteenth Streets, soon to be worth millions. The mayor's largesse extended to lesser landlords, who included such great names as the Goelets and the Rhinelanders, the Roosevelts and the Vanderbilts. When Republicans tried to unseat Fernando Wood on grounds of corruption, William led a list of eminent citizens who relied on city patronage to an open-air rally that effectively silenced Hizzonor's critics. New streets were paved and new multistory tenement houses built to accommodate the population that by the 1850s reached half a million.

Broadway was turned into the city's showplace. Private houses were torn down to make room for shops and hotels. "The mania for converting Broadway into a street of shops is greater than ever," wrote Philip Hone in 1850. "There is scarcely a block in the whole extent of this fine street of which some part is not in a state of transmutation." William perused the city plans, and spent hours studying his rent rolls. "He knew every inch of real estate that stood in his name," wrote a contemporary, "every bond, contract and lease. He knew what was due when the leases expired and attended personally to the matter." He was never handsome. A contemporary, Matthew Hale Smith, described him as "a tall, heavy built man, with a decided German look, a countenance blank, eyes small and contracted, a look sluggish and unimpassioned, unimpressible [*sic*] in his feelings, taciturn and unsocial." Others stressed his intellectual pursuits and called him a man of culture, a student of books and affairs who was a friend of scholars.

His three sons, John Jacob III—John to everybody— William Jr., and querulous, unruly, and alcoholic Henry were too rich and too wellborn to be criticized by city pols. From their mother they inherited the blue blood of the Livingstons and Armstrongs, and from their father the promise of millions. Both John and William Jr. were gentlemen of leisure. Henry was the family's black sheep. Born in 1832 when his father was forty and his mother thirty-two, Henry grew up to be a giant redhead who flew into rages if his father tried to restrain him. He seemed to have inherited the mental illness that affected his uncle John Jacob II and may also have touched his aunt Magdalen. His father was still alive when Henry suddenly married Malvina Dinehart, a farmer's daughter who lived near the Astors' estate at Rhinebeck, New York. The marriage and the couple's decision to buy a farm in the Berkshires of Massachusetts led William Sr. to reduce drastically the share of the family fortune Henry would inherit. Henry and Malvina remained childless, but lived long, happy lives; he died in 1918 at the age of eighty-six.

John Jacob III played the part of the new titular head of the family and its first aristocrat. He exhibited the severe manner of someone who knew his place and expected his interlocutors to know theirs. When the nineteen-year-old Prince of Wales, the future Edward VII, visited New York in 1860, John was on the committee of five who arranged a ball in the crown prince's honor. But John was also a humanist who, to annoy his father and Mayor Wood, supported the Republican candidate of 1860, Abraham Lincoln. He married Charlotte Augusta Gibbes (known as Augusta in the family), and sired only one child, William Waldorf Astor, who, according to *Harper's Weekly,* was "in all probability the richest man of the civilized world." The Gibbeses were an old South Carolina family related to British royalty.

The year old John Jacob died, Augusta bore John their only child. They christened the baby boy William Waldorf in honor of the ancestral home. Two years later they visited Walldorf to oversee the execution of the German provisions of his grandfather's will. Both John and Augusta loved the Old World, and stayed several months in Walldorf before traveling to Italy, France, and Britain. When the Civil War broke out in 1861, John came out strongly in support of President Lincoln and the Union. He was thirty-nine, and, at a time when sons of wealthy families bought their way out of military service, he enlisted. He was the first New Yorker to dig into his pocketbook on behalf of the Union, donating $3,000 for the arming of the tugboat *Yankee,* which relieved the island garrison of Fort Sumter. George McClellan, the appointed leader of the Army of the Potomac defending Washington, D.C., appointed John Astor his aide-de-camp. John rented a house in Washington complete with butler, valet, and cook, but found military life exhilarating when the army moved south to lay siege to Richmond, Virginia. Back in New York, meanwhile, Augusta, an ardent convert to the Northern cause, helped to raise a black regiment. She presented the colors to the regiment with a rousing speech: "When you look at this flag and rush to battle, or stand at guard beneath its sublime motto, 'God and Liberty,' remember that it is also an emblem of love and honor from the daughters of this great metropolis to their brave champions in the field, and that they will anxiously watch your career, glory in your heroism, and minister to you when wounded and ill, and honor your martyrdom with benediction and tears."

The commitment of John and Augusta to ideals in general, and the Unionist cause in particular, was uncharacteristic of the family. His father, William Backhouse, was so opposed to the war he refused to pay the income tax to prosecute it. He took the matter right up to the Supreme Court—and won.

John's brother, William Backhouse Jr., married Caroline Schermerhorn. The family descended from Jakob Janse Schemerhorn, who had settled in New York in 1636 and opened a thriving trade with Mohawks until Governor Stuyvesant accused him of selling arms and gunpowder to the Indians. William and Caroline had little in common and there was little affection in the marriage, which didn't prevent them from having four daughters and, on the fifth try, John Jacob Astor IV ("Colonel Jack"), who went down with the *Titanic* in 1912.

With money and conceit, Caroline made it her lifelong career to make the Astor name synonymous with her wealth, power, and privilege. Ward McAllister, the autocrat of New York chic, said Caroline had "by the acclamation of society itself" risen above everyone else to become the "supreme court of social appeals." From San Francisco's Nob Hill to Newport, the gilded generation's new playground on Rhode Island, the "champagne aristocracy" tried to copy her houses, wardrobes, and affectations. A fortune was no guarantee of admittance: the Goulds, the Harrimans, and the Morgans were not invited to the Astor balls where she reigned, a short

Caroline Astor's Fifth Avenue palazzo

figure in satin, diamond tiara, and pearls. When she decided Lafayette Place was becoming too crowded and bullied her husband into asking his father for a portion of the old Thompson Farm, sister-in-law Augusta joined the scheme and two sumptuous palazzi rose on Fifth Avenue. Who was *the* Mrs. Astor was the subject of titillating gossip.

William Backhouse retired in 1866. His sons were embarrassed to be seen as slumlords, but none of them had his grandfather's commercial talent. John Jacob III was willing to concede the necessity of devoting time to business affairs, even though business bored him. He moved the Astor office from his father's grim Prince Street quarters to West Twenty-sixth Street, only a few blocks from his Fifth Avenue mansion. Behind a simple bronze plaque announcing Astor Estate, agents in round-cut jackets and derby hats slipped in to hand rents to clerks. Chosen for their neat, flowing handwriting, clerks entered the amounts in oversized ledgers. John never insured the tenements built on the Astor land, believing he could better afford the occasional loss by fire of a block of buildings than paying insurance premiums. He was on good terms with William Marcy ("Boss") Tweed, the most notoriously crooked politician of the century, who had risen from the slums of Manhattan to wrest control of the city from Fernando Wood. Tweed had his own "ring" of accomplices who told contractors how much money must be returned in kickbacks. The County Court House, which should have cost $250,000 to build, was completed at the cost of $12 million. In 1871, when the Tweed Ring was at the height of its power, John and five other prominent New Yorkers were induced to make a perfunctory examination of the city's books and to praise Controller Richard "Slippery Dick" Connolly for his honesty. Whether John was naive or was slipped a doctored set of books—he was too rich to be blackmailed by a mere politician—the Astor name was scandalously linked to the plunder of city coffers. The *New York Times,* a newspaper started in 1851 by George Jones and Henry Jarvis Raymond (who once wrote, "There is nothing so mean as one million of dollars except two millions"), nailed the Tweed Ring and the Astor commission's token audit when a disgruntled official handed over actual pages from Connolly's books showing Boss Tweed's men had stolen $30 million. Connolly, the chief embezzler, escaped abroad, taking $6 million with him. Tweed was sent to prison, where he died. By 1880, the Astors' tenement income reached $5 million a year.

John's brother William preferred his yacht and the farm at Rhinebeck on the Hudson River to the city where Caroline reigned—or even better, to put the length of the East Coast between him and his wife. In Florida, he was the founder of the Florida Yacht Club. It must have been humiliating, however, for this grandson of John Jacob to see his real estate dealings turn to dust. Admittedly, his purchase for $7,500 of fourteen thousand acres inland from Daytona Beach in what is today the eastern rim of the Ocala National Forest in Orange County was before the rich and famous turned Florida into a winter playground. He planted orange trees, built a fourteen-room hotel and a store, and allowed the resulting community to be named Astor. Other citrus growers made money, but William's orange groves were never particularly productive. He didn't live to see his grandson Vincent sell the Florida property for $3,100 in 1938.

In New York, meanwhile, John dabbled in railway stock (but missed out on the mergers that created the New York Central Railway), and his wife gave away large sums of Astor money. Orphans, prostitutes, the chronically ill, and Indians who had once sold their souls for a bottle of adulterated Astor liquor benefited from Augusta's beneficence. Her favorite charity was the new Children's Aid Society. Each Christmas she spent $2,000 sending a hundred orphans out West by train. John endowed a six-cents-a-night lodging for street urchins—known ironically as the Astor House.

William Backhouse died in 1875 at the age of eighty-three. At his funeral, Maddie Ward, the granddaughter he and Margaret had brought up after her mother Emily died and her father, Sam Ward, remarried, caught pneumonia; she died shortly afterward at the age of thirty-seven. Her husband, John Winthrop Chanler, followed her to the grave, leaving ten orphans. Their great-uncle, John Jacob III, became their surrogate father. William Backhouse left a million dollars to each of his surviving daughters, $20 million each to John Jacob III and William Jr., and a million to Henry, who, everybody agreed, was not mad but eccentric. As the eldest, John also got Eden Farm north of Forty-second Street and west of Broadway, which became almost as valuable as a gold mine. William Backhouse's will left $500,000 to philanthropies—most of it to the Astor Library.

William Waldorf, John and Augusta's only child, grew up to be a handsome, blue-eyed and sandy-haired youth. Like his father and grandfather, he was sent to Göttingen to study. On his seventeenth birthday, his father wrote to him predicting the imminent collapse of the Confederate armies. At Appomattox nine days later, Robert E. Lee surrendered to Ulysses S. Grant.

William Waldorf married Mary Dahlgren Paul, the daughter of a Philadelphia family with enough money to get by. Mary was a girl of agreeable but not alluring features who preferred the background to the limelight. Mamie, as her friends called her, produced five children; only three of them lived to maturity. She was a capable and popular hostess, but her retiring nature was a disappointment to her husband. Willie, as he was called, was the first Astor to dream of a career in politics. Each time he tried for public office, however, his wealth and his vindictive and prickly personality came under attack. His suggestion that slashing the fare on the city's new elevated trains from a dime to a nickel would benefit the working class caused Jay Gould and August Belmont, the speculators who were making huge profits on the new urban transit, to denounce him. Campaigning for Congress, he kept his gloves on when he shook voters' hands—and lost.

Fellow New Yorker Chester Alan Arthur, who became president after James Garfield was assassinated in 1881, made Willie ambassador to Italy. Nothing appealed more to him than the official dignity, protocol, and etiquette of diplomacy, and his and Mamie's all too short four years in Rome were their happiest time. The Italian nobility liked her and Ambassador Astor became an avid art collector and novelist. Scribner's published his novel *Valentino,* loosely based on the life of Cesare Borgia, and his second historical novel, *Sforza, a Story of Milan.* The election of Democrat Glover Cleveland brought an end to the ambassadorship.

His parents' deaths—Augusta in 1887 and John Jacob III three years later—left him with almost incalculable wealth. The Astors received $9 million a year in New York rentals and the estate was worth $200 million, up from $40 million twenty-five years earlier. Muckraking journalist Burton Hendrick, who gained fame for exposing life insurance swindles, called the Astors "the world's greatest monument to unearned increment" or "a first mortgage on Fate itself." Others estimated Willie's fortune to be between $50 and $80 million in 1890 money.

Willie had been brought up to believe the rules of lineage and primogeniture made him the head of the dynasty. To his distress, his uncle's wife not only held on to the limelight as *the* Mrs. Astor, but also humiliated him and Mamie in New York and in Newport, Rhode Island.

Willie was determined to prove that by birthright he was head of the family, and he wanted Mamie, eighteen years younger than Caroline Schermerhorn Astor, to be acknowledged as the Astors' First Lady. The gentle, shy Mamie knew she had no hope of replacing Caroline, who by dint of flinty willpower remained the Olympian queen. Her calling cards had identified her as Mrs. William Astor, but in response to Willie's agitation for precedence, Caroline thought she'd teach him a lesson by having new cards engraved that simply said Mrs. Astor. Willie insisted his wife should be addressed as Mrs. Astor. Society gleefully watched for the next thunderclap.

Willie and Mamie owned the Beaulieu mansion in Newport; his uncle William and Caroline had bought the opulent Beechwood estate (Vanderbilt's grandson, Cornelius Vanderbilt, owned the yet grander Breakers). In a defensive thrust, Caroline let the organizers of the Casino Ball know she would withdraw her patronage if they dared send one more letter to her addressed "Mrs. William Astor." Willie parried by instructing the Newport postmaster to deliver all mail addressed merely to Mrs. Astor to Beaulieu and not to Beechwood. The row heated up when a newspaper reported that members of Newport's gilded youth supported Mamie's claim to precedence and Caroline was denied her customary church pew. The press called Caroline's supporters "the swells," and Mamie's fans "the howling swells." The gossip sheet *Town Topics* suggested that because Caroline, going on sixty, could not waltz, and Mamie Astor could, the latter was better suited to lead the glittering throng. By the century's end, Caroline Astor and the Gilded Age were seen as passé, and her Newport mansion as a mausoleum. She died in 1908.

—◊—

Willie gave up on the country of his birth as a sensationalist press presented everything he tried to do in politics in the worst possible light. In September 1890, after discreetly making arrangements for his business affairs, he, Mamie, and the children took a ship for England with the express purpose of buying a peerage that would recognize the superiority he had always felt was his. "America is not a fit place for a gentleman to live," he said. On another occasion he claimed his children had been threatened with kidnapping. He slept with two loaded revolvers and didn't seem to have any higher regard for Britain's criminal classes. He armed his London office with iron bars and on his desk had a button that controlled the locks on every door in the building.

A title didn't come cheap during the closing years of Queen Victoria's reign. From the duke of Westminster, Willie bought Cliveden, a vast country estate overlooking the Thames, twenty miles from London, and spent $6 million on refurbishing it to his taste. He spent more millions buying Hever Castle, once the home of Anne Boleyn. To advance his cause in public opinion, he bought newspapers and magazines. One close to his heart was the *Pall Mall Gazette,* an evening newspaper whose editorial stance had shifted from conservative to radical to liberal. Willie's decision to return it to its Tory roots did not sit well with many of the staff, who left to start a rival newspaper. His choice of a new editor was fortunate, however. Harry Cust, heir to Lord Brownlow, member of Parliament and man of letters, published the best new writers—Rudyard Kipling, H. G. Wells, Alice Meynell. Willie, who thought of the *Pall Mall Gazette* as a newspaper by gentlemen for gentlemen, gave Cust magnificent office space and hosted dinner parties for the staff at the Grand Hotel. To accompany the shoptalk, music from an orchestra wafted from behind potted palms. He was eager to contribute articles—he was a published author of two novels, after all—but Cust fobbed him off. Willie's writing, he said, belonged in a literary magazine. To see himself in print and to enhance his prospects of becoming Lord Astor, Willie founded the monthly *Pall Mall Magazine.* The first issue featured a poem by Swinburne and a piece, written by Willie, on Mme. Récamier, the Parisian beauty and wit, and friend of Madame de Staël, of his great-grandfather's generation.

—⁓—

Across the Atlantic, Uncle William and Aunt Caroline's four daughters and one son kept the press entertained. Out of

Caroline's sight, William spent most of his time aboard his
yacht *Nourmahal*, off Florida, in the company of prostitutes.
When one of Caroline's Four Hundred asked after her husband, she would reply, "Oh, he is having a delightful cruise.
The sea air is so good for him. It is a great pity I am such a
bad sailor." When he was home, he embarrassed his wife by
awkwardly propositioning their friends' wives and daughters. Meanwhile, William and Caroline's daughters married
awkwardly, respectably, disastrously, and, in the case of the
youngest, beneath herself.

Emily, the eldest, met James J. Van Alen, a widower,
and announced her intention to marry him. He was not
a bad catch. His father, General James H. Van Alen, had
commanded a cavalry regiment in the Civil War. By in-
vesting $300,000 in the Illinois Central Railroad, he had
made himself a multimillionaire. Emily's father, however,
considered the younger Van Alen a roué. When word got to
Van Alen that Emily's father had said, "Damned if I want
my family having anything to do with the Van Alens," the
would-be son-in-law challenged William to a duel. Seconds
were chosen and a site agreed upon when William decided
it was too stupid to risk his life for a mere Van Alen. He
apologized, and James and Emily were married in 1876.
Five years later, Emily died during the birth of her third
child. General Van Alen took his grandchildren to England
and put them in boarding schools. When he heard his son
was ill, he booked passage to New York, suffered a nervous
breakdown on board the ocean liner, and, after dressing for
dinner, calmly jumped overboard.

The marriage of Helen was more agreeable. The groom
was James "Rosy" Roosevelt of the illustrious if not dramati-
cally wealthy family. Rosy was generous and fun-loving, and
the young couple moved to England, where the Roosevelts
had a country house near Ascot. After Rosy's mother died,
his father remarried and sired another son, Franklin Delano
Roosevelt. Like Emily, Helen died young.

Charlotte Augusta, the third daughter, sorely tested
the family's sense of decorum. She insisted on marrying
James Coleman Drayton, a Philadelphian of threadbare

background. The couple had four children when Charlotte fell madly in love with their neighbor, Hallett Alsop Borrowe, the son of one of New York's leading insurance tycoons. To avoid a scandal, Caroline sent her daughter and son-in-law to London, but Borrowe followed. So did William. Drayton tracked the lovers to a London hotel, and challenged the seducer to a duel. Borrowe declined on the grounds that he had no quarrel with a man who could not keep his wife in his own bed. While this unsavory exchange took place, one of Drayton's seconds to the duel sold the story to the *New York Sun*. Charlotte fled to Paris to join her father. On April 25, 1892, William succumbed to a sudden heart attack in his hotel suite. Not even his death brought a respectful silence as the press on both sides of the Atlantic printed stories to the effect that the family paid off the cuckolded son-in-law so he would shut up. Borrowe's father sentenced his randy son to "internal exile" in Newark, New Jersey. Charlotte got a divorce and, to the relief of the family, moved to England and married a wealthy Scotsman named George Haig.

Carrie, the youngest daughter, who made her debut during the height of her mother's reign, fell in love with Marshall Orme Wilson, the son of Civil War profiteer Richard T. Wilson. Her mother didn't approve and forbade Carrie to see Marshall. Carrie starved herself into bulimia until her mother gave in and agreed to the marriage. Wilson Sr. was a Tennessean who had moved to New York with his wife and four attractive children, establishing them in comfort at 511 Fifth Avenue (formerly the home of William "Boss" Tweed). His daughter Grace married Cornelius Vanderbilt III despite fierce opposition from almost the entire Vanderbilt clan, who thought Grace was an adventuress. Caroline and William's two other daughters married well. May became the wife of the prominent New Yorker Ogden Goelet, and Lelia married Michael Henry Herbert, brother of the earl of Pembroke. Carrie Wilson lived to the age of eighty-seven, two years longer than ancestral John Jacob.

The four Astor sisters' kid brother was nicknamed Jack Ass because although he was handsome and tall, he was also terribly uncoordinated. Brought up by a dominating and doting mother and a father conspicuous by his absence, John

Jacob Astor IV—Jack to everybody—was introduced to society in 1887 with the comment that he was "one of the richest catches and at the same time voted so much less brilliant than his father that it is very questionable whether, were he put to it, he could ever have earned his bread by his brains." His first marriage was a disaster. Ava Willing, the darkly beautiful daughter of one of Philadelphia's finest Quaker families, quickly produced a son and heir, William Vincent. Friends, acquaintances, gossips, and society memoirists all described Ava as a cold, hard, arrogant woman incapable of loving anybody. She was an incarnation of loveliness with a Roman nose and a figure remarked upon by women as much as men at Casino Balls at Newport, where her ball gowns revealed her flawless bare back. She scorned her ungraceful husband and gave herself to her houses, dances, games, and friends. She sparkled at every lighted candle while Jack, as one family biographer put it, "continued to follow her about like a bedraggled and slightly bad-tempered spaniel." Motherhood didn't soften her. She had wanted her only son, known as Vincent, to be an athletic golden boy and was appalled when he grew up rawboned, with huge hands and feet. She could not bear the sight of his ungraceful body and his tendency to knock things over. In the presence of strangers she called him Stupid.

Her husband welcomed the outbreak of the Spanish-American War in 1898 as a god-sent excuse to get away. His title of colonel was honorary, but he financed the mustering and equipment of an artillery battery and took part in the invasion of Cuba. Back in New York, Colonel Jack, as he now titled himself, was on the board of Western Union and other corporations, and answered sixty or more letters a day, half of them requesting financial help, the other half suggesting investment in various schemes. Despite, or because of, his lack of coordination, he possessed an imaginative and resourceful mind. He invented a bicycle brake, and approached the Patent Office with a scheme for pumping warm, moist air from the earth's surface into the atmosphere to make rain. The idea was turned down, but his "pneumatic road improver" won first prize at the Chicago World's Fair. Like his first cousin Willie, Jack published a novel. *A Journey in*

Other Worlds: A Romance of the Future is a science fiction story that conjures up a world forced to conserve energy. Published in 1894, the book outlines a scheme to achieve permanent springtime (but also permanent winter for other regions) by pumping massive amounts of water from one pole to the other until earth rights itself and its north-south axis is perpendicular to its rotation.

The family fortune continued to grow. A sharp financial crisis in 1893 barely affected New York real estate, and the rising influx of immigrants further inflated property values. Colonel Jack and his cousin Willie created a sensation in 1897 by jointly financing the Waldorf-Astoria Hotel, built on the site of Willie's former home on the corner of Thirty-third Street and Fifth Avenue. Featuring a thousand bedrooms and salons and restaurants that quickly became the center of New York high life, it towered over his aunt Caroline's residence just up the block and eventually forced her to move farther up Fifth Avenue.

—⁂—

In England, Willie's paranoia and eccentricity as a host baffled the aristocracy whose ranks he wanted to join. Guests at his estates were required to conform to house rules that were closer to those of a seaside boardinghouse than a stately home. In London he bought a mansion in Carlton House Terrace, a three-minute walk from Buckingham Palace. There, he managed to antagonize the Prince of Wales by accosting a guest at one of Mamie's musical evenings. He had not had the pleasure of making the gentleman's acquaintance, he told the man, asking him to leave. At that Captain Sir Berkeley Milne, R.N., the former commander of the Royal Yacht, retreated to his club and sent a note, explaining he had been dining with Lady Oxford, who had assured him the host at the Astor soiree would not object to his joining her. Clubmen wondered whether they should withdraw the invitation extended to Astor by the Prince of Wales to join the Carlton Club. The prince himself showed his displeasure by inviting Captain Milne to share the royal box. The *Saturday Review* opined that William Waldorf Astor was unfit to tie

Milne's shoe. "Poor Willie," David Sinclair wrote in *Dynasty: The Astors and Their Times.* "For all his sense of dignity and honour, something warped in his personality, some mental imbalance or psychological quirk impelled him to act in a manner which could not have been more calculated to make him look a fool if that had indeed been his intention."

American newspapers reported his British faux pas with such cutting glee that he informed the London bureau of the Associated Press that he had died. In their July 12, 1892, editions, newspapers in New York and Philadelphia carried front-page stories of William Waldorf Astor's death, apparently of pneumonia. Only the *New York Herald* sought confirmation from the Astor Estate office and avoided becoming a victim of the hoax. When his competitors carried W. W. ASTOR IS NOT DEAD corrections the next day, the *New York Tribune* printed a dispatch from London that questioned Astor's mental stability.

Mamie was not cut out for grinding aristocratic intrigue and felt humiliated by her husband's morbid prank. She was homesick and, it seemed, asked her husband not to take the decisive step toward renouncing their American citizenship. Three days before Christmas 1894 she died. She was thirty-six.

The widowed William Waldorf was considered the richest man in the world when, in 1899, he became a naturalized Briton. With his gift for ineptly pouring oil on fire, he answered American press resentment of his "betrayal" by buying the battle flag of the USS *Chesapeake,* the cause célèbre that had led to the War of 1812. When he heard that a group of Americans living in London were thinking of acquiring the flag, and sending it back to the United States, he stepped in, bought the flag, and presented it to the Royal United Service Museum. The gesture embarrassed the leaders of his adopted country. Henry Cabot Lodge, who was in England on a visit, wrote to President Theodore Roosevelt that he had had a long talk with Arthur Balfour, the Conservative statesman and future prime minister: "I was interested to find that he resented Astor's conduct about the flag as much as we." The chance of becoming Lord Astor receded again.

The widower had four children to bring up. Waldorf Jr., Pauline, John Jacob V, and Gwendolyn were given the best English nannies, governesses, and tutors, but a gulf developed between father and children. William Waldorf expected Pauline, who was fourteen when her mother died, to take over as hostess at Carlton House Terrace and Cliveden. "It was not easy to discuss things freely with him, although he was always ready to listen to any problem that worried you, but having given your opinion you could not reopen the subject with an afterthought without risk of being taxed with vacillation and 'not knowing your own mind,'" she would recall.

When Waldorf Jr. married Nancy Langhorne Shaw in 1906, the widower gave them Cliveden as a wedding present. The bride was an American divorcée, one of four daughters of a plantation family on the mend after losing everything in the Civil War—her sister Irene married painter Charles Dana Gibson and was his star model, known as "the Gibson Girl." After an unhappy stint at a New York finishing school, Nancy was a headstrong, intuitive, sometimes irrational young woman who knew how to both amuse and disturb people. She married Robert Gould Shaw, a rich, alcoholic polo player she met in Newport. After three years, a painful, hushed-up divorce followed. On a trip to England to clear her head, she fell in love with Lord Revelstoke. The dandyish head of the Baring banking business dominated the relationship until she learned his lordship had been the lover of Ethel, Lady Desborough, collector of young men.

With his brother, John, and his sister Pauline, the handsome and intelligent Waldorf Jr. had been brought up British—boarding school at nine, followed by Eton, Oxford, and public service. Neither of the boys was close to their father—Pauline was the only one who gave of herself to the aging Willie. Waldorf Jr. developed a compassion for the world beyond the velvet lining of his fortune and saw no conflict in wanting to retain his privileged position and wanting to improve the lot of mankind. He embraced liberal social politics that his father could not fathom.

The American Astors did not attend Waldorf's wedding to Nancy. Ava, Colonel Jack's wife, made an attempt at bringing the families closer. She came to Cliveden, but Nancy found her acid tongue tiresome. Willie would have preferred an English noblewoman to an American divorcée as a daughter-in-law, but Nancy was the best that could happen to Waldorf Jr. Romantic love was not her forte, but she drew her husband out of his shyness and their life together was full and fascinating, if not always happy. "I married beneath me, all women do," was one of her mots.

An era passed in New York with the death, at seventy-eight, of Caroline Schermerhorn Astor. A year after his mother's death, Colonel Jack divorced Ava. Their son Vincent had little affection for his mother. His earliest memory was of being dressed by his nanny in a sailor suit and led to his mother's drawing room. One look at him, and Ava shrieked, "Nanny, take him away! He looks perfectly horrid!"

To celebrate his new single status, the forty-seven-year-old Jack remodeled the Fifth Avenue mansion. He tore out the grand staircase and put a large reception room in its place. The old reception room was turned into a dining room where a portrait of John Jacob I was hung over the fireplace. In January 1911 he gave a ball attended by *le tout* New York. That evening he paid noticeable attention to Madeleine Force, a pretty girl who was three years younger than his son. The seventeen-year-old Madeleine was the daughter of a Brooklyn shipping clerk, but she and her large, buxom mother (referred to behind her back as La Force Majeure) were soon cruising on Jack's new boat. Madeleine was pliable and gratifyingly passionate, two qualities he found irresistible after Ava. Before the trip was over the engagement was announced. A month later the marriage took place in the great ballroom at Beechwood. The honeymoon took them to Egypt and France. When Madeleine discovered she was pregnant, they decided to return to America. Jack booked passage for the maiden voyage on the world's newest and largest luxury liner.

The *Titanic* was four days out of Southampton and nearing Newfoundland during the night of April 14–15, 1912, when she plowed full steam into an iceberg. Eyewitnesses would tell how Jack helped Madeleine into the lifeboat, then asked the officer in charge if he could accompany her, explaining that she was "in a delicate condition." The request was denied. Women and children only. Some wives refused to leave their husbands. Along the tilting deck, crew members tore wives from the arms of their husbands and threw them over the side into the lifeboats. From her lifeboat Madeleine saw the *Titanic* go down. Icy water had seeped into the bottom of the overcrowded boat and reached her knees when, after seven hours, sailors from the *Carpathia* rescued them.

At the first news of the tragedy, Vincent rushed to his father's office in New York. He told the operator at the Marconi Company's wireless offices he would give all the money anyone could possibly want for word of his father's safety. He ran to the offices of the Associated Press, and on his own tried to contact the *Carpathia* on the radio. It took days before it was confirmed that Colonel Jack Astor was one of the *Titanic*'s 1,513 victims.

Vincent inherited the bulk of his father's $87 million estate and cut short his studies at Harvard to assume his obligations as the head of the family. Both Ava and Madeleine were handsomely provided for. Ava had emerged from the divorce with $2 million. Young Madeleine enjoyed a $1.6 million settlement plus the use of Jack's homes in Manhattan and Newport and, as long as she remained unmarried, the interest from a $5 million trust fund. When her son was born, he was named John Jacob VI and given a $3 million trust fund. Ava spent most of her time in England and at the age of fifty married Thomas Lister, Fourth Baron Ribblesdale. Tall and athletic, he was wealthy, and possessed an ancient title together with a country seat and five thousand acres at Gisburne Hall, Yorkshire. The marriage was rocky. At sixty-five, his lordship wanted to snuggle up by the fireplace with a good book. At forty-three, Ava wanted to be the queen of Mayfair.

Americans showed little public sympathy for the plight of Vincent, whose income was $10,000 a day. As the first of the Astors to come into his father's fortune outright, he was also the first to believe the family fortune conferred responsibility and obligations to try to do good. He broke with his great-great-grandfather's tradition of letting others build on Astor land, but his thrusts into real estate development were erratic and naive. He spent hours playing with his model trains. He loved the ocean, and was an enthusiastic yachtsman who studied marine life and brought back rare specimens for the Bronx Zoo. When the United States entered World War I, he gave his yachts to the U.S. Navy, and at war's end returned in command of a captured German submarine.

During the 1920s, Vincent sold squalid Astor tenements and invested in the new Wall Street fad—offshore oil. His hero was his second cousin Franklin Delano Roosevelt, nine years his senior. The Roosevelts were neighbors, in Manhattan and on the Hudson—Hyde Park was near Ferncliff, the Astors' Rhinebeck estate. Both married safe, well-bred girls they had known since childhood: Vincent the statuesque, ash-blonde Helen Huntington, whose father's estate, Hopeland House, was nearby; Franklin his willowy cousin Eleanor. Vincent and Helen moved into 840 Fifth Avenue with a staff of twenty. Every January, they gave a ball in memory of his grandmother Caroline's famous soirees, but the times had changed. Such parties were now charity functions, meaning that anybody who could pay was welcome.

Vincent's success as a developer was mixed. He spent almost $250,000 on the construction of a public market on Broadway and Ninetieth Street, only to sell it at a loss. His projected $75 million Astor Plaza on Park Avenue and Fifty-third Street was taken over by Citibank, which built its own tower on the location. He razed many of his inherited slum tenements and sold others to New York's Municipal Housing Authority for little cash and long-term mortgages. Over time, he disposed of more than $40 million worth of properties until he owned no real estate except the St. Regis Hotel, the *New York Times* annex, and his residences. With his English cousins, he sold the Waldorf-Astoria Hotel. Each branch of the family received $7.5 million for land that had seemed overpriced when William Backhouse Astor had bought it for $25,000 a hundred years earlier. Four years later the new owners sold the hotel for a tidy profit. To his mother's distress, Vincent also parted with the family mansion at 840 Fifth Avenue in 1925. The buyer was the Jewish Society, which demolished the house and erected Temple Emmanuel, New York's costliest synagogue, on the site. In ten years he disposed of half of the some $63 million worth of real estate he had inherited.

He invested $250,000 in Fred Niblo's 1926 movie *Ben-Hur.* The screen version of the Lew Wallace novel, starring Ramon Novarro and Francis X. Bushman, was a sensation that grossed $10 million and gave Vincent a $371,000 profit. Instead of plowing the earnings back into the movie business, he put it toward the purchase of a luxury yacht. The price tag for the new *Nourmahal* was $1.7 million. The 246-foot yacht had a crew of forty, and cost $125,000 a year to run. A Swede was the skipper while Vincent played admiral and entertainment officer on monthlong cruises in the Caribbean or the South Pacific. The yacht brought out his dictatorial side. To a lady pleading to be excused from lunch because of seasickness, he had a note delivered to her cabin saying guests were *obliged* to appear for lunch and if they were not well enough they should be sick over the side. The lady appeared, white-faced, and sat, near tears, through the luncheon, unable to swallow a morsel. Helen hardly ever set foot on the *Nourmahal.* Her passion was music and New York City living. Vincent was tone-deaf and preferred Ferncliff and the yacht. However, they played golf together at Newport, where Vincent had inherited Beechwood and his grandmother's social reputation. Rumors of a looming divorce surfaced in 1922 when Helen took a house in Paris " for an indefinite period," as the *New York Times* put it. Gossip columnists noted there was not even a child to keep the couple together. The divorce would come in 1940 when Vincent met a pretty, vivacious young woman named Mary Benedict Cushing at a dinner party in the home of Rosy Roosevelt. Minnie, as everybody called her, was fourteen years his junior. When his divorce from Helen became final, he married Minnie and slipped away on the *Nourmahal.*

—ᴍ—

Politics intrigued his English cousin. Waldorf Jr. became a Conservative candidate for the House of Commons in 1908. Nancy campaigned with him, telling the predominantly middle-class electorate of Plymouth that her husband was really a Liberal. He lost by five hundred of the fifteen thousand votes cast. Two years later, he won the seat in the House of Commons and instantly set himself apart from the general run of British politicians.

What finally gave sixty-eight-year-old Willie a title were his financial contributions to the British war effort during World War I. He gave $100,000 to the Red Cross in 1914, $175,000 to various public funds, and another $125,000 to benefits for officers' dependents. During the disastrous year 1915, when Germany started the submarine war and it became clear to the Allies that winning the war would be long and bloody, he gave another $100,000* to the Red Cross. When President Woodrow Wilson's assistant secretary of the navy, Franklin Roosevelt, visited Cliveden, Waldorf Jr. showed him outbuildings that had been turned into a 110-bed hospital.

Not everybody applauded when William Waldorf Astor's name appeared on the 1916 New Year's Honors List. His son and daughter-in-law had not been consulted. "I was furious and so was Waldorf," Nancy wrote. "The first we knew of it was when someone rang Waldorf up and asked him what he was going to call himself now." Waldorf, who as a son of a peer would have to give up his seat in the Commons and move to the House of Lords, was bitterly opposed. When Willie asked Nancy if she agreed with her husband and she said yes, her father-in-law remembered old John Jacob's leapfrog will and not only inserted a codicil in his own will leaving half his fortune to Waldorf and Nancy's son when he came of age, but cut off Waldorf altogether. In her memoir, Nancy would suggest there was more than politics behind her distaste for

*The Federal Reserve began its Consumer Price Index in 1913, the same year federal income tax was instituted. It calculates a 1913 dollar to be worth $16.83 in 1999 money.

the trappings of aristocracy. It was unseemly somehow for an American, albeit a naturalized British citizen, to become William Waldorf, First Viscount of Astor. Elements of the British press were equally uncomfortable. Wrote the *Spectator*: "There is a widespread conviction that the grant of honours in exchange for money, though the transactions are disguised, amount to corruption, which . . . if it is allowed to continue will bring democracy into putrefaction." Cynics were sure that Astor's elevation to the peerage would not encourage American support for the war. One wicked tongue suggested he might choose a butcher's cleaver for his coat of arms. When he did select a heraldic crest, the figures he chose were a fur trapper and an Indian under the goshawk of Pedro de Astorga. He attended the House of Lords twice, once in 1916 to take his seat, and again the following year when he received his viscountcy.

William Waldorf's death in 1919 made Waldorf Jr. the Second Viscount. In a by-election to fill his House of Commons seat, Nancy became the first woman to be elected to Parliament. She was impatient with centuries-old rules of the Commons. Winston Churchill told her to her face that he found the sight of a woman in the Commons both an intrusion and an embarrassment. Over the next decade, Lady Astor, as she was universally known, displayed such a flair for politics she remained a conservative M.P. until 1945, concentrating on issues affecting women and children. She acted in the forefront of events and was loved and hated, admired and deplored. It was she who told Churchill that if she were his wife she'd poison his tea, to which he famously replied, "My dear Nancy, if I were your husband, I'd drink it."

In the 1920s, Lady Astor was one of the leading hostesses, entertaining duchesses, prime ministers, and intellectuals at the London town house on St. James's Square and at Cliveden, which she redid with the assertion that the Astors had no taste. Her friend George Bernard Shaw wrote a play about her, *The Millionairess,* that Katharine Hepburn turned into a West End success.

Politically, Waldorf and Nancy turned sharply to the right, and contributed to the appeasement of Hitler and to the atmosphere of genteel, eccentric defeatism that permeated British politics in the 1930s. The "Cliveden Set" included Prime Minister Neville Chamberlain's most clamorous supporters: Ellen Wilkinson, a radical member of the Labour Party; George Bernard Shaw, the aging playwright and critic of all social and moral theories; and the ultra right-winger Marquess of Londonderry, a descendant of foreign secretary Viscount Castlereagh, who in 1813 had sent the Royal Navy to attack Astoria. Among the Americans in attendance was Charles Lindbergh, who gave the most fearsome assessment of Germany's Luftwaffe and a correspondingly dismal picture of the weakness of the Anglo-French air forces. Also under the Astors' hospitable roof were the Duke and Duchess of Windsor, who were friends of top Nazi and Fascist officials and visited Hitler in 1937. Also there were Joseph P. Kennedy and William Bullitt, President Roosevelt's ambassadors to England and France, who both advised FDR to keep the United States out of a war that Hitler would win.

In America, Vincent had backed Roosevelt in the 1932 presidential election and supported the early stages of the New Deal. He, too, had turned to the right and as a partner in *Today* magazine, and later *Newsweek,* became a vigorous critic of the president.

—⚉—

The outbreak of World War II saw the Astors on both sides of the Atlantic rally. After Hitler invaded Poland in September 1939 and Britain and France declared war on Germany, Shaw wrote to Nancy saying the Allies should call off the war and tell Hitler that if he oppressed the Poles insufferably, Poland would be a greater trouble to him than half a dozen Irelands had ever been to Britain. Nancy's reply has not survived, but she was woman enough to admit she had been wrong. Throughout the war, she denounced delays in payments to soldiers' wives, discrimination in allowances paid to men and women suffering war injuries, and denial of the right of British women married to aliens to regain their nationality, including the plight of fifteen hundred wives of

German nationals left stateless. During the Battle of Britain she refused to surrender to mass hatred and told a crowd in bombed-out Birmingham, "Hate is a deadly poison. Kill the Germans, don't hate them."

Working secretly for cousin FDR, Vincent got into the spy business while the United States was still neutral. He and several staunchly pro-British friends began monitoring the activities of embassies and agents in the United States and Canada. With the help of trusted employees at Western Union, they intercepted international cables and even opened diplomatic bags. Working hand in glove with British intelligence, they tampered with the mails, obtained confidential information from the Chase National Bank on foreign accounts funding foreign agents, and forwarded their findings directly to the White House. Through FDR, Prime Minister Winston Churchill asked Vincent to shadow the Duke and Duchess of Windsor. By now an embarrassment to the British government, the pair were ordered to the Bahamas and told to keep a low profile. When, against Churchill's orders, they bought a cabin cruiser and began touring the Caribbean, Vincent shadowed them from the *Nourmahal,* and reported their movements to Roosevelt. After Pearl Harbor, Vincent reenlisted in the navy and, from a desk at the Eastern Sea Frontier Headquarters, organized Atlantic convoys.

John Jacob VI, who had been born after his father's death aboard the *Titanic,* took no part in the war. Vincent was furious. He accused his half brother of faking mental disability in order to be rejected for active service, and tried to have FDR overturn the Draft Board decision. Jack was an intelligent, inconsiderate eccentric with a chaotic streak in him. He was a womanizer who thought nothing of embarrassing his three wives with other women.

Nancy Astor was sixty-six when the war ended, a tiny but imperious woman with stormy relationships with her sons and daughters-in-law and with the Conservative Party, which considered her a liability. Waldorf's failing health gave her the fig leaf not to run for reelection. Docking in New York in 1945, she called herself an extinct volcano, but threatened to run for Congress. After all, she had been born in Virginia. Waldorf died in 1952. Nancy traveled a lot, as sharp-tongued as ever (she answered the welcome of Northern Rhodesia's Governor Sir Stewart Gore-Browne by saying, "Welcome to you, as one slave owner to another!"). She died of a stroke at age eighty-five. Her youngest son, Sir John Jacob Astor VII, married Ana Iñez "Chiquita" Carcano, who danced with President John F. Kennedy in the White House in 1961.

—〰—

There are still Astors in America, descendants of the son Madeleine bore Colonel Jack after he went down with the *Titanic*. Vincent, however, was the last of the direct male line. His marriage to Minnie lasted thirteen years and ended in divorce in 1953. That same year he wed the twice-married and recently widowed Brooke Marshall. Like his marriages to Helen and Minnie, the Vincent-Brooke union remained childless. After his death in 1959, Brooke became *the* Brooke Astor of New York. "By my marriage to Vincent I bear the name of a truly remarkable man: John Jacob Astor, founder in this country of my husband's family," she would say in 1981. "He married Sarah Todd in the German Reformed Church. Sarah's family were quite a cut above Astor. She was connected by marriage with several sea captains, and also Henry Brevoort, who was a man of standing and influence in New York. My husband used to say that one of the reasons for the various Astors' success was that they always married above themselves."

On a June morning in 1988, Gavin, the Second Baron Astor of Hever, the father of John Jacob VIII, Third Baron of Hever, was in Walldorf, Germany, to unveil a bust of his great-great-great-grandfather. The American consul, representatives of Astoria, Oregon, and members of the British family were also there to enjoy the concert, dancing, food, and fireworks that marked the 209th anniversary of John Jacob's setting out into the world, promising God he would be honest, industrious, and never gamble.

Notes

—ɯ—

Although John Jacob Astor died rich and famous, not one of his children, sisters, or brothers ever published a memoir about him or even passed on an anecdote that might throw light on his character. Astor himself left no corpus of writing that would make his contributions readily available to latter-day historians of ideas. Seventeen years after his death, James Parton, a journalist sometimes described as the father of American biography, wrote the first Astor biography, *Life of John Jacob Astor* (New York: American News, 1865). Parton interviewed many people and collected all the then-current stories. "No one can vouch for the accuracy of any of them but all books written about John Jacob bear the Parton stamp," wrote Virginia Cowles in *The Astors* (New York: Alfred A. Knopf, 1979), adding that since Astor's rise was due to his ability to form warm friendships with important people, he probably had more wit and charm that he is credited with.

The New-York Historical Society is the repository of the J. J. Astor and Alfred Gallatin papers. The Library of Congress and the New York Public Library also hold Astor papers. The 1817 court case against Astor over the *Caledonia* affair is in the National Archives and Records Administration appellate case files. The author of the present book has relied on Parton and archival material in New York, Philadelphia, Boston, and Washington. New sources include biographies on Thomas Jefferson, James Monroe, and the Adams family. Documentation supporting quotes in the narrative is cited below.

Introduction

Philip Hone, "All he touched," quoted in James Morton Smith, ed., *The Republic of Letters: The Correspondence Between Thomas Jefferson and James Madison, 1776–1826,* 3 vols., New York: W. W. Norton, 1995, p. 101. President Zachary Taylor, "The greatest scoundrels," quoted in David Sinclair, *Dynasty: The Astors and Their Times,* New York: Beaufort Books, 1984, p. 105. Astor's gift for seeing "how one form of commerce could be linked," quoted in Kenneth Wiggins Porter, *John Jacob Astor, Business Man,* vol. 2, Cambridge, Mass.: Harvard University Press, 1931, p. 940. J. J. Astor IV, "I asked for ice," quoted in Sinclair, op. cit., p. 207. Brooke

Astor, "His story makes," in Brooke Astor address to New York German Society, April 22, 1981.

1 The Hard Years

Pierre Adet, "Mr. Jefferson likes us," December 31, 1796, quoted in Arthur D. Howden Smith, *John Jacob Astor: Landlord of New York,* Philadelphia: Lippincott, 1929, p. 942. Smith, op. cit., p. 942, "I took a walk," letter from J. J. Astor to Washington Irving, November 25, 1836, quoted in Virginia Cowles, *The Astors.* New York: Alfred A. Knopf, 1979, p. 14.

3 Into the Woods

Wadsworth, "His wagon had broken," quoted in Porter, op. cit., p. 36. Astor, "Dear Peter," Astor to Peter Smith, November 15, 1794, Ms. Book, Baker Library. "The goods destined," in Washington Irving, *Astoria: Adventure in the Pacific Northwest,* 1836, reprint, London: KPI, 1987, p. 7. Washington Irving, "On these occasions" and "They ascended the rivers," in Irving, op. cit., p. 10. Philip Turnor, "Give men," quoted in James K. Smith, *David Thompson: Fur Trader, Explorer, Geographer,* London: Oxford University Press, 1971, p. 26. Astor's first documented fur trade, for "two thousand dollars," in John Upton Terrell, *Furs by Astor: The Full Story of the Founding of a Great American Fortune,* New York: William Morrow, 1963, p. 74. Washington Irving, "Voyageurs frolicked," ibid., p. 101. "He gives cash," *New York Packet,* in Sinclair, p. 37.

4 Politics

Thomas Jefferson, "Hereditary from father to son," quoted in Joseph J. Ellis, *American Sphinx: The Character of Thomas Jefferson,* New York: Alfred A. Knopf, 1998, p. 138. Thomas Jefferson, "Americans should never," quoted in Alexis de Tocqueville, *De la démocratie en Amérique,* Paris: Robert Laffont, 1986, p. 223. William Dunlap on Gallatin's "dark hair, coarse and bushy," quoted in Raymond Walters, Jr., *Albert Gallatin: Jeffersonian Financier and Diplomat,* New York: Macmillan, 1957, p. 217. "Do not assume," James Madison to Thomas Jefferson, February 15, 1795, quoted in James Morton Smith, op. cit., vol. 2, p. 872.

5 Rounding Out the Century

"Gentlemen. Please to make" letter, quoted in Arthur D. Howden Smith, op. cit., pp. 22–23. "I Can not Describe," Astor to Peter Smith, quoted in Terrell, op cit., p. 97. Robert Prescott, "A German person," Prescott to Robert Liston, August 31, 1797, quoted in ibid., p. 106. Albert Gallatin suggesting that Canadian dealers had "a most dangerous influence," quoted in Sinclair, op. cit., p. 46.

6 China Profits

Emperor Qianlong, "We possess all things," quoted in *The Pulse of Enterprise, 1800–1850,* Amsterdam: Time-Life Books, 1992, p. 107. "He was dashing," Ellis, op. cit., p. 174. The wording of the Burr water company charter quoted in *New York: A Collection from Harper's Magazine,* New York: Gallery Books, 1991, p. 498. "Why, Mr. Astor" in Porter, op. cit., vol. 1, p. 923.

7 Realpolitik

Boston newspaper, "We are to give money," quoted in *The Economist,* December 23, 1999. Thomas Jefferson, "Seek for and pursue," quoted in Dayton Duncan and Ken Burns, *Lewis and Clark: The Journey of the Corps of Discovery,* New York: Alfred A. Knopf, 1998, p. 8. Thomas Jefferson, "The river Missouri," letter to Congress, quoted in ibid. Thomas Jefferson, "Captain Lewis is brave," in letter to Benjamin Rush, February 28, 1803, quoted in ibid.

8 Punqua Wingchong

Albert Gallatin, "They are so few," Gallatin to Thomas Jefferson, December 18, 1807, quoted in Walters, op. cit., p. 199. John Lambert, "The embargo had now," quoted in *New York: A Collection from Harper's Magazine,* op. cit., p. 220. "Surrendered all essential decision," Ellis, op. cit., p. 238. The embargo "is certainly," Thomas Jefferson to Albert Gallatin, August 11, 1808, Gallatin Papers, New-York Historical Society. Senator Latham Mitchell, "Punqua Wingchong, a Chinese merchant," quoted in Porter, op. cit., vol. 1, pp. 420–421.

9 Family

James Truslow Adams, "There was not," quoted in Dana Lee Thomas, *The Money Crowd,* New York: Putnam, 1972, p. 22. Astor, "Dear Peter," quoted in Porter, op. cit., vol. 1, p. 387. Girard, Astor "passed through," quoted in Sydney Greenbie and Marjorie Greenbie, *Gold of Ophir: The China Trade in the Making of America,* New York: Wiley-Erickson, 1937, p. 150. Girard, "I am surprised," in Harvey O'Connor, *The Astors,* New York: Alfred A. Knopf, 1941, p. 9. Washington Irving's description of Hannah Gallatin "in the drawing room," quoted in Walters, op. cit., p. 214. "Had better send for his daughter," Albert Gallatin to John Jacob Astor, quoted in Porter, op. cit., vol. 2, p. 1040. Gulian C. Verplanck, "I recollect dining," quoted in *New York: A Collection from Harper's Magazine,* op. cit., p. 397.

10 *The Good Ship* Enterprise

Astor on Captain Ebbets, "Enjoyed both the esteem and confidence," quoted in Terrell, op. cit., p. 152. Washington Irving's description of the Kodiak Indians and Governor Baranov in op. cit., p. 395. "Here were two," in Jeanette Mirsky, *The Westward Crossings: Balboa, Mackenzie, Lewis and Clark,* New York: Alfred A. Knopf, 1946, p. 354. "Weary of his job," Terrell, op. cit., p. 152. John Quincy Adams quoting Rumiantzov, "Our attachment," from Adams to Robert Smith, September 30, 1810, in

John Quincy Adams to Secretary of State (Robert Smith), Oct. 12, 1810, *Memoirs*, ed., Francis Adams, 7 vols., New York: Macmillan, 1913–1917, vol. 2, pp. 179–180.

11   A Perfect Triangle

"Whether we remain," Thomas Jefferson to Joseph Priestley, January 28, 1803, in *The Writings of Thomas Jefferson,* ed. Paul Leicester Ford, New York: Putnam's Sons, 1892–1899, p. 295. Henry Dearborn on George Clinton, he "speaks well of Astor," quoted in Terrell, op. cit., p. 143. Jefferson, "examined these sheets," quoted in Duncan and Burns, op. cit., p. 209. Gratiot, "I am indebted," quoted in Terrell, op. cit., p. 323. "In boldness of enterprise," Hiram Martin Chittenden, *The American Fur Trade of the Far West,* 1903, reprint, New York: Press of the Pioneers, 1935, p. 114. Jefferson to Astor, "I remember well," quoted in Washington Irving, op. cit., p. 24. "The four commissioners," in Terrell, op. cit., p. 145. Jackson, "Surprise and admiration," quoted in Washington Irving, op. cit., p. 33. "Possibly, he thought Canadians," in Arthur D. Howden Smith, op. cit., p. 137. "The adroit and buoyant," Washington Irving, op. cit., pp. 1–2. "On these occasions," ibid., pp. 109–110. Thomas Nuttall, "Sir, don't you think," quoted in Terrell, op. cit., p. 172.

12   Outbound

Jonathan Thorn, "The collecting of materials" and "They were determined," quoted in Washington Irving, op. cit., pp. 39–40. Jonathan Thorn, They appeared "like spectres," quoted in Terrell, op. cit., p. 180. "Fortunately for all," Washington Irving, op. cit., p. 43. Alexander Henry, "A very filthy race," quoted in Elliott Cones, ed., *The Ms. Journals of Alexander Henry and of David Thompson,* Minneapolis: Ross and Haines, 1897, p. 750. Gabriel Franchère, "Toward midday," quoted in David Thompson, *Columbia Journals,* Montreal: McGill-Queen's University Press, 1994, p. 100. David Thompson, "$\frac{1}{2}$ a mile," Thompson MSS, bk. 27, vol. 11, Toronto: Ontario Department of Public Records and Archives. "April 15: Set off," Thompson, op. cit., p. 84. "Arms, legs" and "The ship had disappeared," Washington Irving, op. cit., p. 90.

13   The Hunt Journey

John Upton Terrell, "Lisa had only 20 men," quoted in Terrell, op. cit. p. 190.

14   No News

Albert Gallatin, "The reduction," Gallatin to Thomas Jefferson, November 11, 1809, Gallatin Papers, New-York Historical Society. "A horse was," Washington Irving, op. cit., p. 393.

15   Mr. Madison's War

Albert Gallatin to Thomas Jefferson, "The series of misfortunes," quoted in Walters, op. cit., p. 253. Astor, "As soon as," quoted in Terrell, op. cit., p. 205. "At a time when foreign commerce," Parton, op. cit., p. 58. Northwesters expressed "their fears," Washington Irving, op. cit., p. 390. "It is of great," Astor to Gallatin, December 22, 1814, Gallatin Papers, New-York Historical Society. Astor to Girard postscript, "We have just," MS, Girard College, Philadelphia, Girard Papers, 1814, No. 354. Astor to Monroe, "Dear Sir, Senice I had," Ms., Library of Congress, Monroe Papers, vol. 19, Writings to Monroe, November 1813–March 1815. Astor, "Let Mr. King," Ms. Book, Baker Library, Harvard University, Astor Papers, Letter Book I, 1813–1815, pp. 280–281. Robert Stuart, "You can very readily," quoted in Sinclair, op. cit., p. 104. Astor, "Dear George, I have received," Ms. Book, Baker Library, Astor Papers, Letter Book I, 1813–1815, p. 290. James Gallatin, "The band played," in Richard H. Horne, ed., *The Great Peace Maker: The Diary of James Gallatin.* London: Robson and Sons, 1872.

16 So long as I Have a Dollar

Astor to Daniel McKenzie, "While I breath," quoted in Terrell, op. cit., p. 239. Astor to George Ehninger, "By the peace," quoted in ibid., p. 240. Astor to Wilson Price Hunt, "After their treatment," quoted in Washington Irving, op. cit., p. 421. "Of course you know," Astor to Albert Gallatin, October 9, 1815. Gallatin Papers, New-York Historical Society. Astor, "It appears to me," quoted in Porter, op. cit., vol. 1, p. 964. Monroe to British ambassador, "Partly at the insistence," quoted in Terrell, p. 240. "The moment Comcomly," Alexander Ross, *Fur Hunters of the Far West,* 1855, reprint, Chicago: R. R. Donnelley, 1924, p. 16. "As to Comcomly," in Washington Irving, op. cit., p. 417. "Whatever the reason," Arthur Howden Smith, op. cit., p. 180. Ross, "Late one evening," op. cit., pp. 300–301. "The tragic list," in ibid., p. 304. "How vain," in ibid., p. 305. James Monroe, "Mr. Astor, of New York," quoted in Terrell, op. cit., p. 240. Astor, "What would you," quoted in Parton, op. cit., p. 242. "Our statesmen have become," in Washington Irving, op. cit., p. 425. James Madison, "Nothing but seasons," in Madison, *Letters and Other Writings,* vol. 3, Philadelphia: J. B. Lippincott, 1865, p. 116.

17 John Jacob Astor & Son

Description of William as "the richest and less attractive," quoted in Sinclair, op. cit., p. 133. Christian Bunsen, "I am now," quoted in ibid., p. 94. Washington Irving, "There was a busy," quoted in *New York in the Age of the Constitution, 1775–1800,* ed. Paul A. Gilje and William Pencak, Cranbury, N.J.: Associated University Presses, 1992, p. 14. Astor to Charles Gratiot, "I have thought," Ms. Book, Baker Library, Astor Papers, Letter Book II, p. 113. Major Puthuff to Governor Cass, "I wish to God," quoted in Terrell, op. cit., p. 251. The *Missouri Gazette,* "In 1817," quoted in Terrell, op. cit., p. 340. "I was changing," Astor to Albert Gallatin, March 14, 1818, Gallatin Papers.

18 Paris

Astor, "Supposing it may be useful," September 12, 1818, Astor Papers, Baker Library, Harvard University. Irving on John Jacob II "in very bad health," quoted in Terrell, op. cit., p. 364. "Knowing full well," in Sinclair, op. cit., p. 99. "Americans noted the frenzy," in Stephen Longstreet, *We All Went to Paris: Americans in the City of Light, 1776–1971,* New York: Macmillan, 1972, p. 79. "Powdered queues," in ibid., p. 86. "All Europe is threatened," Astor to James Monroe, April 5, 1820, New York Public Library, Monroe Papers. The Patterson-Napoleon marriage contract, "If the marriage," quoted in David Stacton, *The Bonapartes,* New York: Simon & Schuster, 1966, p. 29. Bo (Jerome Bonaparte) to William Patterson, "Mama goes out," quoted in ibid., p. 221. Betsy Napoleon, "The men are all merchants," quoted in ibid., p. 224. Edward Gibbon, "To the perfection," quoted in Longstreet, op. cit., p. 93. Betsy Napoleon, "Quite true," quoted in Eugene Lemoine Didier, *The Life and Letters of Madame Bonaparte,* New York: C. Scribner's Sons, 1879, p. 61. Betsy Napoleon to William Patterson, "I form no plans" and "They are less wealthy," quoted in Stacton, op. cit., pp. 219–220. Betsy Napoleon, "Mr. A and daughter," quoted in Didier, op. cit., pp. 162–163. James Gallatin, "Really Mr. Astor," quoted in Sinclair, op. cit., p. 42. "Either Astor had suffered," in Terrell, op. cit., p. 289. "For the interest," Astor to Albert Gallatin, October 18, 1822, Gallatin Papers, New-York Historical Society. Astor to Betsy Napoleon, "I told her," quoted in Didier, op. cit., p. 61. Betsy Napoleon to Patterson, "The Bonapartes are all alike," quoted in ibid., p. 72. Astor to Dorothy Langdon, "Eliza is very well," quoted in Porter, vol. 2, op. cit., p. 1176. Ramsay Crooks to Astor, "To address Messrs Berthold and Chouteau," quoted in Chittenden, op. cit., p. 318. "He is said in July," in Porter, vol. 2, op. cit., p. 1945.

19 This Land Is My Land

"Many are the stories," in Chittenden, op. cit., pp. 346–347. Taylor, "The greatest scroundels," quoted in Sinclair, op. cit., p. 105. Thomas Biddle, "So violent," quoted in Chittenden, op. cit., p. 30. "The Indian" and "It may indeed," in Chittenden, op. cit., p. 25 and p. 380. "Wherever the trade," Astor to General William H. Ashley, April 22, 1822, quoted in Porter, op. cit., vol. 2, p. 811. Ramsay Crooks to Pierre Chouteau, "I regret truly," quoted in Chittenden, op. cit., p. 30. "The chief elements," in Chittenden, op. cit., p. 375. "Here I cannot pass," Astor to Albert Gallatin, October 18, 1822, Gallatin Papers. Robert Stuart to David Stone, "Permit me," quoted in Chittenden, op. cit., p. 325. "He had no illusions," in Terrell, op. cit., p. 373. Astor to Ramsay Crooks, "On the whole," quoted in ibid., p. 376. "Imagine my surprise," in Charles Larpenteur, *Forty Years a Fur Trader on the Upper Missouri: The Personal Narrative of Charles Larpenteur, 1833–1872,* New York: F. P. Harper, 1898, p. 65. Kenneth McKenzie to Pierre Chouteau, "On my arrival," quoted in Terrell, op. cit., p. 416. The Blackfoot-Assiniboine treaty text, "We sent greeting," quoted

in ibid., p. 417. Astor to Pierre Chouteau, "Your voyage," quoted in ibid., p. 436. Pierre Chouteau to Astor, "I am convinced," Astor Papers, New-York Historical Society, iii.

20   Estimable Grand-Papa

Astor, "The only hard step," quoted in Porter, op. cit., vol. 2, p. 1122. Halleck, "Mr. Astor," quoted in Sinclair, op. cit., p. 216. "A little indulgence," Pierre Chouteau to Ramsay Crooks, August 17, 1831, American Fur Papers 1813–1843, Detroit Public Library, Burton Historical Collections. "In the hands," Crooks to Chouteau, October 1, 1831, ibid. Thomas Forsyth to Lewis Cass, "Mr. [J. P.] Cabanne," quoted in Terrell, op. cit., p. 399. James Parton, "One of the ablest," in *Harpers's Magazine,* May 27, 1863. *Harper's* on Astor's goals "to get all," quoted in Sinclair, op. cit., p. 150. Astor to Ramsay Crooks, "With regard," Detroit Public Library, Burton Historical Collections, Letters of Ramsay Crooks, Astor and the American Fur Company, 1813–1843. Henry Brevoort, "An untoward event," quoted in Sinclair, op. cit., p. 139. Astor to Pierre Chouteau, "I think now," Astor Letters, Pennsylvania Historical Society, Philadelphia. William Astor to Vincent von Rumpff, "I was much," quoted in Terrell, op. cit., p. 465. David Stuart to John Lawe, "Pray, give yourself," and Ramsay Crooks to Pierre Chouteau, "The business seems," quoted in ibid., pp. 461–463. Astor to Pratte & Company, "Wishing to retire," Astor Letters, Pennsylvania Historical Society, Philadelphia.

21   The Bigger Picture

Astor letter from London, "I very much fear," quoted in Chittenden, op. cit., p. 365. "In literary circles," Porter, op. cit., vol. 2, pp. 1050–1051. "It is a picture," quoted in Pierre Irving, *Life and Letters of Washington Irving,* 1863, reprint, Detroit: Gale Research, 1967, vol. 3, p. 113.

22   Writing about It

Washington Irving, "He was too," quoted in Porter, op. cit., vol. 2, p. 1054. Washington Irving, "Steam boat aground," journal entries dated September 11 and 27, 1832, in Washington Irving, *Journals and Notebooks,* ed. Nathalia Wright, vol. 5, Madison: University of Wisconsin Press, 1969–1986, vol. 5 (1832–1859), p. 54. Astor feeling "the want of occupation," quoted in Porter, op. cit., vol. 2, p. 1053. "A complete depository," Washington Irving to S. G. Drake, October 10, 1837, Irving Papers, New York Public Library. Washington Irving to Pierre Munro Irving, "John Jacob Astor," quoted in Johanna Johnston, *The Heart That Would Not Hold: A Biography of Washington Irving,* New York: M. Evans, 1971, p. 332. "Columbus and John Jacob Astor," James Fenimore Cooper, *Correspondence of James Fenimore Cooper, Edited by His Grandson,* New Haven, Conn.: Yale University Press, 1922, p. 588. Washington Irving, "Astor was hovering," quoted in Stanley T. Williams, *The Life of Washington Irving,* New York: Oxford University Press, 1935, p. 83.

Washington Irving to Pierre Munro Irving, "One or two years," quoted in ibid., p. 84. Washington Irving, Fur traders "have always," quoted in Chittenden, op. cit., p. 240. Henry Wadsworth Longfellow, "John Jacob stand out," quoted in Sinclair, op. cit., p. 124. *New York Mirror* review, October 22, 1836. London *Spectator* review, October 22, 1836. *Quarterly Review* piece, November 1836. The *Southern Literary Messenger* review, January 1838. "He [Astor]," Sinclair, op. cit., p. 68. "Deeply pained," in Hubert Howe Bancroft, *Works,* San Francisco: History Company, 1888, xxviii. "It has been" and "Pen pictures," in Chittenden, op. cit., p. 242. "Astoria is neither," in Robert Spiller, Willard Thorp, Thomas J. Johnson, Henry Seidel, Richard Canby, M. Ludwig, and William M. Gibson, eds., New York: Macmillan, 1974, p. 774. Washington Irving, "Old Mr. Astor," quoted in Porter, op. cit., vol. 2, p. 1054.

23   A Third Fortune

"Not another speaker," in Philip Hone, *The Diary of Philip Hone, 1828–1851,* New York: Dodd, Mead, 1889, p. 289. James Gordon Bennett, "Anyone who can pay," quoted in Lucy Kavaler, *The Astors: A Family Chronicle of Pomp and Power,* New York: Dodd, Mead, 1966, p. 36. "Some of it," Fanny Kemble, *Journal of a Young Actress,* ed. Monica Gough, New York: Columbia University Press, 1990, p. 14. "Evidently Astor," Porter, op. cit., vol. 2, p. 919. Joseph Green Cogswell, "I went out," in Wilson, op. cit., p. 81. Derek Wilson, *The Astors, 1763–1992,* New York: St. Martin's Press, 1993, p. 35.

24   Richest Man in America

Horace Greeley, "It is our deliberate," quoted in William Harlan Hale, *Horace Greeley: Voice of the People,* New York: Harper and Bros., 1950, p. 106. It was said "old Mr. Astor," quoted in Porter, op. cit., vol. 2, p. 1048. Fitz-Greene Halleck, "Mr. Astor," quoted in Cowles, op. cit., p. 59. Walt Whitman, "Beut feeble," quoted in Bliss Perry, *Walt Whitman,* Boston: Houghton Mifflin, 1906, p. 13. Astor to John James Audubon, "You come at a bad time," quoted in Porter, op. cit., vol. 2, p. 1057. Thomas L. McKenney to Dolley Madison, "Your old friend," quoted in Meade Minningerode, *Certain Rich Men,* New York: G. P. Putnam Sons, 1927, p. 33. "This old gentleman," in Hone, op. cit., p. 291.

25   Heirs and Graces

Philip Hone, "John Jacob Astor," quoted in Sinclair, op. cit., p. 146. *Hunt's Merchant Magazine,* "There are few men," quoted in O'Connor, op. cit., p. 5. "The mania," in Hone, op. cit., p. 15. "He knew every inch," in Cowles, op. cit., p. 72. "A tall, heavy built man," in Matthew Hale Smith, *Sunshine and Shadow in New York,* Hartford, Conn.: J. B. Burr, 1868, p. 126. *Harper's Weekly,* "In all probability," John G. Gates, *The Astor Family: A Unique Exploration of One of America's First Families,* Garden City, N.Y.: Doubleday, 1981, p. 76. Augusta Astor, "When you look at this flag," quoted in Sinclair, op. cit., p. 175. Ward McAllister on

Caroline Astor, quoted in Matthew Josephson, *The Robber Barons: The Great American Capitalists,* New York: Harcourt, Brace, 1934, p. 329. Burton Hendrick, "The world's greatest monument," quoted in Cowles, op. cit., p. 137. Caroline Astor, "Oh, he is having a delightful cruise," quoted in Elizabeth Lehr, *"King Lear" and the Gilded Age,* Philadelphia: Lippincott, 1935, p. 65. Jack Astor's introduction as "one of the richest," quoted in Sinclair, op. cit., p. 135. Jack "continued to follow," in Cowles, op. cit., p. 135. "Poor Willie," in Sinclair, op. cit., p. 258. Henry Cabot Lodge to Theodore Roosevelt, "I was interested," quoted in Cowles, op. cit., p. 154. Pauline Astor, "It was not easy," Archive of Lord Astor of Hever, Notes Written by Pauline Astor. Ava Astor, "Nanny, take him away," quoted in Wilson, op. cit., p. 288. Nancy Astor, "I was furious," quoted in Christopher Sykes, *Nancy: The Life of Lady Astor,* Chicago: Academy Chicago, 1972, p. 193. *Spectator,* "There is a widespread," quoted in Sinclair, op. cit., p. 270. Winston Churchill, "My dear Nancy," quoted in Sykes, op. cit., p. 144. Nancy Astor, "Hate is a deadly poison," ibid., p. 507. Brooke Astor, "By my marriage," in Brooke Astor address to New York German Society, April 22, 1981.

Bibliography

—⊶—

Adams, Henry. *The Life of Albert Gallatin*. Philadelphia: Lippincott, 1879.

Adams, John Quincy. *Writings*. Ed. Worthington C. Ford. 7 vols. New York: Macmillan, 1913–1917.

Astor, John J. *Business Letters, 1813–1828*. Benson, Vt.: Chalidze Publications, 1991.

Astor, John Jacob, IV. *A Journey in Other Worlds: A Romance of the Future*. New York: D. Appleton, 1894.

Bancroft, Hubert Howe. *Works*. San Francisco: History Company, 1888.

Bauer, K. Jack. *Zachary Taylor: Soldier, Planter, Statesman of the Old Southwest*. Baton Rouge: Louisiana State University Press, 1985.

Bemis, Samuel Flagg. *John Quincy Adams and the Foundation of American Foreign Policy*. New York: Alfred A. Knopf, 1969.

Brannon, Gary. *Last Voyage of the Tonquin: An Ill-Fated Expedition to the Pacific Northwest*. Waterloo, Ont.: University of Waterloo, Escart Press, 1985.

Bristed, Charles Astor. *The Upper Ten Thousand: Sketches of American Society*. New York: Stringer and Townsend, 1852.

Brooke, John. *King George III*. New York: McGraw-Hill, 1972.

Chittenden, Hiram Martin. *The American Fur Trade of the Far West*. 1903. Reprint, New York: Press of the Pioneers, 1935.

Cooper, James Fenimore. *Correspondence of James Fenimore Cooper, Edited by His Grandson*. New Haven, Conn.: Yale University Press, 1922.

Coues, Elliott. *New Light on the Early History*. Minneapolis: Ross and Haines, 1965.

Coues, Elliott, ed. *The Ms. Journals of Alexander Henry and of David Thompson*. Minneapolis: Ross and Haines, 1897.

Cowles, Virginia. *The Astors*. New York: Alfred A. Knopf, 1979.

Didier, Eugene Lemoine. *The Life and Letters of Madame Bonaparte*. New York: C. Scribner's Sons, 1879.

Duncan, Dayton, and Burns, Ken. *Lewis and Clark: The Journey of the Corps of Discovery*. New York: Alfred A. Knopf, 1998.

Ellis, Joseph J. *American Sphinx: The Character of Thomas Jefferson*. New York: Alfred A. Knopf, 1998.

Franchère, Gabriel. *Relation d'un voyage à la cote du nord-ouest de l'Amérique septentrionale, dans les années 1810, 11, 12, 13, et 14.* Montreal: C. B. Pasteur, 1820.

Gates, John G. *The Astor Family: A Unique Exploration of One of America's First Families.* Garden City, N.Y.: Doubleday, 1981.

Gilje, Paul A., and Pencak, William, eds. *New York in the Age of the Constitution, 1775–1800.* Cranbury, N.J.: Associated University Presses, 1992.

Gonzales, Juan. *Harvest of Empire: A History of Latinos in America.* New York: Viking, 2000.

Greenbie, Sydney, and Greenbie, Marjorie. *Gold of Ophir: The China Trade in the Making of America.* New York: Wilson-Erickson, 1937.

Hale, William Harlan. *Horace Greeley: Voice of the People.* New York: Harper and Bros., 1950.

Henry, Alexander. *Travels and Adventures in Canada and the Indian Territories.* Toronto: George N. Morang, 1901.

Hone, Philip. *The Diary of Philip Hone, 1828–1851.* New York: Dodd, Mead, 1889.

Irving, Pierre. *Life and Letters of Washington Irving.* 1863. 4 vols. Reprint, Detroit: Gale Research, 1967.

Irving, Washington: *Astoria: Adventure in the Pacific Northwest.* 1836. Reprint, London: KPI, 1987.

———. *Journals and Notebooks.* Ed. Nathalia Wright. 5 vols. Madison: University of Wisconsin Press, 1969–1986.

Jefferson, Thomas. *The Writings of Thomas Jefferson.* Ed. Paul Leicester Ford. 10 vols. New York: Putnam's Sons, 1892–1899.

Johnston, Johanna. *The Heart That Would Not Hold: A Biography of Washington Irving.* New York: M. Evans, 1971.

Josephson, Matthew. *The Robber Barons: The Great American Capitalists.* New York: Harcourt, Brace, 1934.

Kavaler, Lucy. *The Astors: A Family Chronicle of Pomp and Power.* New York: Dodd, Mead, 1966.

Kemble, Fanny. *Journal of a Young Actress.* Ed. Monica Gough. New York: Columbia University Press, 1990.

Kennedy, Roger G. *Burr, Hamilton and Jefferson: A Study in Character.* New York: Oxford University Press, 2000.

Larpenteur, Charles. *Forty Years a Fur Trader on the Upper Missouri: The Personal Narrative of Charles Larpenteur, 1833–1872.* New York: F. P. Harper, 1898.

Leary, Lewis. *Washington Irving.* Twayne's United States Authors Series. Boston: G. K. Hall, 1981.

Lehr, Elizabeth. D. *"King Lear" and the Gilded Age.* Philadelphia: Lippincott, 1935.

Longstreet, Stephen. *We All Went to Paris: Americans in the City of Light, 1776–1971.* New York: Macmillan, 1972.

Madison, James. *Letters and Other Writings.* Vol. 3. Philadelphia: J. B. Lippincott, 1865.

Minningerode, Meade. *Certain Rich Men.* New York: G. P. Putnam Sons, 1927.

Mirsky, Jeanette. *The Westward Crossings: Balboa, Mackenzie, Lewis and Clark.* New York: Alfred A. Knopf, 1946.

Morgan, Ted. *FDR: A Biography.* New York: Simon & Schuster, 1985.

O'Connor, Harvey. *The Astors.* New York: Alfred A. Knopf, 1941.

Parton, James. *Life of John Jacob Astor.* New York: American News, 1865.

Perry, Bliss. *Walt Whitman.* Boston: Houghton Mifflin, 1906.

Porter, Kenneth Wiggins. *John Jacob Astor, Business Man.* 2 vols. Cambridge, Mass.: Harvard University Press, 1931.

Remini, Robert. *Daniel Webster: The Man and His Time.* New York: W. W. Norton, 1997.

The Pulse of Enterprise, 1800–1850. Amsterdam: Time-Life Books, 1992.

Ross, Alexander. *Adventures of the First Settlers on the Oregon or Columbia River.* London: Smith Elder, 1849. Reprint, Norman: University of Oklahoma Press, 1953.

———. *Fur Hunters of the Far West.* 1855. Reprint, Chicago: R. R. Donnelley, 1924.

Shepherd, Jack. *The Adams Chronicles: Four Generations of Greatness.* Boston: Little, Brown, 1975.

Sinclair, David. *Dynasty: The Astors and Their Times.* New York: Beaufort Books, 1984.

Smith, Arthur D. Howden. *John Jacob Astor: Landlord of New York.* Philadelphia: Lippincott, 1929.

Smith, James K. *David Thompson: Fur Trader, Explorer, Geographer.* London: Oxford University Press, 1971.

Smith, Matthew Hale. *Sunshine and Shadow in New York.* Hartford, Conn.: J. B. Burr, 1868.

Spiller, Robert, Thorp, Willard, Johnson, Thomas J., Seidel, Henry, Canby, Richard, Ludwig, M., and Gibson, William, M., eds. *Literary History of the United States.* New York: Macmillan, 1974.

Stacton, David. *The Bonapartes.* New York: Simon & Schuster, 1966.

Sykes, Christopher. *Nancy: The Life of Lady Astor.* Chicago: Academy Chicago, 1972.

Taillandier, Saint-René. *Dix ans de l'histoire d'allemagne.* Paris: Didier, 1875.

Terrell, John Upton. *Furs by Astor: The Full Story of the Founding of a Great American Fortune.* New York: William Morrow, 1963.

Thomas, Dana Lee. *The Money Crowd.* New York: Putnam, 1972.

Thompson, David. *Columbia Journals.* Montreal: McGill-Queen's University Press, 1994.

Tocqueville, Alexis de. *De la démocratie en Amérique.* Paris: Robert Laffont, 1986.

Walters, Raymond, Jr. *Albert Gallatin: Jeffersonian Financier and Diplomat.* New York: Macmillan, 1957.

Williams, Stanley T. *The Life of Washington Irving.* New York: Oxford University Press, 1935.

Wilson, Derek. *The Astors, 1763–1992: Landscape with Millionaires.* New York: St. Martin's Press, 1993.

Index

—ᴍ—